BRITISH GOVERNMENT IN INDIA

Lord Wellesley as Governor General, 1800

From a Painting by R. Home

BRITISH GOVERNMENT IN INDIA

The Story of the Viceroys and Government Houses

By

THE MARQUIS CURZON OF KEDLESTON, K.G.

Viceroy and Governor General of India
Jan. 1899–May 1904, and Dec. 1904–Nov. 1905

> *'Dost thou not know that the greatest part of Asia is subject to our arms and our laws? that our invincible forces extend from one sea to the other? that the potentates of the earth form a line before our gates? and that we have compelled Fortune herself to watch over the prosperity of our Empire?'*—Timur [Tamerlane] to Sultan Bajazet.
>
> GIBBON: *'Decline and Fall of the Roman Empire,'* cap. lxiv.

VOLUME ONE

CASSELL AND COMPANY LTD
London, New York, Toronto and Melbourne

Published 1925

Printed in Great Britain

PREFACE

Historia vero testis temporum, lux veritatis.—Cicero, *De Oratore*, Lib. 11. 9

THIS book is a debt, too long overdue, both to Calcutta and to India. While I was there as Viceroy between the years 1899 and 1905, I resolved to write the history of Government House—that stately building, by far the finest Government House in the Empire, designed upon the model of my own home of Kedleston in Derbyshire—which had sheltered the rulers of India for exactly one hundred years; and I collected the material from many sources, official and private, for the purpose. When I returned to England I continued my researches and began to write the book. After a while I was drawn back into the vortex of public life, and my opportunities for literary work diminished. Then came the Great War, since which date, having been almost continuously in office, it was only at rare intervals and spasmodically that I was able to resume the task.

Meanwhile I continued to receive from my successors in the Viceroyalty appeals to complete the undertaking. Nor did these abate when the seat of the Government of India was moved from Calcutta in 1912, and the palace of the Governor General was handed over to the Governors of Bengal. Rather did they press that their official residence should still find its historian in one who had occupied it in its glory, and was acquainted with its history and traditions.

I have therefore taken advantage of odd moments of leisure to finish the work which I began nearly a quarter of a century ago. So far from suffering, it has, I think, gained by the delay. For during the interval researches have been made, and books have been published, which throw much fresh light on the history of Calcutta during the 19th century, and before; so that a far more complete and accurate story can now be told than would have been possible at an earlier date.

The building which was the original *raison d'être* of this book is the Government House of which I have already spoken; and not

v

the least interesting part of the story may be found to lie in the narrative of the long and embittered struggle between Lord Wellesley and the East India Company over its erection—a story which is for the most part hidden away in official documents, and has never before been fully told. As to the subsequent history of the house, a great deal that appears in these pages has only been collected with much labour from private sources.

It was difficult to write the history of this Government House without tracing the often puzzling pedigree of its predecessors, as also of the Council Houses in which the Governors General and their colleagues transacted the public business of the Government for one and a half centuries. Nor would it have been desirable to omit the enchanting resort of Barrackpore, where, in the days when Hill-Stations were unknown, and the Viceroy never left Bengal except for a rare and in those days prolonged tour in the Upper Provinces, he spent as much if not more of his time than in Calcutta itself. Special attention has also been given to some topographical problems, such as the Indian residences of Warren Hastings, which have long agitated the minds of students, but which in these pages I hope to have finally solved. There may be some readers also who will care to read the story of how the Black Hole site was recovered and commemorated only twenty years ago ; while for such as prefer to turn their gaze to more recent history and to the future, the chapter on the great Victoria Memorial Hall may provide both a surprise and an incentive.

But these Volumes are in truth much more than a history either of these subjects or of the various Government Houses in and about Calcutta which have been tenanted by the representatives of the Crown in India. It was impossible to pursue the studies required for this purpose, without learning a great deal, not merely about these residences, but about the lives and personalities of the men who occupied them. Many of these were long before my day, but even about them fresh knowledge was to be gleaned. The last ten Viceroys I have known personally, and I can speak of them from first-hand information. I should be able therefore to draw here a picture of Viceregal life as it was lived at Calcutta throughout the 19th century, although it will now be so no more. Great figures will pass across the stage, great events will be referred to, of which

Government House was the scene and source, and in both cases maybe we shall peep behind the curtain of official reticence.

At this stage, however, a further vista opened before me. For as I pieced together the records of the Governor Generalship, it appeared to me that there was a good deal to be said about the history of that institution, about its functions and duties, that was not to be found in any current work, and could only be fairly told by one who had filled the post himself. The story of the men is also the story of the office ; and the story of the office is that of British Government in India, not, as commonly related, in terms of battles and conquests or even of administrative and legislative acts, but in its constitutional development as a great and powerful piece of executive machinery, by which Great Britain has for a period of a century and a half successfully moulded and controlled the destinies of millions of the human race. How the two parts of this great machine, in India and in England, have operated, either in combination or not infrequently in conflict, what have been the reactions between Calcutta and Whitehall, and how the power of the Viceroyalty has at different times waxed and waned, it will be the object of these pages to expound.

And then, while dealing with the men, I asked myself whether, instead of treating the administrations of the successive Governors General, so to speak, as things apart—as is the way with the customary biographies—it might not be desirable to follow the long sequence, just as one might survey in a picture gallery the portraits of a line of ancestors or a dynasty of kings, comparing one with another, tracing the points of difference or resemblance between them, and seeking to arrive at some final conclusions concerning the part which individually or collectively they had played in the progressive evolution of the whole.

It has been far from my mind to describe and weigh the public policy of any Governor General. For such an appreciation or such a criticism we must turn either to the standard histories of India or to the lives of the statesmen concerned. Rather have I sought to paint the man as he appeared in his life in India, to show how he felt and comported himself, what were his characteristic attributes, how he impressed his contemporaries, and what mark he left on the events of his time. It is perhaps a rash thing for a Viceroy thus to pass in review his predecessors. But on the other hand who should be better qualified to do it, for who can know so well as he the difficulties and the trials, the disappointments and sorrows, no less than the opportunities and the compensations? Perhaps in the course of this examination my narrative may throw a light on some dark places ; while it will have been written in vain if it does not disclose to the British public how their principal servants in India have endured as well as wrought, have suffered as well as served.

Thus my book will be found to fall in the main into two parts. The first volume will perhaps have a more particular interest for those who know and have lived in Calcutta. The bulk of the second may appeal to a wider audience, since it may claim to be a side chapter of history that for the most part has not hitherto been written. Together they are my last tribute—the sole which it is now in my power to offer—to the memories of that great office and to the undying magic of India and its peoples.

CONTENTS OF VOLUME ONE

CONTENTS

CHAPTER VI

THE INDIAN HOUSES OF WARREN HASTINGS

CHAPTER VII

THE BLACK HOLE AND ITS MONUMENT

CHAPTER VIII

THE VICTORIA MEMORIAL HALL

CONTENTS

CHAPTER IX

FORMS, CEREMONIES, AND ENTERTAINMENTS

LIST OF ILLUSTRATIONS

INTRODUCTORY

I find by all you have been telling
That 'tis a house but not a dwelling.—Pope.

Mirari beatæ
Fumum et opes strepitumque Romæ.—Horace, *Ode* iii, 29.

THERE are few subjects more interesting than the history of a great house. The circumstances of its building, the alterations made in it by successive owners, the scenes which it has witnessed, the atmosphere which it exhales, combine to invest it in time with an almost human personality, that reacts forcibly upon its occupants, and may even affect the march of larger events. Sometimes a single individual will seem to have left an enduring imprint on the house. At others it sets a similar stamp upon those who have dwelt within its walls. In the case of a great family mansion, which has passed for generations from one scion to another of an ancient stock, the house becomes an epitome of the family history, and is the outward and material symbol of its continuity. We may trace in its architecture and furnishing the habits and tastes of successive generations. We may even, without being unduly fanciful, observe the influence that these features have exercised upon the characters of its inmates, imparting to them a sobriety or a liveliness of nature which in some cases at least appears to be the direct emanation of the dwelling itself. Great writers have not been slow to elaborate so promising a theme. Who can forget the House of Usher of Edgar Allan Poe, the Gabled House of Nathaniel Hawthorne, or the grim and fated mansions which Sheridan Le Fanu loved to depict?

But a great Government House or official residence possesses an interest different from and in some respects superior to these. What it may lack in continuity of occupation, or in genealogical interest or in mystery, it makes up for by the quick kaleidoscope of its story and the diversity of incident of which it can boast. And when the tenants follow each other at the interval of a few years only, coming *en masse* and going *en masse*, the scope for drama is immensely increased. The house has, so to speak, a new lease of life, and a fresh opportunity for adventure, with each recurrent wave every four or five years : and as one fugitive occupant after another disappears, it alone survives as a witness to their career or fortunes. They vanish in the generations of man almost as swiftly as a meteor in the sky. But their trail still lingers behind them in the places which they inhabited ; and the walls are left to tell with silent eloquence the tale.

I know of no building to which such reflections apply with greater force than Government House, Calcutta. Since it was built by Lord Wellesley at the beginning of the 19th century, until its final abandonment as the residence of the Viceroy in 1912, it was occupied by twenty-four Governors General of India, or an average of little more than four years each. Some of them were among the foremost men of their time. Within its walls grave decisions were taken, momentous scenes enacted, important movements born. When the house was built, the British Empire in India was like a little patchwork of crimson spots on the map of the Indian Continent. When it was abandoned, that colour had overspread and suffused the whole.

Where the two Hastings and Wellesley and Hardinge and Dalhousie had conquered and annexed, their later successors organised and made firm. But from the same Government House, and from the same desk in that house, all these men issued the orders that first created and then consolidated an Empire. As I sat at the table I could picture to myself the wide brow and aristocratic lineaments of Wellesley, the austere dignity, the frail but overpowering energy, the laborious application of Dalhousie, the patient and pathetic serenity of Canning, the imposing presence of Mayo, the courtly charm of Dufferin. Even when the lustres lit up the great Ball Room on the night of some splendid entertainment, I could see Lord and Lady Hastings advance with an excess of old-world ceremonial, or the form of John Lawrence, uncouth and careless, stride up the floor.

During the seven winters that I spent in Government House I came to know a good deal about those who had preceded me, partly because, the Government of India being a Government that does its work for the most part on paper, I was able, when I chose, and was often obliged, whether I chose or not, to read their printed views in Minutes or Despatches; partly because, of my own accord, I made a special study of their published Lives or Journals, as well as of the Memoirs and narratives of the time; so that in the end they ceased in my imagination to be a mere procession of solemn figures marching " after the high Roman fashion " across the stage, and became instead a company of fellow-workers and counsellors, who had done the same thing that I was trying to do, and who, from the stores of their experience or wisdom, offered to me invaluable advice or warning.

I realised also the close connection of Government House with the great city around it. Just as the Empire of India had grown out of the orders that emanated from its walls, so had the capital city, of which Government House was the hub, spread and grown in like proportion. Wellesley's Calcutta was a very different place from that which I knew. But whereas his Government House was a little too large and grandiose for the city of 1800, the latter in 1900 had grown up to and even outstripped its official centre, and found its counterpart in the prodigious and ever increasing expansion of the power that radiated from the seat of Indian Government over the Eastern world. The atmosphere of Calcutta, with its teeming population, its immense mercantile interests, and the breeze and buoyancy of its life, had a great and invigorating influence upon Government House. It was perpetually beckoning the Government of India from its bureaux, and the Viceroy from his study; and whereas Lord Wellesley's official activities were for the most part confined to Government House, scarcely a day passed in which the modern Viceroy was not called upon to perform some public or ceremonial duty in the city or its surroundings.

I grew to be very fond of Calcutta, and was almost as familiar with its features as I was with the records of Government House. I do not speak merely of the museums and galleries and public institutions, which were more or less under the official patronage of the Viceroy, and which he was called upon to visit: I speak of the place as a whole. There was hardly a squalid street or leafy lane in the suburbs which I did not penetrate in my afternoon drives in a mail phaeton with my wife, who loved the place as much as I. We knew the red dust of the rutty roads, the acrid smoke that hovered towards sundown over the festering *bustis*, the bowers of bamboo and plantain that overhung and blended with the green scum on the surface of the stagnant pools.

In the course of these wanderings we visited and explored nearly every house or enclosure that concealed behind its discoloured walls or in its often untidy compound any memorable legend of the past. Where Warren Hastings lived and loved, where he and Francis fought,[1] where the dances were given to which young men came down from the interior to pick up a newly arrived and not always a youthful bride from England, where Macaulay wrote, where Thackeray was born, where Rose Aylmer was buried—all these places were as familiar to us as the corridors of Government House. As some of the later chapters of this book will show, there was not a surviving relic of the still older Calcutta, the city of Old Fort William, of Clive and Holwell and the Black Hole, that I did not investigate and where possible renovate or conserve. Nor were we concerned with the residences or recollections of our countrymen only. Native life and habit and buildings were not less absorbing in their claim. One afternoon I can never forget, when alone in the crowded streets near Kalighat, our carriage was stopped by the effusive demonstrations of the native crowd, and we were escorted in triumph and on foot to the reeking shrine of the sanguinary Goddess.

Neither, even at this distance of time, is it possible to forget the solemn pageantry of the evening, as we returned by the river bank in the fading twilight, when, through a pall of mist and smoke, the tall masts and spars of the big sailing-ships made patterns in ink against the sky, when the newly lit street lamps twinkled like fireflies along the Strand, and amid the gathering gloom the crimson sun sank down to his grave in the black and rushing waters.

In the course of these peregrinations Old Calcutta became almost as familiar to me as New. I could picture the Agent and the Conscript Fathers of the earlier Factory walking in solemn procession to Church on Sunday, and the Governor General of a later date taking the same road in his State Coach and six. The streets became crowded with palanquins and the river alive with snake boats and barges. Famous figures, in cocked hats and white wigs and queues, started at

[1] For a hitherto unpublished account of the duel by Warren Hastings himself, see Chapter XII.

every turn to life.   The present seemed to recede and to be swallowed up in the past.   When I returned to Government House, it was peopled with ghosts who flitted down the passages and glimmered in the marble halls.   It is not surprising that in such surroundings and with such opportunities I should have prosecuted the researches, some of which are detailed in these Volumes, or that the study of Government House should have developed into the study of Calcutta, and both into a study of British Government in India and the men who wielded it.

Years later, as I pen these words, the recollections of that time are as fresh in my mind as though I had left them but yesterday ; and the writing of this book has been to me far less a labour than a relaxation.

BRITISH GOVERNMENT IN INDIA

CHAPTER I

EARLY GOVERNMENT HOUSES

Tantæ molis erat Romanam condere gentem.—VIRGIL, *Æneid*, I. 33.

THE Government House of Lord Wellesley was by no means the first residence from which the Government either of Bengal or of India was administered by Englishmen. It had a number of predecessors, whether these were the official headquarters of the Company or the residence of its official head ; and the attempt to discover and distinguish between them is one of the most prolific of the many sources of uncertainty in which the student of Old Calcutta is involved. We must first discriminate between the official rank and position of the persons to whom we refer.

From 1633 to 1682 the Bengal establishment of the East India Company was subordinate to the Government of Fort St. George, Madras, and the headquarters of its Agent were Balasore or Hugli. William Hedges (1682–4) was the first Governor not under Madras. His successor, however, John Beard senr., (1684–5) was again subordinated to Fort St. George, as were Job Charnock (1686–93), Francis Ellis (1693–4), Charles Eyre (1694–9) and John Beard junr. (1699–1700). Sir Edward Littleton, whose Commission was dated from 12th January, 1699, but who only assumed office in July, had the curious title of President or Chief for the Bay of Bengal, and Minister or Consul for the English Nation (English East India Company)—a position which he held until he was deposed by order of the Court in January 1707. But he only once visited Calcutta, and he was the only President for the separate affairs of the English East India Company.

Of the Governors resident at Calcutta, the first independent Governor after William Hedges was Charnock's son-in-law, Sir Charles Eyre, who was President and Governor of Fort William in Bengal (London

B   I

East India Company) from May 1700[1] to January 1701. He was followed by John Beard junr., whose Commission was from the older London East India Company, and who ruled 1701–5. His successor Anthony Weltden, and a line of twenty-one followers including Lord Clive, bring us down to Warren Hastings in 1772 —all of these having borne the official title of " President in the Bay and Governor and Commander-in-Chief of Fort William in Bengal, for the United East India Company." Hastings, who had held the post from 13th April, 1772, became in 1774 the first Governor General of Fort William in Bengal under the Regulating Act, passed in England in that year. He assumed the new office on the same day as his colleagues, including Philip Francis, namely 20th October, 1774. These are the functionaries, with their strange mixture of employers and titles, with whose official residences we have first to deal.

In the earlier days of British settlement at Calcutta or Sutanuti, *i.e.* Cotton mart, as the village was called where Charnock established himself for the third time on 24th August, 1690, to speak of a Government House would have been in the nature of a joke. Charnock himself, and his successor Ellis, lived in a thatched hut, near the river bank, probably not very distinguishable from the *bustis* in the native quarter of modern Calcutta. There he smoked and drank and did his huckstering with the natives, and lived with his native wife,[2] the unconscious forerunner and father of dominion. This domicile, which one would dearly have liked to see preserved in a museum—was accidentally burned down in December 1694 (Charnock had died 10th January, 1693), and its contents were sold by auction—then called ' outcry '—for Rs. 575. It is described as having been at a considerable distance from the Factory.

Such was the comfortless private abode of the founder of Calcutta. But for business purposes he had acquired the *pukka* (*i.e.* brick and mortar) *cutcherry* or office of the local *jagirdar*, belonging to the Mozumdar family, and there he lodged the Company's official staff and records. Whether this building was embraced in the perimeter of the Fort that was presently to follow, is not clear.

---

[1] The date of his appointment was 20th December, 1699—the interval representing the length of time required for the Commission to reach India.

[2] It seems to be more than doubtful whether Charnock ever married her according to the rites of any Christian Church. For in the register of St. Mary's Church, Madras, where his three daughters were baptised, no mention is made of their mother's name—a thing almost invariably done in the case of legitimate children.

The next step was taken when, seven months after the death of Charnock, who had left matters in considerable confusion, Sir John Goldsborough " Commissary General and Chief Governor of the English East India Company " came up from Madras to reorganise affairs. The Court of Directors had sanctioned the construction of a factory, as far back as February 1689, but how little had been done in that direction we have seen. Goldsborough now purchased a house for the Company, which was a poor structure of brick and mud, and ordered it to be surrounded by a wall, *i.e.* to be converted into a fort, as soon as permission could be obtained. Charles Eyre, whom he had appointed agent in place of the incompetent Ellis, moved into this abode, which may therefore I suppose be regarded as the first Government House of Calcutta. Its site is said to have been the strip of land north of the present Custom House, where the ' Long Row ' stood in the later Fort. But it had no lengthy existence, for in 1706 it was pulled down, having been badly injured by storms. A marble tablet, with an inscription indicating the site, has been affixed to the wall of the Custom House.[1]

The permission to fortify, which it had been impossible to obtain in 1693, was tacitly conceded by the Nawab of Bengal (in his own interest) in 1696, and Charles Eyre and John Beard junr., proceeded, though with considerable circumspection, to build the embryo of the subsequent Fort. Gradually the walls and bastions were raised, Beard himself residing on the site of the future North-west bastion overlooking the river. The position of the Fort was the space between Fairlie Place and Koila Ghat Street in modern Calcutta. On its Eastern side was Dalhousie Square (then and afterwards known as the Park or as Tank Square, while the Tank that still adorns its centre, though then of much smaller dimensions, was called the Great Tank or Lal Dighi, the Red Tank).[2] On the West the River Hugli, which laved the walls of the Fort, was at least 250 yards further inland than its present channel. The entire building occupied the ground now

[1] This is one of the numerous tablets, which, after careful investigation, I set up in this part of Calcutta, together with brass lines let into the ground or pavement, to indicate the outlines and principal contents of Old Fort William. With their aid the general features of the Fort—in so far as they are not obscured by modern buildings—can be clearly traced. A fuller account of them is given in a later chapter on the Black Hole Monument.

[2] This name does not appear, as frequently supposed, to have been derived from the reflection of the red brick masonry of the Fort in the water. For we read of Red Tanks elsewhere in Bengal, for instance at Chandernagore, and it may be that Lal in this context does not mean *red* at all. The Park seems also to have been known as Lal Bagh.

covered from North to South by the East Indian Railway Office, the Custom House, the Calcutta Collectorate, the Opium Godowns, and the General Post Office. By the end of 1699 the Court of Directors felt that matters had advanced sufficiently to justify them in declaring Bengal a Presidency, their Agent (Sir C. Eyre) President and Governor, and the embryo fortification Fort William, in honour of the King.

Locally however the progress was so slow that it was not till 1702 that Governor Beard was able to set about the building of an adequate Government House in the Southern part of the extended Fort, on a site South of Government House No. 1. But in 1704 only one storey had been roofed in, and Sir E. Littleton, calling in at Calcutta on his way up the river to discuss where he should reside, " thought that a house in the town would be more convenient to him, there being but few good rooms furnished in the Fort."

In 1706, however, the structure was at last completed, and was henceforward generally known as the Factory or the Governor's House. The Court of Directors asked for a plan of the building, which was sent to them. Only three years later Captain Alexander Hamilton—the much-travelled gossip, whose caustic comments on the Calcutta of this epoch are the foundation of much of the history and some of the legend that have ever since prevailed—visited Calcutta and described the edifice in the often quoted terms :

" The Governor's House in the Fort is the best and most regular piece of architecture that I ever saw in India."[1]

This laudatory description appears to have been not unmerited, if we may judge from the plan of Lieut. Wells in 1753, which is reproduced here, and also from the reconstruction that was possible when the foundations were unearthed in 1891, but still more from contemporaneous illustrations, two of which are also reproduced. The house occupied three sides of a rectangle, looking towards the East. But the main façade, 245 feet long, looked towards the river, with which it was connected by a colonnade, running down from the main entrance to the water gate and the *ghat* or landing-stage in the centre of the outer river wall.

This was the exit by which Governor Drake, Commandant Minchin and others made their ignoble flight on the morning of 19th June,

[1] "New Account of the East Indies," Vol. II, p. 9.   1844.

1757, on the day before the capture of the Fort and the tragedy of the Black Hole. The gate by which Siraj-ud-Dowlah effected his entry on the evening of the following day was the smaller river-gate further to the North, and near to the North-west bastion, behind which stood the great flagstaff of the Fort.

The Factory building itself was two storeys in height, all the main apartments being upon the upper floor. On entering by the main doorway on the riverside, you turned to the left and ascended by the great staircase to the central hall, from which the principal buildings, lit by very long windows, branched out on either side. On the Eastern face a raised verandah or arcade ran round the three sides of the interior quadrangle. The Governor's apartments were situated in the South-east wing, but were of no great size, and in the later years, before 1756, were rarely occupied by him, being in all probability used as offices alone. On one of these wings appears to have stood a square tower at the four corners of the roof of which life-size statues are depicted (I think fancifully) in one of the engravings.

The two illustrations of the building here reproduced date respectively from 1736 and some date between 1737 and 1754. In the former, which was engraved by George Van der Gucht from a painting (now in the India Office) by Messrs. George Lambert and Samuel Scott,[1] the tall spire of St. Anne's Church is seen still standing in the background ; and the Factory House itself looks very smart, having been repaired during the three preceding years (1732–5) at a cost of Rs. 53,000.

In the second picture, which was drawn by J. Van Ryne and published in London in 1754, we see the squat cupola that replaced the tall church spire after the latter had collapsed in the cyclone of 1737. A reduced and emasculated version of the second engraving appeared in the " Universal Magazine," and was reproduced by Rev. J. Long in his article in the " Calcutta Review " of December 1852. A Mr. Grose was the last visitor who has left a published reference to this Government House before its destruction. In 1750 he thus

[1] George Lambert (1710–65) was the first President of the Society of Arts, founder of the Beefsteak Club, and for many years principal scene-painter at Covent Garden Theatre. Samuel Scott (1710–72) was a marine painter of some eminence. These two artists were commissioned by the East India Company to paint a series of pictures of the most important settlements of the Company in the East Indies and on the way thither. But it does not appear that they ever visited the Indies, so that their pictures, although based on reliable data, are not of first-hand value. The entire series was engraved by G. Van der Gucht (1696–1776).

described it : " The Governor's House was within the Fort and was a handsome regular structure." [1]

It was on the grass outside the Eastern verandah of this house that Holwell and the survivors of the Black Hole were brought out and laid down on the morning of 21st June, 1756, and it was in the inner hall that the interview took place between the Nawab and Holwell, who was given " a large folio volume " to sit upon, and was interrogated about the treasure of which the Nawab had been disappointed to find so little in the Fort.

This is the last picture that we have of the old ' Factory.' When Clive and Watson recaptured Calcutta in the following year, the interior of the Fort and the Fort itself had undergone a complete change. There is nothing to show that the Governor's House was ever reoccupied, or that it admitted either of repair or re-occupation. We know that the space under the East curtain wall between the main gate and the Black Hole was converted into a temporary church, that for a few years soldiers were quartered in some of the other buildings, and that in 1767 the rest of the interior was converted into a Custom House. But of the old ' Factory ' there is no mention, and in the next map of Calcutta that we possess, that executed by Colonel Mark Wood in 1784–5, it has completely disappeared, and the interior of the Fort is a jumble of buildings that bear no resemblance to the original plan.

I have already referred to the repairs that were undertaken in this Government House at an earlier date in 1732–5. During that time the Governor, John Stackhouse, lived in a hired house for which the Company paid a rent of Rs. 2,400 a year. It may have been the experience of a less stuffy atmosphere than the interior of a walled enclosure on the side removed from the river that indisposed him or his successors to return to the Fort. Indeed it is possible that the leased house may have been purchased at this date. Anyhow, a new residence was acquired for the Governor before 1742,[2] and henceforward he seems to have resided in a large three-storeyed house, marked on the contemporary maps as the Company's House, which

---

[1] " Voyage to the East Indies," Vol. II, p. 237 (2nd Edition), 1772.

[2] This date is fixed by the existence of a plan of Calcutta in the year 1742, which was added to at a later date, to illustrate the attack upon Calcutta on 18th June, 1756, and was afterwards published in a corner of Thuillier's map of Calcutta, 1852–6. " The Governor's House " is plainly marked upon it in the position described in the text, as it is also in the plans of 1753 and 1756.

OLD FORT WILLIAM, FROM THE RIVER (1736)

stood outside the old Fort to the South of it on the river bank, in a detached and airy position. The illustrations already referred to show this house to have been surrounded by a large compound, and connected by an avenue of trees with its own *ghat*. On the land side an unoccupied space of ground separated it from the Park and the Tank (Dalhousie Square), so that it stood in a position of almost unique advantage, very suitable for the official head of the Settlement. A neat gateway, as may be seen from the engravings, led from the ground into the Park, and it was from hence that the Governor is described as having walked to the Church, which stood at the Western end of Writer's Buildings, the Company having sent out in 1728 to say that if the Governor wanted a Chaise and pair, he must pay for them himself.

This house, which we will call Government House No. 3, was presumably the residence of Governor Roger Drake before the fall of Calcutta. In February of that year (1756) orders were issued to strengthen it by building a verandah round it. A few months later, it played a certain part in the defence and capture of the Fort. On the afternoon of 18th June, it was occupied as an outpost by a small force of the Company's troops, in order to prevent an attack from that quarter; but these were dislodged about 8 p.m. by a strong fire from the enemy, who had established themselves in the house next to it on the South. What happened to it on the return of the English in 1757 is not clear, and whether Clive resided there during his first term of office is more than doubtful. Others have suggested that he lived in "Mr. Eyre's house," close to the Old Fort, on the site now occupied by Messrs. Finlay Muir and Co.'s offices.

On 26th August, 1767, we find the Civil Architect sending a letter to the Board to the effect that "he has surveyed the whole of the Government House, which he finds in so decayed and ruinous a condition as to require an immediate and thorough repair." If the reference is to the house which I have called Government House No. 3, I do not think the repairs were ever undertaken; and soon after the grounds were converted into a Bankshall or Marine Yard, which gave its name to the surrounding street or streets. Col. Mark Wood's plan of 1784-5 shows a 'New Wharf' depicted at the Northern, and a 'New Dock' at the Southern extremity of its river front, although the latter, constructed for the repair of pilot vessels, is commonly said not to have been built till 1790.

Anyhow it soon fell out of use, and was filled up in 1808. The modern representative of the dock, though far in the bed of the old river, is the present Police *ghat*. The site of the old ' Governor's House ' is divided between the Military Account Offices and one of the Opium Godowns.

The Governorship of Henry Vansittart (1760–4), between Clive's first and second administrations, provides us with our next enigma. In December 1759 the house of one M. Carvalho was purchased for Lt. Col. Eyre Coote (afterwards Sir Eyre Coote). In January 1761 Vansittart took possession of this house (it may have been because of the dilapidated condition of the Governor's House on the river) [1] ; but where it was, or what became of it afterwards, there is nothing to show ; although it does not require a very vivid imagination to conjecture that it must have been situated in the little *cul-de-sac* running Southwards out of Dalhousie Square, nearly opposite the Dalhousie Institute, which is still known as Vansittart Row. As however I know no more about it, I can hardly describe this as Government House No. 4.

Wherever the house, the Governor does not seem to have been content with it—or in any case the fashion of ' Garden Houses ' or country retreats a little way out of Calcutta as a relief from the pestilential smells and abominable unhealthiness of the already congested town was fast setting in—for about the same time a Garden House was bought by the Company for the use of the Governor. This house was the property of William Frankland, one of the Members of Council who had escaped from the Fort on 8th June, 1756, on the pretext of escorting the women to the river,[2] and it was bought for Arcot Rs. 10,000. The Court of Directors, however, in the less

---

[1] Another possible theory is that the house on the river was demolished after the recovery of Calcutta and that it is of Vansittart's house that the Civil Architect reported so unfavourably in 1767. Miss Blechynden (" Calcutta Past and Present ") thinks that the Governor's house on the river was identical with Mr. Drake's house which the Council reported on 21st December, 1758, that they had " purchased for the sum of Rs. 12,000 to be used as an import warehouse, when the old Fort was clearing out to be converted into barracks for the military." But it is difficult to see how this house could belong to Mr. Drake, when it had been described on maps since 1742 as the Company's House, and the Governor's House, thereby clearly implying that it was the property of the former and the official residence of the latter. I think therefore that Mr. Drake's house must have been his private property and have stood elsewhere. He had been deposed on 20th June, 1758 ; so that it was not unnatural that he should be parting with his property on leaving India.

[2] He was the son of a former Governor (1726–8) and a great-grandson of Oliver Cromwell.

OLD FORT WILLIAM, FROM THE RIVER (1754)

trying temperature of Leadenhall Street, had no bowels of compassion, and when they heard of the transaction they replied on 19th February, 1762, in the most acid vein :

" Most certainly the purchasing of Mr. Frankland's house, for, as you mention, the refreshment of the Governor when the multiplicity of business will permit him to leave the town, at the expense of the Company's Rs. 10,000 is, notwithstanding your allegations to the contrary, a superfluous charge, and must, as in reason it ought, be borne by the Governor at his own private expense ; this is the more necessary and reasonable since the noble appointments settled upon the Governor by our directions last season, which are intended to take in all the expenses he may be put to on the Company's account."

In these circumstances the baffled Vansittart had no alternative, if he desired his country breezes, but to buy the house himself—which he did. In the year following we come across him again presiding as Governor at the Council meeting on 9th June, 1763, when Stanlake Batson struck Warren Hastings in the face. At the end of 1764 he left India and became Member of Parliament for Reading and a Director of the Company. Five years later he met a watery grave, the frigate " Aurora " in which he had sailed from England in September 1769, as one of the three Commissioners sent out by the Court to enquire into the administration of the Company, having gone down with all hands in the Indian Ocean. In the next generation his son became Chancellor of the Exchequer in Lord Liverpool's phenomenal administration and was created Lord Bexley in 1823. Vansittart's purchase was the house well known a little later on as the residence of Sir Elijah Impey between the years 1774 and 1782, and of Bishop Heber for a few months in 1824. In those days it was surrounded by a large deer park (hence the name Park St.), which covered the space between that street and Chowringhi. Now it is the Loretto Convent in Middleton Row ; but a tablet upon its walls recalls its diversified history—an epitome of the strange and abrupt vicissitudes with which Indian life too soon makes us familiar.[1]

With the mystery of the houses occupied by the Governors of this transitional epoch is bound up the great name of Clive. His two periods of office were from 27th June, 1758, to 28th January,

---

[1] There is in my opinion no ground for the statement which has been made in some quarters that this Garden House was ever known as Belvedere.

1760, and from 3rd May, 1765, to 29th January, 1767. Where did he live in each?

If any Government House had survived the siege and its sequel, it is of course possible that Clive may have inhabited it. Miss Blechynden (pp. 69–71) quotes from a private diary, dated October 1795, as indicating that when he first arrived in Calcutta in January 1757, he may have occupied the house behind St. Anne's Church described as Mr. Eyre's in the maps of 1742 and 1753. Perhaps this was so. But Eyre's house was pulled down in the course of the same year; and it is now, I believe, regarded as certain that during his first term of office Clive occupied a house belonging to Huzuri Mull,[1] which after he had left for England was in 1761 rented as a Custom House; and a marble tablet has, I am informed, been placed upon the building to this effect.

When he came back for a second term, tradition points strongly to his residence in the house in Clive St. (which is said thereby to have acquired its name) afterwards rented by Philip Francis in 1776 at the enormous figure of £100 per month, because it was "the best house in the town," and occupied fifty years ago by the Oriental Bank, and later by the Royal Exchange, which itself disappeared in 1915. Other authorities however claim that Clive's residence was No. 9 Clive Street, now occupied by Messrs. Graham and Co. From these indications it has been generally supposed that in the interval after the recovery of Calcutta there was no official Government House, and that individual Governors established themselves where they pleased.

From a phrase however that occurs in a Minute by Warren Hastings, which I shall quote presently, I do not think that this was the case. Referring to the buildings on the Esplanade, known as the New Council House, to which I shall next turn, and which he himself occupied for a few years as Governor, he says that it was "the habitation of former Governors," from which it is not possible to draw any other conclusion than that it was occupied by Clive, Verelst, and Cartier.

Before leaving the subject of Clive and Garden Houses, it seems opportune here to notice that Dum Dum was the place where he is

---

[1] Huzuri Mull, the friend and executor of the famous Omichund (Amin Chand), was a native of enormous wealth in the time of Holwell, Clive and Hastings. He possessed great property and was the donor of many benefactions.

said to have courted the country air and repose. Nearly sixty years later, in November 1824, Bishop Heber thus described a visit to the spot :

" The Commandant [1] General Hardwicke, with whom we spent the day, resides in a large house, built on an artificial mound of considerable height above the neighbouring country, and surrounded by very pretty walks and shrubberies. The house has a venerable appearance, and its lower storey, as well as the mound on which it stands, is said to be of some antiquity, at least for Bengal, where so many powerful agents of destruction are always at work that no architecture can be durable—and though ruins of buildings of apparently remote date are extremely common, it would perhaps be difficult to find a single edifice 150 years old. The building is of brick, with small windows and enormous buttresses. The upper storey, which is of the style usual in Calcutta, was added by Lord Clive, who also laid out the gardens and made this his country-house." [2]

The building was probably an old Dutch or Portuguese factory, erected on the site of an older *kila* or block-house.[3] Clive's walks and shrubberies, laid out in the formal Dutch style, have now disappeared. But the house would appear to have been added to by Clive, less as a retreat for himself than as a Sanitarium or convalescent home for the servants of the Company after illness. In recent years it has been the headquarters of the local Volunteers.

We are now approaching in our survey the period when, as European Calcutta spread further Southwards, and the paddy fields and fever-haunted jungles of Govindpur gave place to the lawnlike stretch of the Maidan, houses both official and private were built on the site, then as now known as the Esplanade, although the name is now confined to the broad road that runs East and West from Chowringhi to the river, whereas 150 years ago it covered the whole expanse that stretched right up to the glacis of the new Fort William—an area then unbroken by a single enclosure or even by a single tree. The fourth and fifth Government Houses—to whose history, also not devoid of some mystery, I now turn—stood upon the Northern fringe of this expanse, and were almost exactly upon the site of the later palace of Lord Wellesley, by which it was succeeded and replaced.

---

[1] *I.e.* of the Bengal Artillery.
[2] " Narrative of a Journey in India," Vol. I, p. 44.
[3] Miss Blechynden (p. 235) says that R. C. Sterndale, "who once occupied the house," thought that the *kila* had probably been the stronghold of robbers, who formerly plied their boats on the Great Salt Water Lake that then ran up as far as Dum Dum.

On this expanse the plans of 1785 and 1792 and contemporary descriptions show two buildings of very similar style, standing in a considerable enclosure facing the Esplanade. The more Westerly building was the new Council House, which was erected in 1764–5 to take the place of a temporary Council Chamber that had been used after the recovery of Calcutta, but had proved unsuitable for the purpose. It has hitherto escaped notice that this new Council House on the Maidan, as depicted in the drawings of Baillie and Daniell,[1] was a very close reproduction of the destroyed Factory in Old Fort William, or Government House No. 2. It stood upon the property of the Company,[2] and was built by their architect— whence no doubt the design. It was a handsome edifice occupying three sides of a quadrangle, facing the esplanade, but separated from it by a low wall, surmounted with an iron railing, and it stood in what is now the South-western corner of Government House compound, immediately abutting on Council House Street, to which it seems likely that it gave its name. Though erected for a Council House and though dedicated to that use exclusively from the years 1775 to 1800, this building, in the absence of any official residence for the Governor, was employed by him for that purpose in the years between 1772 and 1775. We have Warren Hastings' statement (16th June, 1779) that it was also so inhabited by his predecessors, and in a Minute dated 9th February, 1775, we have the fuller statement of his own occupation. He says :

" On his accession to the Government (*i.e.* in 1772) he was accommodated in the present Council House, which was entirely occupied by him for a dwelling, and the offices of Government were then kept in the old Council House, since fallen to ruins . . . At last the Governor General for the convenience of public business gave up his house, the present Council House, to the offices, and rented for himself the house where he now resides belonging to Mahomed Reza Khan."

The Council House on the Esplanade must therefore take its place as Government House No. 4, a fact that has not been realised in any previous publication. For its history in the capacity of a Council Chamber, reference must be made to the next chapter.

---

[1] *Vide* the illustration in Chapter II.

[2] Lord Wellesley said at a later date that it was the only ground possessed by the Company in Calcutta—a remark which could certainly not have been made at the date of its original acquisition.

I now turn to the larger building immediately adjoining the Council House on the East, which was leased by the Company from Mohammed Reza Khan[1] at a rent of 1,000 Rs. per month. That this rent was subsequently more than once enhanced we learn from a letter written by Chaplain William Johnson in 1785, in which it is stated that the Governor General paid Rs. 1,500 p.m. or Rs. 18,000 p.a. for the house : and, later, from the defence put forward many years after by Lord Wellesley to the censure passed upon him by the Court of Directors for having bought the ground and demolished the house upon it, in order to make way for his own magnificent creation. From this it appears that in 1798 Mohammed Reza Khan had died, and the owner was his son Nawab Dilawar Jung, and that the rent at that time paid for the building by Government was Sicca Rs. 1,624 per month, or £2,437 per annum. What Lord Wellesley thought of the house I shall state later on. It will be better for the moment to discuss earlier references.

The ground plan of this house shows a building covering three sides of a quadrangle (very similar indeed in shape to the Council House adjoining). Its external appearance was that of a considerable two-storeyed mansion, the rooms of which were protected on the Southern side from the sun by an arched verandah on the ground floor and a closed verandah above. From either side of it there projected towards the Esplanade two long one-storeyed wings or arms, presumably containing offices or quarters of the staff, and enclosing between them a courtyard of fair size, shut off from the Maidan by a low wall with pillars and railings upon it, and pierced by two tall pillared gateways.

The flat roof of the mansion had a white plastered balustrade with urns on the sky-line, and a single projecting room, probably a sleeping chamber, in a tower or belvedere, with a sloping roof. Between this house and the Council House next door was a garden thickly planted with trees. Closely adjoining it upon the East was another considerable house (both in the ground

---

[1] Mohammed Reza Khan was the wealthy and powerful native of Murshidabad, under whom the English, after their assumption of the Diwani of Bengal and Orissa in 1765, had placed the revenue and criminal administration of the Presidency. In 1770 he was arrested with his family and brought to Calcutta by Warren Hastings (owing to the intrigues of Nuncomar) on suspicion of having embezzled vast sums of money, but was reinstated as the result of the enquiry. Thenceforward he and his son after him resided at Chitpore, and were known as the Chitpore Nabobs, dispensing a profuse hospitality and exercising considerable influence.

plans and in the illustrations) which will presently reappear in my narrative.

When exactly this house, which is now about to take its place as Government House No. 5, was built (presumably by the Nawab) for its illustrious official tenant, we do not know. Many years afterwards the well-known J. S. Marshman of Serampore, writing an anonymous article in the " Calcutta Review " of June 1845,[1] stated (p. 439) that

" After the capture of Calcutta, a new residence was erected for the President, on the spot where the present Government House now (1845) stands ; and it was there that he was in the habit of entertaining his guests at dinner in the month of May at one in the afternoon without punkahs and placing a little hookah on the table before each individual, when the cloth was removed."

Whether this reference was to the Council House or to the Nawab's house is not clear. In any case the latter was already the official residence of John Cartier (1769–72), the immediate predecessor of Warren Hastings, as the following passage will show.

Relations between the English at Calcutta and the Dutch at Chinsura were at this time of a very friendly description, and in 1770 the Dutch Director went down the river to pay a State visit to the newly appointed British Governor. He took with him the Dutch naval officer, afterwards an Admiral, who called himself J. S. Stavorinus ; and the latter, to whose close observation we owe many valuable side-lights on the Calcutta of the period, recorded the visit in terms which I will quote in full :

" At four o'clock upon the following morning, upon the turning of the tide, we again proceeded downwards, and at seven we came to Chitpur, situated about a Dutch mile above Calcutta, where we stopped for the Deputies from the English Council, who were to come to receive the Director and his Company. Half an hour afterwards they arrived, and paid a visit of welcome to the Director in his budgerow. The chief of them was the second in command at Calcutta, Mr. Russel.

" After a stay of about a quarter of an hour, they conducted the Director on shore ; and followed by the rest of the Company, they entered a handsome summer-house, close to the river, which belonged to Mr. Russel.

" We found breakfast prepared for us here, and after stopping about an hour, we left this place, in five coaches sent by the Governor for that purpose. Six of his lifeguards on horseback, dressed in blue, with gold lace, rode by the side

---

[1] Entitled " Notes on the Left or Calcutta Bank of the Hooghly."

of the coach in which the Director was.   At ten o'clock we were set down in Calcutta at the house prepared for the reception of the Director V.[1]   It was a very handsome building, provided with many and roomy apartments, all furnished in the European style, and hung with damasked silk.   It was the property of the little nabob, or minister, Mahomed Rezachan, who had purchased it of an English gentleman for Rs. 120,000, and always resided in it when he was at Calcutta ; but as he was not now in the place, the English Government had made use of it.   On the area before it stood a company of eighty sepoys, under arms, commanded by the European officer, as a guard, in honour of our Director ; which continued to do duty as such all the while he remained in Calcutta.

"When the Director alighted before the house, a salute of nineteen guns was fired from Fort William.

"As soon as we had entered the house, the Director despatched one of his chubdars with a message to the English Governor, who resided in the Government House, next to that in which we were, to enquire if it were convenient for His Excellency for us to wait upon him in a body.   Soon after, however, accompanied by all the Members of the Council of Calcutta, the Governor came over in person to welcome the Director.   After the first complimentary ceremonies were over, Mr. V. said that the object of this national visit was to congratulate Mr. Cartier upon his accession to the Governorship, adding as a particular compliment, that he hoped Mr. Cartier would so well manage affairs as to be able to return to Europe in a few years ; to which that gentleman replied with a smile, and expressed his thanks by an amicable interchange of civilities.

"These compliments were made and returned by the Director in French, and by the Governor in English, the latter not understanding French, nor the former English, while Mr. Russel performed the office of interpreter.   This visit of ceremony lasted more than an hour.   The Governor then departed with the gentlemen of the Council.   Half an hour afterwards, the Director V. went with us to pay a visit of ceremony in return to the Governor, which lasted about three-quarters of an hour; at the conclusion of which he conducted us out, accompanying us to the steps; in the same way as the Director had done upon receiving his visit just before.

"About half-past twelve o'clock, having been formally invited to dinner by the Governor, we went again to the Government House.

"Here we found, in a large and airy saloon, a table of sixty or seventy covers. The service was entirely of plate.   The Director was seated at the upper end on the right hand of the Governor, having on the other side the General of the English land-forces, being the third person in the Council of Calcutta, or rather the second, exclusive of the Governor.   The other gentlemen in company were

[1] This was George Louis Vernet, Dutch Director at Chinsura, who built the Dutch (now the English) Church there in 1767—as commemorated in a medallion over the entrance door—and who had shown much friendliness to the English, when second of the Dutch Factory at Calcapore, in the fateful days of 1756.

placed promiscuously at table. Full half of the guests were officers of the troops, for whom the Governor keeps every day open house.

"When the cloth was taken away a *hooka*, which is a glass filled with water, through which the smoke of tobacco is drawn, and of which I shall speak further, was set before every one of the company, and after having smoked for half an hour, we all rose from table, and separated each to his respective dwelling." ·

Now to what conclusions are we led by this interesting account? The Dutch are taken to a handsome house, formerly belonging to an Englishman, but then the property of Mohammed Reza Khan; it is next door to Government House (but as the Council House adjoined the latter on the West, it can only have been the large house shown in Baillie's and Daniell's drawings on the Eastern side, standing within the present compound of Government House at the corner of that end of Old Court House Street, which is now called Government Place); the English Governor is residing in the Government House, and it is sufficiently large to admit of an official dinner of sixty to seventy covers. All of these are significant statements, the real application of which it is impossible to misunderstand.

Three years later, on 19th October, 1774, Philip Francis and his fellow Councillors from England, General Clavering and Colonel Monson, together with the new Judges of the Supreme Court, landed at Chandpal Ghat, in circumstances of which Macaulay has written in terms of some rhetorical exaggeration:

" The members of Council expected a salute of 21 guns from the batteries of Fort William. Hastings allowed them only 17. They landed in ill-humour. The first civilities were exchanged with cold reserve. On the morrow commenced that long quarrel which after distracting British India was renewed in England, and in which all the more eminent statesmen and orators of the age took active part on one side or the other."

Here we are only concerned, not with the larger consequences, but with the incidents of the day, left on record by the pen of Francis' brother-in-law and companion, Alexander Mackrabie:

" The procession to the Governor's House beggars all description, the heat, the confusion, not an attempt at regularity, no guards, no person to receive or to show the way, no state. But surely Mr. Hastings might have put on a ruffled shirt.

---

[1] " Voyages to the East Indies." By J. S. Stavorinus. Vol. I, pp. 142–44.

"The ceremony of introduction gone through, the audience broke up, and we changed the scene though not the climate. At two the whole party, increased by this time to 150, met again at the Governor's house to dine."

Now from the fact that Hastings, in his explanatory letter to the Court of Directors of 3rd Deccember, 1774, more than once referred to the place of reception as "my own house and not the Council house," it has been, perhaps not unnaturally, inferred that he received and entertained his affronted colleagues at a private residence, owned or rented by him, in some part of Calcutta, and this house has been identified by some writers with Belvedere,[1] by others with a house said to have belonged to Hastings in Esplanade Row—of which more anon—and by others with the house known later on as Mrs. Hastings' house in Hastings Street. To me, I confess it would have appeared in any case most unlikely that Hastings should, even if he possessed a private house, have had one large enough to entertain 150 persons at dinner, or that being in official residence as Governor at Government House, a building capable, as we have seen of accommodating a large party, he should have stepped out of it, on a purely official occasion, in order to receive his official guests elsewhere. It would seem far more natural to suppose that the entertainment was held, where all such functions were held—*viz.* in the official residence of the Governor. Further, the fact that he called it " his house " was not intended to imply ownership as distinct from occupation, as is shown by his not infrequent use of the term in direct reference to the official residence of the Governor General. That the entertainment to Francis and his colleagues was given in the rented Government House I entertain therefore not a shadow of doubt and this question may, I think, be regarded as settled. Viewing the incident, however, in its wider aspect I entirely share the view of Lord Thurlow that it was the greatest misfortune both to India and to England that the vessel that carried out the three Councillors, had not gone to the bottom.[2]

Our next witness is the vivacious Mrs. Fay, who came to Calcutta in 1780, and wrote as follows :

" Esplanade Row, as it is called, which fronts the Fort seems to be composed of palaces, the whole range, except what is taken up by the Government and Council Houses, is occupied by the principal gentlemen in the settlement."

[1] Busteed, " Echoes from Old Calcutta " (4th Edition), 1908, p. 67.
[2] " Creevey Papers," Vol. I, p. 61.

C

In March 1781, William Hodges, R.A. who was a friend of Warren Hastings and painted pictures for him, arrived in Calcutta and—publishing his book later in 1793—thus wrote—

" For its magnificence Calcutta is indebted solely to the liberal and excellent taste of the late Governor General (*i.e.* Warren Hastings) and it must be confessed that the first house was raised by Mr. Hastings which deserves the name of a piece of architecture ; in fact it is even in a purer style than any that has been built since, although it is on a smaller scale than many others."[1]

It has always been supposed that the reference here is to one or other of the Government Houses which were occupied by Hastings in Calcutta.   But as he built none of them himself, nor, as I shall show in my chapter on his Indian residences, any other house in the town or its suburbs, except Hastings House in Alipore, I have no doubt in my own mind that it is not to any Calcutta house but to the latter that Hodges refers.

Our next witness is the Frenchman M. de Grandpré, who, coming to Calcutta in 1789, while Lord Cornwallis was Governor General, thus wrote of the residence of the latter :

" The Governor General of the English Settlements East of the Cape of Good Hope resides at Calcutta. . . . As there is no palace yet built for him, he lives in a house on the Esplanade, opposite the citadel.   The house is handsome, but by no means equal to what it ought to be for a personage of so much importance.   Many private individuals in the town have houses as good ; and if the Governor were disposed to any extraordinary luxury, he must curb his inclination for want of the necessary accommodation of room.   The house of the Governor of Pondicherry is much more magnificent."[2]

As it has never been suggested that Lord Cornwallis owned or lived in any other house than this Government House, except it be the Government House in the Fort which I shall next describe, it cannot be doubted that the allusion is to the building on the Esplanade ; and I think indeed that I have now sufficiently established that the whole of the references which I have quoted above (except that of Hodges) relate to the same edifice, which was apparently known in Calcutta as Buckingham House, presumably because Buckingham House in London was at that time the Royal residence, but which I have denominated Government House No. 5.

---

[1] " Travels in India during the years 1780-1-2-3."   By W. Hodges, R.A., 1793.
[2] There is in existence at Calcutta a mortgage deed dated 18th May, 1789, in which this house is described as " in the tenure or occupation of the Rt. Hon. Charles Earl Cornwallis, Governor General.'

That this building, though it served as a Government House for a quarter of a century, was, in face of the great increase both in the official and unofficial community of Calcutta, very ill adapted for its purpose is more than probable. But it is amusing to read the lurid colours in which its failings were depicted by the imperious Proconsul who was destined to destroy it, in the justification of his conduct which he offered after his return to England in 1806. Lord Wellesley submitted :

"*First*.—That the apartments contained in the building occupied by the Governor General and denominated Government House, both with respect to their construction and accommodation, were inferior to the apartments in the ordinary houses of individuals, exposing the health of the Governor General to the most serious injury from the effects of the climate.

"*Second*.—That the building did not furnish any accommodation for the family[1] of the Governor General, or for the public officers immediately attached to his person.

"*Third*.—That the building did not contain any apartments suited to occasions of public ceremony, or for the reception of the augmented number of the inhabitants of the capital of the British possessions in India, reducing the Governor General to the necessity of hiring buildings conducted by individuals for places of entertainment, whenever public or other occasions required that he should assemble the principal officers and inhabitants of the settlement.[2]

"*Fourth*.—That from the decayed state of the building, the sum of Sicca Rs. 79,000 or £9,875 was requisite for putting it in a state of suitable repair ; that the proprietor could not, with justice, have been required to defray this charge in addition to the heavy expenses which he had recently incurred for repairs and alterations, and consequently that the expense of the further repairs required must have been made at the charge of the Government.

"*Fifth*.—That the amount of the rent paid for the building being Sicca Rs. 1,625 or £213 per month far exceeded the value of the building."

The fiat of the autocratic little man having gone forth, Government House No. 5 disappeared from the scene in 1798, and its site was entirely swallowed up in the magnificent creation of its destroyer.[3]

---

[1] The term "family" did not mean the relatives, but the staff of the Governor.

[2] Although the house had sufficed, as we have seen, in earlier days for dinner parties of 80–150, Lord Wellesley's account of the situation as it existed with the greatly augmented society at the end of the century, was perfectly true ; and we read of Lord Cornwallis and Sir John Shore as giving their public breakfasts and balls in the Old Court House—until it was pulled down in 1792—and later in the ballroom attached to the theatre at the North-west corner of Lyons' Range, now the premises of Finlay Muir & Co.

[3] Rev. J. Long writing in 1852 said, "The remains of its bathroom may be seen in the South-west corner of Government House compound near the Treasury." Whatever these remains may have been, they were certainly not the bathroom of this Government House ; for, as I have shown, the Council House occupied this part of the enclosure, and the old Government House was much more to the East.

It will have been noticed that the question has more than once been raised in this narrative as to the house or houses in Calcutta which Warren Hastings may have owned or rented during his tenure of office. He undoubtedly had a considerable taste for buying and selling real estate, and the question as to what residences he occupied at different times, whether as Governor, as Governor General or as a private individual, is one of the most puzzling that confronts the student of Old Calcutta.   As this will involve a rather minute examination of evidence and is somewhat apart from the question of official residences, or Government Houses, I will postpone it for separate treatment in a later chapter of this volume.

Here, however, confining myself to the purely official aspect of my enquiry, I must revert to a yet further series of proceedings by that remarkable man.   In an earlier part of this chapter I have referred to the purchase of a Garden House for Governor Vansittart, as having been disallowed by the Court of Directors, who compelled the unfortunate Governor to refund the money himself. A little later Governor Cartier, who entertained the Dutch Director at Buckingham House in 1770 took him a ride to his country seat at Belvedere. But this house also, it is clear, was only the private residence or Garden House of Cartier,[1] who followed the uniform practice of having what would now be described as a week-end resort out of town. It was reserved for Warren Hastings to convert this into an official tenure. In the interval the Company had relented, and in a Minute dated 9th February, 1775, the Governor General wrote as follows :

" On receipt of the instructions of the 29th March, 1774, which also allotted one of the Company's country houses for the use of the Governor-General, the Company possessed none such. These houses had all been disposed of at a public sale about the year before, for reasons which appear on the Minutes of the Board of Inspection. The Governor General, however, willing to avail himself of an indulgence, which, in the manner it was bestowed, he regarded as a particular mark of favour, endeavoured to procure a country house for his use which would be suitable to his convenience and to the dignity of the first officer of the Company's Government in India. For this reason he purchased the house occupied by his predecessors, Mr. Verelst and Mr. Cartier called ' Belvidere,' for the sum of Sicca Rs. 60,000, and is in actual possession of it.   But he does not wish to bring the Company under any engagements

---

[1] When he made over charge to Hastings in 1772, he retired to another Garden House, known as Elysium, in Garden Reach.   In that neighbourhood, also, at a later date, Sir John Macpherson, when Acting Governor General, had a Garden House.

respecting it till their positive directions on the subject shall be received ; and in the meantime he proposes that the Board should only allow him a yearly rent for this house, equal to the common interest (10 per cent.) of the purchase money."

The Board agreed to this proposal, and accordingly Belvedere, which was afterwards the Government House of the Lieutenant Governor of Bengal and is now retained for the Viceroy's annual visit to Caleutta, became for the first time an official residence of the Governor General. During the short-lived conflict with Clavering and Francis in 1777, one of the letters of Hastings to Barwell (dated 24th June) is written from Belvedere. Inasmuch, however, as the Board only allowed him a rent for the house, and as he subsequently in 1780 sold it himself, it is clear that it actually remained his property, and that the Company did not take it off his hands.

I have already described the circumstances in which Warren Hastings, after evacuating the Council House, was forced to rent the adjoining house (Government House No. 5) from the Nawab. Resenting, however, both the inadequacy of the building and the necessity of living in leased quarters, he again addressed the Board in a Minute dated 16th June, 1779, in which, after dwelling upon the inconveniences which he had experienced from residing in a " house which is much too small for the accommodation of my family and for transacting my business " he continued :

" When the Company were pleased to allow me the use of a house in town and another in the country, they doubtless intended that they should be in every respect suitable to the station of their Chief Magistrate. I have put them to no greater expense in these articles than rupees 1,500 per month.[1] The inconveniences which I have hitherto suffered in so circumscribed a habitation as my house in town are now becoming intolerable by the increase of my family and the necessity of their residing at Calcutta during the rainy season. I believe the Board will rather be surprised that I have so long endured these inconveniences than that I now apply to them for relief ; and in this opinion I am now induced to propose, that the house, the property of the estate of the late Colonel Fortnom, be taken for the Company on a lease of one year to commence from the 1st of July at the rent of sicca rupees 1,200 per month for the accommodation of the Governor-General or such other purpose as may hereafter be thought proper, if it should not suit the person who may in future fill that office."

[1] *I.e.* £2,250 per annum.

The Company accepted this proposal, and the property so bought was that in Hastings Street, now a part of the business premises of Messrs. Burn & Co., which was afterwards known as Mrs. Hastings' house, where after his marriage with her in August 1777, Hastings continually resided when in town, giving his official entertainments only at Buckingham House.

A further account of this residence will be found in the chapter dedicated to the subject of Hastings' houses in and around Calcutta. There also will be found a reference to another town residence which he would seem to have occupied before he acquired the Hastings Street property.

The next Government House, which I will call No. 6, is one that has attracted curiously little attention in the pages of historians, and appears to be generally unknown as a Government House at all. Actually it was anterior in construction to some of those which I have described. This is the house in the second or modern Fort William, which was first planned by Clive on what we should call Vauban lines in 1757, after the insecurity and unsuitability of the old Fort had been demonstrated by the events of the preceding year, and which after a long and sorry tale of incompetence and peculation was finally completed at a cost of two millions sterling, not as is commonly stated by the guide books in 1773, but only in 1781. Clive's original idea was that all the principal Europeans and the Governor General along with them should have houses inside the new Fort to which they might retire in the event of another attack or rebellion. Accordingly the plans provided for a Government House of moderate dimensions in the interior of the Fort, which though it has long since ceased to fulfil the object of its founder and has been converted into a Soldiers' Institute and Garrison Library and rechristened the Outram Institute,[1] is still occasionally called by its old name. I append a ground plan of the Fort with the situation of this edifice marked upon it, and also a sketch plan of the house as originally designed.

This Government House, as we find from Gazettes and other official records, was occupied on several occasions by the Governor General.

In September 1786, when Lord Cornwallis arrived at Calcutta

[1] Sir James Outram had founded a similar Institute, bearing his name, at Dum Dum : and before he left Calcutta in 1860 he made over some 500 of his own books to the Soldiers' Library at Fort William, which then honoured itself by taking his name.

OLD GOVERNMENT HOUSE (1788)

in succession to Warren Hastings, he was met at the waterside by a party of the Bodyguard and walked thence to the Fort, where his reception was public. After his commission had been read he retired to breakfast, presumably at the Government House in the Fort.

When not required for the Governor General, this house seems to have been occupied by the officer in command at Fort William. Thus we have a letter from Colonel Pearse, the friend of Warren Hastings, to the latter, dated 8th January, 1787, in which, writing from Fort William, he says that he is " residing in the ' Great House.' "

When Lord Wellesley returned to Calcutta by sea from Madras in 1799, he proceeded to the gates of the Fort, and thence to the Government House " upon arrival in the Fort." [1]

During the next few years, while the new Government House was in course of erection, the Gazette contains a number of references which seem to imply that it was to this house that Wellesley had recourse, when he came down to Calcutta from Barrackpore, where he resided for the greater part of the time when not on tour. Thus on 6th February, 1800, when he attended in state a Thanksgiving Service at St. John's Church, in honour of the recent victories of British arms, he is described in the Gazette [2] as having

" proceeded on foot from the Government House to the Church at about half an hour past six o'clock in the morning through Council House Street, which was lined by the Bodyguard, the Native Troops in Garrison at Fort William, and the Calcutta Native Militia."

And again, when on 20th April, 1802, Lord Wellesley made a State Entry—probably for the first time—into the new Government House, the Gazette of the day before reported that :

" His Excellency the Most Noble the Governor General will proceed to Calcutta on Tuesday morning. He will enter the Government House by Old Court House Street, towards which the troops off duty will be formed in a street from the gate of the present Government House." [3]

It is of course possible that on one or other of these occasions Lord Wellesley may have been residing in the Treasury Buildings, opposite the South-west Gateway of the new Government House, as we know that he was staying there on the night of the great Ball on 26th January,

---

[1] " Calcutta Gazette," 15th September, 1799.
[2] " Selections from Government Records," by W. S. Seton-Karr, Vol. III, pp. 257-9.
[3] *Ibid.*, Vol. III, p. 100.

1803. But the context seems to fit better a procession from the Fort : and on the night of the Ball he may have turned out merely for convenience sake, since he had certainly been in residence in his new palace for some time beforehand.

I do not know of any Governor General of later date who has similarly occupied the Fort House. Lord Canning certainly did not carry out Clive's original intention by taking refuge there during the Mutiny.

Although the building was rarely used by the head of the Government, it was not infrequently employed by him for State guests of especial distinction. When Lord William Bentinck (the future Governor General) visited Calcutta in July 1805, as Governor of Madras, the Government Gazette of 4th July recorded that at 6 p.m. His Lordship

" attended by the State boats and the band of the Governor General landed at the Water Gate of Fort William and was received by the Commanding Officer, the Garrison Staff, and several officers of the Governor General's staff. His Lordship was then conducted through a street of troops to the Government House in the Fort which had been prepared for his reception."

Sir E. Paget, who took over the Command in Chief from Lord Hastings in 1823, also resided for a short time in these quarters, which he described as " a magnificent house," before moving into Belvedere.

Bishop Heber's temporary occupation of the same house as the guest of Lord Amherst on his first arrival in Calcutta in October 1823 is better known, because of a passage in his Journal which I will quote :

" From Kidderpore we passed by a mean wooden bridge over a muddy creek, which brought us to an extensive open plain like a race-course, at the extremity of which we saw Calcutta, its white houses glittering through the twilight, which was now beginning to close in, with an effect not unlike that of Connaught-place and its neighbourhood as seen from a distance across Hyde Park. Over this plain we drove to the Fort, where Lord Amherst has assigned the old Government House for our temporary residence. The Fort stands considerably to the south of Calcutta and west of Chouringhee, having the Hooghly on its west side. The degree of light which now remained rendered all its details indistinguishable, and it was only when we began to wind through the different walks, and to hear the clash of sentries presenting arms as we passed, that we knew we were approaching a military post of great extent and considerable importance. We at length alighted at the doors of our temporary abode, a large and very handsome building in the centre of the Fort, and of the vast square, grassed over and divided by broad roads of *pucka* or pounded brick, with avenues of tall trees, stocked with immense flights of crows which had not yet ceased their evening concert when we arrived. We found at the door two sentries, resembling Europeans in everything but complexion, which indeed was far less swarthy than that of the other natives whom we had hitherto seen, and were received by a long train of servants in cotton dresses and turbans ; one of them with a long silver stick, and another with a short mace, answering to those of the peons who had received us at the landing-place.

"The house consisted of a lofty and well-proportioned hall, 40 feet by 25 feet, a drawing-room of the same length, and six or seven rooms, all on the same floor, one of which served as a chapel, the lower storey being chiefly occupied as offices or lobbies. All these rooms were very lofty with many doors and windows on every side ; the floor of plaister, covered with mats ; the ceilings of bricks, plaistered also, flat, and supported by massive beams, which were visible from the rooms below, but being painted neatly, had not at all a bad effect. Punkhas, large frames of light wood covered with white cotton, and looking not unlike enormous fire-boards, hung from the ceilings of the principal apartments, to which cords were fastened, which were drawn backwards and forwards by one or more servants, so as to agitate and cool the air very agreeably. The walls were white and unadorned, except with a number of glass lamps filled with cocoanut oil, and the furniture, though sufficient for the climate, was scanty in comparison with that of an English house. The beds instead of curtains had mosquito nets ; they were raised high from the ground and very hard, admirably adapted for a hot climate." [1]

Some of the trees and the crows have not yet disappeared from the Fort. But the splendid avenue which led from the Chowringhi Gate to the Government House was swept away by the terrible cyclone of 5th October, 1864, and has never been replaced.

In the ensuing year this house was turned to a more melancholy use, for having been lent by Lord Amherst to the Chief Justice, Sir Christopher Puller, it was the scene of his premature death on 26th May, 1824.

A few years later, Lord W. Bentinck, not unmindful perhaps of the hospitality which he had himself once enjoyed in this building, lent it as Governor General to a prominent civilian for his honeymoon [2] —a precedent which has been followed by every successive Governor General for decades in the analogous case of the pretty Bungalows in the Park at Barrackpore.

[1] "Narrative of a Journey in India," Vol. I, p. 24, 1828.
[2] " Thirty-Eight Years in India," by W. Taylor, 1881.

In 1841, when Lord Auckland was about to leave India, his sisters went to inspect the Government House in the Fort with the idea that, after Lord Ellenborough's arrival, they might in the interval before the sailing of their own ship, take up their temporary habitation there.[1] Miss Eden described it as " a melancholy looking house but cool and quiet, and with a little clean furniture will do very well." But nothing came of the plan, for the two parties continued to live happily together in Government House during the twelve days that intervened before Lord Auckland sailed.

When Lord Dalhousie, after being four years in India, took up, in 1852, the impoverished and disgraceful condition of the furniture of the Government Houses in Calcutta and at Barrackpore—of which more will be said in an ensuing chapter—and appointed a Committee to enquire and report, they dealt with the Government House in the Fort in the following scathing terms :

" This is a very substantially built upper-roomed house, though not conveniently arranged in point of accommodation. The rooms on the upper floor are lofty and large, but of the lower apartments no use seems ever to have been made. . . . The furniture that is in this house without exception is of the oldest and meanest description, quite unfit for any gentleman's lodging, and, in our opinion, all ought to be removed and replaced forthwith, if the house is intended to be used. It is better at all events that there should be nothing in the house at all than such discreditable appointments as are now there.

" The house is for the most part unoccupied, but if, as we believe it to be, it is meant to be available chiefly for the reception of strangers of distinction, its arrangements are strangely unsuited for the purposes expected of it, for, taken on the whole, the furniture in it is the worst we have had the occasion to report on belonging to the Government."

Lord Dalhousie however decided not to spend any money upon this house, for reasons which I will give in his own language :

" It certainly has been occasionally, though very rarely, used by guests of the Governor General ; but it has been much more frequently occupied, when occupied at all, by officers of the personal staff, or by those to whom it has been lent for a time. During the past year it has been chiefly occupied by wives of officers serving in Burmah.

" Since, then, the Fort house is little used ; since it is not conveniently situated for guests of the Governor General ; and since, by arrangements which I contemplate, the accommodation for guests in this house (*i.e.* Government House) may be somewhat increased—I think I shall best fulfil the expressed

[1] " Letters from India," by Hon. Emily Eden, Vol. II, p. 276.

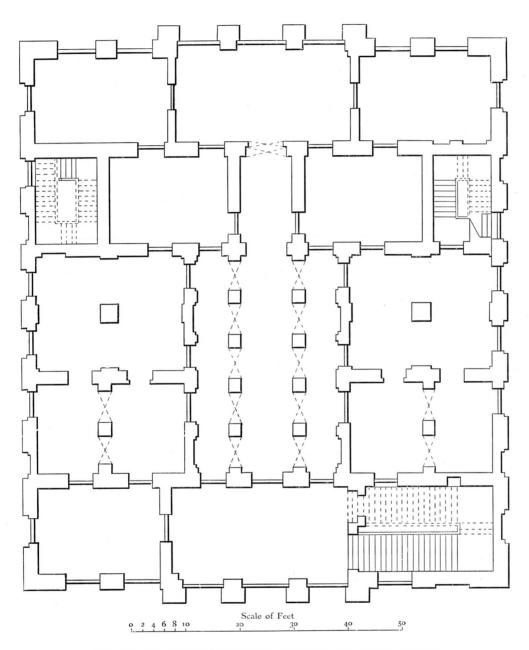

Scale of Feet
0 2 4 6 8 10   20   30   40   50

PLAN OF GOVERNMENT HOUSE IN THE FORT

expectations of the Honourable Court that due economy will be observed in regard to the new furniture by providing no furniture at all for the Government House at the Fort.

"The house may be applied to far more useful purposes there. What these may be shall be separately considered."

Thus was sealed the doom, as an official residence, of this Government House. But once again, and for the last time, was it so employed, in circumstances which Lord Dalhousie would have been the last to foresee. For only four years later, when the Mutiny broke out, the King of Oudh, whom Lord Dalhousie had deposed, and of whose possible doings Lord Canning's Government was very apprehensive, was brought up from Garden Reach, and was installed as a State guest *malgré lui*—one might more correctly say as a State prisoner— in the Fort House until the danger was overpast. He was there from July 1857 to June 1859.

I have not included in this chapter, and cannot count here as a separate Government House, the residence in the Treasury, which we learn from the official account that Lord Wellesley was occupying on the night of the great Ball in his new palace on 26th January, 1803. The Treasury, still so called, is the block of buildings, formerly known as the Accountant General's Office, situated at the corner of Council House Street and Esplanade Row West, outside the South-west Gate of Government House. Lord Wellesley may have occupied a suite of rooms here for a time during the building of Government House ; or he may merely have shifted from the latter on the occasion of the entertainment, for sake of convenience. In one work I have found it stated that 'the house adjoining the Treasury Buildings occupied by the Marquis Wellesley, was connected with it by a kind of bridge or covered gallery.[1] While the new Government House was in course of erection the Governor General occasionally—as has been shown —stayed in the Fort. But his usual residence was at Barrackpore, where he did his work with his Secretaries and Staff, far away from the *fumum et opes strepitumque Romæ*, and his activities at which place will be dealt with in a later chapter.

We now approach the circumstances in which, breaking away from all the traditions or inconveniences of his predecessors, Lord Wellesley boldly swept away the Government House and Council House which

[1] Burford's " View of Calcutta," 1830.

he found on the Esplanade, acquired a very wide stretch of ground
by purchase, and proceeded to erect thereupon what is without doubt
the finest Government House occupied by the representative of any
Sovereign or Government in the world.[1] As these proceedings
involved the imperious Governor General in a conflict with his official
superiors and were one of the causes of his retirement from India ;
and as, in their larger consequences, they went far to stamp an Imperial
character upon the Government of India—whose scope and tone
expanded in ratio to its splendid habitation—it will be fitter that they
should be fully discussed. I will dedicate to them accordingly a
separate chapter.

[1] The French are proud of their new Palais du Gouvernement at Saigon in Cochin China, and the
Portuguese of their ancient dilapidated palace at Goa. I have stayed in both, and can assert that no
comparison is possible.

CHAPTER II

COUNCIL HOUSES

To speak his thought is every freeman's right
In peace, in war, in council and the fight.—Pope. Trans. of Iliad, xii. 249.

"And Absalom and all the men of Israel said, The counsel of Hushai the Archite is better than the counsel of Ahithophel. For the Lord had appointed to defeat the good counsel of Ahithophel."—II Samuel, xvii. 14.

THE present seems to be an appropriate occasion for discussing the vexed question of the site of the various buildings that have at one time or another been acquired for or used as the Council Chambers of Government at Calcutta. Among the local problems that have been bequeathed to us by the omissions, the carelessness, or the contradictions of our authorities, both contemporaneous and modern, there is none more bewildering than this ; and if I shall have rather mercilessly to dissect the claims of some aspirants to the title, I shall yet hope to leave a residuum of demonstration sufficiently clear to carry us to a reliable conclusion.

(I) Prior to the capture of Old Fort William in 1756, there is nothing in the papers of the East India Company or, so far as I know, in any authority to indicate where the meetings of Council were held. Presumably it was in the large building that constituted the principal feature of the Fort, and was variously designated as the Governor's House and the Factory. But of this we have no certain knowledge.

(II) After the fall of Fort William in 1756, and its recovery in 1757, when most of the buildings in the interior were found to have been demolished, it was necessary to make fresh provision. The death by drowning in the Hugli, in May 1758, of Mr. Richard Court, a senior merchant of the Company, and one of the survivors of the Black Hole, who for " behaving very well " had been nominated to Council, but had barely lived to enjoy his honours, placed a house at the disposition of the Company ; and we read in Consultations of 22nd June, 1758, that

" There being at present no proper places for the public offices from which circumstances many inconveniences arise in carrying on the business of the Settlement, and as it will be proper likewise to have a room to hold our Councils in contiguous to the Secretary's and Accountant's Offices,   Agreed the dwelling house of the late Mr. Richard Court be purchased for the Honourable Company and appropriated to the above uses." [1]

But here our difficulty begins, for we do not know where and which was Mr. Richard Court's house.   It is not marked as such in Lieutenant Wells' map of 1753, presumably because at that date it had not been acquired by Mr. Court.   Mr. Long is even more tantalizing in his annotations, for whereas he appended a footnote to the above extract that " this house was situated in the street called after it Council House Street," in his article in the " Calcutta Review" of 1852 he wrote, between inverted commas, quoting from some unnamed authority :

" Clive Street was once the grand theatre of business, and there stood the Council House, and every public mart in it."

Elsewhere in the same article, alluding apparently, but with equal error, to a later epoch he said,

" We have heard that the Council was formerly held in the house which still stands between MacKenzies' and Hollings' Offices, the scene of many stormy discussions between Hastings and Francis."

The scene of these controversies was undoubtedly, as I shall show presently, elsewhere.

But the Offices in question would appear to have been in Lal Bazaar,[2] widely removed from the probable site of a Council House ; so that this legend must, I think, be dismissed.

I used to be told in my time that the building on the East side of Council House Street near Fancy Lane, occupied by the Private Secretary's Office, was the site of this elusive Council Chamber ; and I think that this story must have been derived from Dr. Busteed, who said " Tradition, I do not know with what truth, places the oldest Council House, north of the Exchange,[3] on a site now occupied by the Office of the Private Secretary."[4]

[1] Long's " Selections from the Unpublished Records of the Government of India," Vol. I, No. 352, p. 144.
[2] Cotton's " Calcutta Old and New," p. 318.
[3] This must however be a mistake, for the Exchange was the South-west corner building of Tank or Dalhousie Square, and the Private Secretary's Office, though it was shifted three times in the thirty years before 1900, can never have been to the North of it.
[4] " Echoes of Old Calcutta," 2nd Edition, p. 112.

Miss Blechynden has another site, for she says that Mr. Richard Court's house, where the Council met, "was probably a house near the hospital," [1] *i.e.* the Old Hospital, which in 1757 stood to the North of what is now St. John's Churchyard at the corner of Council House Street and Hare Street.

Mr. Firminger in one of his earliest publications favoured a third site; for in 1905 he wrote: "The Older Council House must have been close to where the Imperial Record Department now carries on its labour" [2] (*i.e.* on the West side of Council House Street, nearer the Esplanade).

All these theories appear to rest upon the assumption that it was from this unidentified Council House that Council House Street was named. It has always seemed to me, on the other hand, to be more probable and indeed certain that the street, originally prolonged through what is now known as Government Place, took its name from the first real Council House, erected specifically for the purpose, in the years immediately following 1764; for the latter stood at its South-eastern corner.

The shortlived Council House of 1758 was famous, if for no other incident, because on 9th June, 1763, it was the place where, one of the Members of Council, Stanlake Batson, lost his temper and struck Warren Hastings in the face.[3] That it had a shortlived official existence is however indisputable, for on 15th October, 1764, we find the following among the Proceedings of Council:[4]

"The present Council room being from its situation greatly exposed to the heat of the weather, and from its vicinity to the Public Office very ill calculated for conducting the business of the Board with that privacy which is often requisite, it is agreed to build a new Council room at a convenient distance from the Offices, and that it shall be done under the inspection of Mr. Fortnum, the Civil Architect."

To this Mr. Long appended the following footnote:

"The Old Council room was shut in by houses to the south. There were no punkahs then, men had to endure heat in their white jackets with the slight degree of air the chauries gave. On the trial of Nankumar the heat was so

[1] "Calcutta Past and Present," p. 74.
[2] Thacker's "Guide to Calcutta," p. 40.
[3] Batson was suspended, and Governor Vansittart and Hastings refused to sit with him even after he had apologised and been reinstated by the votes of the majority.
[4] Long's "Selections," Vol. I, No. 764, pp. 384-5.

great one day that one of the Judges had to go out six times to put on six changes of linen."

This is a rather irrelevant reference, since Nuncomar's trial was held in the Old Court House, on the site now occupied by St. Andrew's Church.

The Bengal Records of 1772 contain a Report on the ruinous state of the "Old Council House" with an estimate for repairs at the cost of Arcot Rs. 62,000, and a plan for a new Council House at a cost of Arcot Rs. 1,55,000. This however was refused by the Court of Directors.

In 1773 the abandoned Council House was advertised for sale as " a *cutcha* building . . . with a detached building for a godown, cook-room, etc., and a compound, part surrounded with a railing, containing four *beeghas* 11 *cottaks* of ground."[1]   In February 1775 Warren Hastings described it in a Minute as having " fallen to ruins," and added that soon after his accession to office (in 1772) the Offices of Government were removed to Mr. Keir's house, which was rented for the Company at 1,000 Rs. a month. This house however, proved to be both inconvenient and insufficient for the purposes required. Presumably this was the house on the Esplanade, the property of Archibald Keir, which was afterwards in 1781 let to the Company for the monthly rent of Rs. 2,500, to house the Supreme Court, who sat there for the first time on 2nd January, 1782. The locality of the dilapidated Council House was still an unsolved problem when, just as these pages were going into print, there was unearthed an extract from the " India Gazette or Calcutta Public Adventurer " of 3rd March, 1781, to the following effect :

" To be let or sold, The House known by the name of the Old Council House, next door to the old Export Warehouse. For particulars please to enquire of Mr. Edward Mulling at the Commercial Council House."

Here accordingly I am at last able to set this uneasy and long-lived ghost to rest ; for the old Export House was a building erected against the South bastion of Old Fort William, on the site of what is now known as Koila Ghat Street ; and therefore it is clear that somewhere in that street, probably at or near to its junction with Bankshall Street, stood the building which has been the centre of so

---

[1] J. C. Price, " Notes on the History of Midnapore."

OLD COUNCIL HOUSE (1788)

much conjecture and so prolonged a controversy. It may very well be one of the buildings that are marked in Upjohn's Map of Calcutta (1794) in what he designates Tankshall Street (now Koila Ghat Street)—a misprint for Tackshall Street, the Dutch name for the Custom House, which stood at its river extremity.

I now pass to the new Council House built in accordance with the order of 1764. About its size and appearance there can be no manner of doubt—although even these proofs have been misinterpreted by some. The building is depicted in the maps of Wood (1784) and Upjohn (1794), and is illustrated in the coloured drawings of Daniell (1788) and Baillie (1794). It lasted from circ. 1765 to 1800, when Lord Wellesley ordered its destruction.

I have already given a description of this building in my chapter on the Early Government Houses of Calcutta, because we have there seen, on the authority of Warren Hastings himself, that it was for some time (in the absence of any official residence owned by the Company) occupied as a Government House both by himself and his predecessors. Lord Clive (1765–1767), Verelst and Cartier presumably resided there, or at least used it for official purposes, and I imagine that during that period Council must have met there also. If this be so, it was the unquestionable scene of the many and dramatic encounters between Warren Hastings and Francis, where to the numerical majority wielded by the younger man, the elder opposed the inflexible resolution and serene patience that were destined ultimately to triumph. The famous answer of Hastings and Barwell to the illegal assumption of authority by General Clavering, the Governor General of a day, dated 20th June, 1777, was issued by them from the Revenue Department and speaks of the " meeting of the Council in that Department." But as Hastings explained in his sketch of the proceedings of those five days, this meant no more than that he and Barwell met there, Clavering and Francis having " met at the General Council Table " in the official Council House on the Esplanade. It was in a private room of this Council House that, in August 1780, Francis, after a meeting of the Council, drew Hastings aside, and handed to him the written challenge which resulted in the famous duel between them a few days later at Alipore in which Hastings laid his enemy low.

As I have previously remarked, this building presented a remarkable

D

resemblance in shape and appearance to the Factory or Government House in Old Fort William, of which it must have been to some extent a conscious imitation.

When Lord Wellesley decided, on his own authority, in 1798 to demolish this Council House and to purchase and pull down the adjoining Government House, he acted upon reasons which, as regards the former, he subsequently explained in his reply of 1806 to the censure of the Court of Directors in 1805.[1] In paragraphs 143 and 146 of this memorandum he declared, in language almost identical with that which Warren Hastings had applied to its predecessor, that the Council House

" did not afford the necessary accommodation for the meeting of the Council and for the public officers attached to the Government, exposing the members of the Government and the public officers immediately attached to it, to serious personal inconvenience, and subjecting the transaction of the public business to material obstruction."

He went on to say :

" That the Council House was an old[2] and extremely decayed building, and that from the long period of time which had elapsed since the principal part of the Council House had been erected, from the various alterations which it had undergone, and from the bad quality of the materials of which it had in general been constructed, the building was actually in danger of falling, and that the expense of reconstructing the Council House, even on the same confined scale, would have subjected the Company to a charge of Sicca Rupees 1,20,000 or £15,000, an expense which must have been incurred in the course of a few years.   The expense alone of repairing the Council House would have been Sicca Rupees 43,243 or £5,405."

It is difficult not to suspect the Governor General of some conscious exaggeration in the above representation. But anyhow the Council House was doomed, and it disappeared from view. Where Lord Wellesley's Council met while his new Government House was in course of erection we are not told. Nor apparently did it very much matter ; for as we learn from other sources the Most Noble the Governor General was in the habit of excusing his own attendance, and ordering his colleagues to report their proceedings to him for confirmation or the reverse. I have always thought this

---

[1] *Vide* Miscellany in the "Asiatic Annual Register" of 1807, pp. 48–54.
[2] It was only 33 years old.

South View of the Council-House and Government-House, Calcutta.

W. Baillie sculp. 1794

N.º 5

COUNCIL HOUSE AND GOVERNMENT HOUSE (1794)

one of the most typical illustrations of his imperious and arbitrary character.

It may here be mentioned that the original plans for the new Fort William on what is now the Maidan, commenced by Clive at the end of 1757, included a Council House as well as a Government House. The latter, as I have shown elsewhere, was built and was occasionally occupied by the Governor General and by distinguished guests. But I can find no record of a Council Chamber having been constructed or used : though any one of the main rooms of the Government House would have been large enough for a Council meeting of the small size that then existed. While the new Government House was being erected, Council may have met here, or more probably in the Treasury Buildings.

(IV) When the new Government House was finished, the Council Chamber seems to have been located there—and for more than a century afterwards—in a room on the first floor of the North-east wing. Mrs. Graham, visiting India in 1810, describes it as in the North-east angle.[1] Von Orlich in 1843 said, it is true, that " the *lower* storey contained the Council Chamber and other public rooms," but if by this he meant the ground floor, he was mistaken.[2]

In this Council Chamber, twenty-three Governors General, from Lord Wellesley onwards, presided over the deliberations of the Executive, and during the past half century, also, of the Legislative Council of the Government of India, and behind each for the last 90 years of this period, the features of Warren Hastings looked down from the wall with silent calm upon the proceedings of successors who reaped where he had sown and prevailed because of what he had suffered.

Not yet however is the tale of supposititious Council Chambers exhausted, and before leaving the subject I must examine the claims of three other pretenders to the title.

The first of these is the house, No. 51 Bentinck Street (formerly Cossaitollah Lane, *i.e.* the Butchers' quarter) occupied till recently by Messrs. Llewellyn and Company, but now doomed, which is variously said to have been the Government House and the Council Chamber of Warren Hastings, and of the first Lord Minto. I knew the house, having visited it while in India, and I have declined to

[1] " Journal of a Residence in India," 1812, p. 137.
[2] Capt. L. Von Orlich, " Travel in India," 1845, Vol. II, p. 185.

give it any place in the list of early Government Houses, because I am unaware of any shred of evidence, beyond legend, that it was ever used either as a residence or as a Council Chamber either by Hastings or by Lord Minto. When the former succeeded John Cartier as Governor in April 1772, the new Council Chamber on the Esplanade was already in existence; and although he used it for some time as an official residence, it is probable that the Council met there also. When Lord Minto came out in 1807, the Council was already accommodated in the North-east wing of Government House. Is it credible that either should have removed the meetings of Council from these quarters to relatively small apartments in a private house in a poky lane?

The second claimant is the house, No. 9 Esplanade Row, which is also said in some quarters to have been the residence and to contain a Council Chamber of Warren Hastings. The former point is discussed in the chapter dealing with his residences. As to the latter, there is no evidence to show that the Council ever met here, nor, for the reasons already given in the case of 51 Bentinck Street, is it in the least likely.

The third and last of the pretenders is a handsome room on the first floor of the building occupied in my time by the Legislative Department of the Government of India, a little to the East of the South or main entrance to the Town Hall. I was taken to see this apartment shortly after my arrival in Calcutta—it is a fine room with panelled walls and rather ornate plaster mouldings of a Georgian type—and I was informed that here too Hastings and Francis had contended. Enquiry, however, showed that the building of which it forms a part was originally occupied by the Home Department, and was converted in the years 1857–8 (the first map in which it appears is Simm's map of Calcutta of 1857), into the headquarters of the Legislative Department, which was first created in the rearrangement that followed upon the Mutiny. This Council Chamber cost about Rs. 35,000, and was probably built for the Legislative Council of the Governor General that was then called into being. There is no record, however, to show that this Council sat there, and when it was superseded by the larger Council created by the India Councils Act of 1861, the latter met, as it has continued to do ever since, in the Council Chamber in Government House.

GOVERNMENT HOUSE (1813)

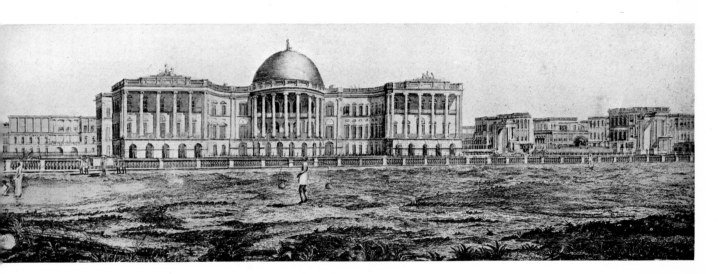

GOVERNMENT HOUSE (1825)

A new use, however, was found for the empty Council Room, for when the Bengal Legislative Council was constituted in 1862 (Bengal having become a Lieutenant Governorship), it sat in this room, and continued to do so for many years until Sir Ashley Eden (Lieutenant Governor 1877–82) constructed a new Council Chamber for his Government at the West end of Writers' Buildings (on the site once occupied by the first Calcutta Church of St. Anne). This is the octagonal building immediately behind the replaced Holwell Monument. It was first occupied in the winter of 1883–4, and the empty room in the Legislative Department, where the Law Member has since presided over Committees, and sometimes does his work, thereupon resumed its rôle of confusing and leading astray the school of willing misreaders of the history of the past.

On many occasions in the last half century, as has elsewhere been noted, the Legislative Council of the Government of India has burst its somewhat restricted boundaries in the Council Chamber in Government House, and has overflowed into the larger halls in the centre of the building. The discussions on the Ilbert Bill in 1884, which attracted large crowds, were held in the Marble Hall, a precedent which was again followed in the time of Lord Minto (1905–10). In my day the debates on more than one Budget, and on several of the contentious measures of the Session of 1904, were for a similar reason held in the Throne Room, which is better lighted than the Marble Hall. The Viceroy presided at the Western end and the spectators were arranged in rows at the opposite extremity.

From this survey it will be seen that since the purchase of Richard Court's house in 1758, there have been, in my opinion, only three official Council Chambers of the Government of India of whose identity we can be certain, namely (1) Old Council House, whose site I have identified ; (2) the Council House on the Esplanade : (3) the Council Room of Wellesley and his successors in Government House ; and that of the numerous claims advanced on behalf of other pretenders, there is not one that will stand the test of a critical examination.

Perhaps it may be said that the whole question of the Council Chambers of the Indian Government is one of local and topographical rather than general concern. The answer is that to the Calcutta people, for whom in the main these initial chapters are written, the early history of the city, now being rapidly submerged under the altered conditions and larger requirements of modern life, is a matter of absorbing interest ; while neither the historical student nor even the average Briton can be deaf to the appeal of sites where great men disputed and struggled in their efforts to found, to extend, and to maintain an Empire. Indeed when we think of those early Council Chambers, where first the Factors of the Company debated in stifling heat but with inflexible formality about prices and freights and bales, until gradually political issues with their trail of intrigue and corruption dominated the scene ; or whether we reconstruct the stormy controversies of a later stage, when Hastings and Francis and Clavering and Monson and Barwell indulged in their fierce and wellnigh mortal encounters ; or whether we contemplate the more dignified setting and orderly procedure of the 19th century Councils in the new Government House, and the long succession of famous men who contended around that table ; or again descend to the period when elected representatives of the Indian communities, often men of high character and conspicuous intelligence, were admitted to the Imperial Legislative Council and crossed swords there in debate with their European colleagues,—it is difficult to imagine any spot in the British Empire, with the exception of 10 Downing Street in London, the walls of which, could they speak, would tell a tale more dramatic in its intensity or more pregnant in its results. And now that the Government of India has folded its tents and stolen away, the deserted forum of Imperial debate is in course of becoming an ancient monument whose record can never be studied without pride or without emotion, but which, unless it be set down, will soon, in the swiftly changing panorama of Indian life, lapse into irretrievable oblivion.

CHAPTER III

BUILDING OF THE NEW GOVERNMENT HOUSE, 1798–1803

What! is not this my place of strength, he said,
    My spacious mansion built for me,
Whereof the strong foundation stones were laid
    Since my first memory.
            —TENNYSON. "Palace of Art."

LORD WELLESLEY, then Earl of Mornington (he was not created an Irish Marquis until 2nd December, 1799), landed in Calcutta on 17th May, 1798, and assumed office the next day. He was not long in making up his mind as to the requirements of his Government. The Court of Directors at a later date declared that the decision was arrived at in June. In the documents from which I have already quoted,[1] and which contained his final reply to his critics, after stating the case against the then existing Government House and the then existing Council House, he went on to say—

"Under these circumstances, it was considered to be expedient to adopt an arrangement which should afford a suitable residence to the Governor General, and should, at the same time, combine objects of utility and of ultimate economy, by concentrating the public offices in the vicinity of the Government House, and by effecting a general reduction of the expense to be incurred by the Company for the rent of public buildings.

"The Governor General, therefore, determined to purchase the house hitherto appropriated for the Government House, to direct that house, as well as the Council House (which was the property of the Company), to be taken down, and a suitable Government House to be erected on the site of those buildings."

On 2nd October, 1798, the Chitpore Nawab, Dilawar Jung, who was the owner of the then existing Government House (Council House, as we have seen, was already the property of Government), signed a deed of release and assignment for Rs. 1,07,733 or £13,450 for two pieces of ground. The old Government House must have

---

[1] Miscellany in the "Asiatic Annual Register," 1807.

been taken down shortly afterwards. Council House appears to have been left standing until 1800, when it too disappeared. Leaving over for the moment the question as to the degree in which Lord Wellesley acted without the knowledge and sanction of the Court of Directors, and was therefore justly blameable by them—which will be better discussed at the end of this chapter, when his activities at Government House have been carried to a conclusion—I will describe the steps by which he proceeded to carry out his plans on the spot.

Captain Wyatt [1] an Engineer Officer, and E. Tiretta, [2] the Company's Civil Architect, were called upon to prepare plans for the building. Captain Wyatt's design was preferred, and accordingly he was the architect responsible for the new Government House. The Chief Engineer, Major General Cameron, was then instructed to furnish an estimate of the cost, which, after including marble and iron-work, was found to amount to Sicca Rupees 5,29,211 or £66,150. Some sections and plans of the proposed Government House are still in existence, drawn by J. Best, who was an Assistant in the Drawing Office of the Chief Engineer.

Captain Wyatt's design was adapted from the plan of my own home, Kedleston Hall in Derbyshire, which was built for my great great grandfather, the first Lord Scarsdale, by the famous architect Robert Adam, in the years 1759–1770. Or rather the first plans of Kedleston were prepared by the almost equally well-known architect James Paine, and were published in the collection of his Drawings ; but, Paine having retired from the work before it had advanced very far, it was then handed over by my ancestor to Adam, recently returned

---

[1] Captain Charles Wyatt had originally entered the army as an Infantry Officer, but was transferred to the Corps of Engineers as Lieutenant in 1781. He received the Honorary rank of Captain some time before 1799 and the permanent rank from 10th December, 1800. In January 1799 he was attached, no doubt because of the important work with which he was now entrusted, to the office of the Secretary to Government in the Secret Department, and was rewarded for his services by being appointed a Commissioner of Police in May 1800. In May 1801 Lord Wellesley nominated him to assist in negotiations for the acquisition of Barrackpore Park, and in June 1803 appointed him member of a Committee to report on Calcutta improvements. Lord Wellesley described his position at this period as " Superintendent of Public Works." In October 1806 he retired from service in India. It appears from a letter written by Lord Wellesley to Lord Grenville (Dropmore MSS. Hist. MSS. Com., Vol. VII, p. 215) that Captain Wyatt was a nephew of the well-known English architect James Wyatt.

[2] Edward Tiretta was an Italian about whose adventurous career there is an interesting Note in Dr Busteed's " Echoes of Old Calcutta " (4th Edit.), p. 341. He had been an associate of the notorious Jacques Casanova in Europe; but having made many countries ' too hot ' for him, he drifted to India, where he became in turns respectable, versatile, wealthy, and bankrupt. He left his name to a bazaar which he acquired in Chitpore Road, and which appears in all the maps of the period, and also to a Burying Ground, which he bought in order to inter his young French wife. For many years he held the post of Superintendent of Streets and Buildings, or as it is here called, Civil Architect to the Company, and he appears to have been distinguished *inter alia* for the extraordinarily bad English that he spoke.

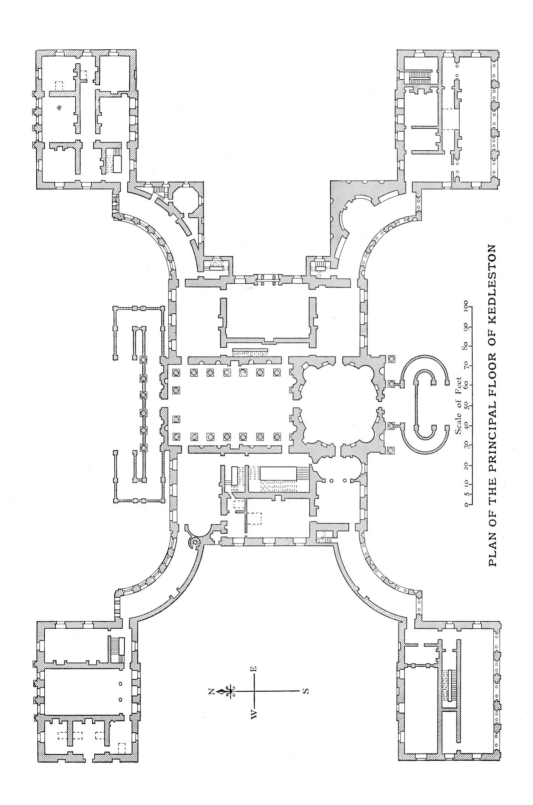

PLAN OF THE PRINCIPAL FLOOR OF KEDLESTON

Scale of Feet
0 5 10 20 30 40 50 60 70 80 90 100

N
E
W
S

from his tour to the Dalmatian Coast, and thrilling with ambition to reproduce the classical forms and grandiose proportions of the architecture of the Roman Empire. Many scores of drawings, sketches and plans of Kedleston by Adam's own hand, some of them executed but others never carried out, are in the possession of my family or in the Soane Museum in London ; and this house was certainly regarded then, and I believe has been regarded since, as the masterpiece of the architect's earlier style.

But it was not for the decorative features or the beauty of the style that the Kedleston model was adopted for Calcutta. I have never been able to ascertain whether Lord Wellesley or any of his friends or family had actually seen Kedleston. It was visited later on, among other notabilities, by Warren Hastings. But in the second half of the 18th century its fame was on many lips, it had been twice visited and described by no less a person than Dr. Johnson, and it figures in the pages of Boswell and Mrs. Thrale. Plans, sections, elevations, drawings of every part of it had appeared in many publications, notably in Paine's work and in "Vitruvius Britannicus," [1] and were reproduced in every current text book of Architecture ; so that no personal or intimate knowledge of the English mansion was needed to reproduce its essential features in Calcutta.

There can be no doubt that it was the remarkable suitability of the general design to the conditions of a tropical climate that caused its adoption by Captain Wyatt. The scheme of a great central pile with curving corridors radiating from its four angles to detached wings or pavilions, each of which constituted a house in itself, was admirably adapted to a climate where every breath of air from whatever quarter must be seized, and where a perpetual current relieves the petty aggravations of life. In England the many mansions of the nobility and gentry that were built upon this plan in the Palladian *furor* that lasted from Vanbrugh and Kent to the brothers Adam and Chambers, were as a rule uncomfortable and inconvenient, the splendour of the State rooms in the central block involving too frequently the sacrifice of the bedrooms and domestic quarters, and the banishment to long distances of the offices and servants' habitations. But in India, where the Government House of what was destined at no distant date to become an Empire required a succession

---

[1] "Vitruvius Britannicus, or the British Architect," by Woolfe and Gandon, Vol. IV, p. 7. 1767.

of great halls and State apartments, and where a legion of native servants renders distance and inconvenience of relatively minor importance, no better model could in all probability have been chosen. Even there the plan was not without its serious inconveniences, as anyone who wished to proceed from one wing to the other, and could only do so by traversing the State rooms in the centre, and this at no small expenditure of time, speedily discovered. Many a Governor General, and perhaps still more his wife and family, have bewailed this drawback. But from the point of view of ventilation and healthiness I cannot imagine a superior arrangement ; while the many frontages, facing all points of the compass, rendered it possible to cope with every condition of temperature.

So many erroneous accounts have been published of the degree to which the Indian building adhered to or departed from its English prototype, that I may perhaps explain definitely in what respects they correspond or differ. Appended are plans of the first floors of the two houses—of Kedleston as it was originally planned by Paine and Adam, and of the Calcutta house as built by Wyatt. They resemble each other in the broad external features of shape, design and orientation, in the extreme dimensions from East to West, which are identical in the two, in the concentration of the main State rooms in the middle pile, in the placing there of a great marble hall supported by columns, and in the superimposition of a dome above the Southern façade. But they differ radically both in material and arrangement. Kedleston was built mainly of a grey or yellowish sandstone, hewn in Derbyshire quarries, and only partly of brick. The Calcutta house is built entirely of brick covered over with white plaster, the colouring of which is renewed every year. They differ also in completeness of design, only two of the projecting pavilions having been finished at Kedleston, whereas Calcutta has all four ; in the addition of a semicircular projecting portico and colonnade on the South front at Calcutta[1] ; in the height of the corridors (at Calcutta they are three-storeyed and their roof-line is level with that of the wings, at Kedleston they are two-storeyed and therefore lower in elevation) ;

---

[1] I have no doubt that this feature, which was never executed at Kedleston, is taken directly from one of Paine's designs. His book (" Plans, Elevations and Sections of Noblemen's and Gentlemen's Houses," 2 vols., 1783) would be in the possession of the Calcutta architects as well as " Vitruvius Britannicus." *Vide* especially Vol. IV Plate 46 of the latter work, and Plan XLV of the Principal Storey of Kedleston in Paine's Vol. II.

and in the general external proportions, which are more imposing at Calcutta, but more harmonious and artistic at Kedleston.

There is an equal difference in the interior arrangements ; notably in the existence of two storeys above the ground floor in the principal rooms of the central block at Calcutta, whereas at Kedleston the marble hall and the circular saloon beyond it are carried right up to the roof, and are lit by skylights, in the former case in the coved ceiling, in the latter case at the top of the great dome ; in the absence at Calcutta of any grand staircase and the substitution for it of four petty staircases at the four angles of the central block—a subject of constant criticism and even ridicule at the hands of the European visitors to the Calcutta Government House in the first quarter of the 19th century ; and in the provision in the Indian house—so necessary for the Indian climate—of big verandahs on the Southern face.

Thus the differences greatly exceed the points of identity ; although the resemblance is sufficiently close to strike anyone who knows the two buildings. In respect of interior furniture and decorations, there can be no comparison between the two mansions, Kedleston being replete with the exquisite fittings and decorations that are characteristic of the Adam style. Perhaps it may be regarded as an illustration of the small points on which even the larger issues of life depend, that it was the alleged correspondence of the two houses that first turned my attention, when a boy, to India, and planted in me the ambition, from an early age, to pass from a Kedleston in Derbyshire to a Kedleston in Bengal.

There was no ceremonial laying of the foundation stone of the Calcutta palace, the Governor General having left for Madras in connection with the Mysore compaign ; but on 5th February, 1799, the first brick was laid by " one of the supervisors," Mr. Timothy Hickey of the Engineer Department. This gentleman is otherwise unknown to fame ; but he may have been a brother or relative of the other T. Hickey, an artist then residing in Madras, to whom Lord Wellesley sat for a presentation portrait while he was in that Presidency, and who was the painter of the Mysore series of pictures that were acquired by Lord Wellesley and afterwards hung successively at Barrackpore, in Government House, Calcutta, and more recently at Belvedere.

For a time we hear nothing more of the progress of the works, until in April 1801 a Committee, of which Major General Cameron was the President, and the ubiquitous Tiretta a member, was appointed by Lord Wellesley, " to survey the new Government House previous to the commencement of the plaster-work of the building." Its report is before me as I write. It complimented Captain Wyatt upon his professional skill and found both timber-work[1] and masonry to be very good and the materials excellent.

Early in 1802 the building must have been sufficiently advanced to allow of official parties being held within its walls, for an advertisement in the "Calcutta Gazette" of 29th April, 1802,[2] prescribed the entrance and exit of carriages by the great gates. Two very material differences may however be noted from the usages of a later time—palanqueens were instructed "to remain within the enclosure in front of the house," and the hour at which the gates were opened was 7 a.m.

By August 1802 official entertainment was possible, for on the 9th instant the Governor General

" entertained at breakfast in the New Government House Major-General Baird[3] and the Officers of the Army who returned from Egypt, together with all principal ladies and gentlemen of the Settlement, and several of the principal inhabitants of the Danish Settlement at Serampore."[4]

On 22nd September the Governor General held a Levée (in the morning) on the day appointed for the Proclamation of Peace between " His Majesty, the French Republic, His Catholic Majesty and the Batavian Republic ";[5] and at 5.30 p.m. the Proclamation, announcing the joyful event, was read a second time by the Sheriff from the big staircase of Government House—a practice since abandoned in favour of the steps of the Town Hall, where I remember attending in 1901 the Proclamation of the accession of King Edward VII.

On 18th January, 1803, the building, which had then been almost four years in construction, was reported to be complete, and a second

---

[1] It appears from the Report that the beams, doors, and window frames were of *saul* wood, while the floors of the upper storey were of teak.

[2] Seton-Karr's " Selections," Vol. III, pp. 101-2.

[3] Well known already to Lord Wellesley from the storming of Seringapatam. The Governor General had sent him to the Red Sea in command of an Indian Force, British and Native, to take part in the Egyptian campaign against Napoleon.

[4] Seton-Karr's " Selections," Vol. III, p. 332.

[5] " Asiatic Annual Register, 1803," p. 36. The chronicler deemed it of sufficient importance to add " On this occasion His Excellency appeared for the first time in the insignia of the Ottoman Order of the Crescent," which had been forwarded to him from the " Grand Signior " at Constantinople in recognition of the part played by India in the Egyptian campaign.

GOVERNMENT HOUSE
CALCUTTA

Scale of Feet

0 10 20 30 40 50   100

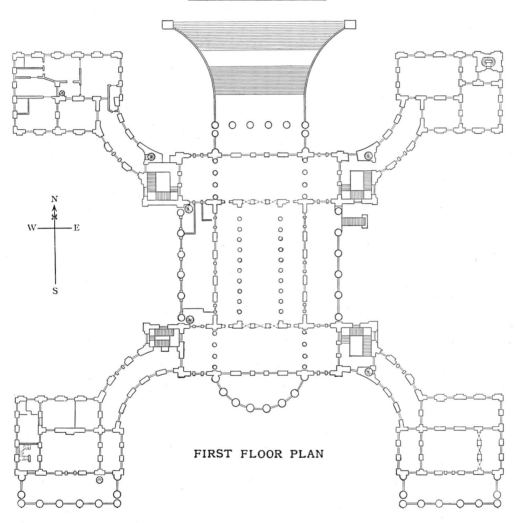

N

W—E

S

FIRST FLOOR PLAN

Committee, again with General Cameron as President, but without the versatile Tiretta, who had now been succeeded as Civil Architect by Mr. Blechynden—was appointed to examine the building. Again the Committee paid a high tribute to Captain Wyatt, and again it complimented all concerned upon the skill and attention devoted to the work ; the actual cost of which was now reported to be Sicca Rupees 5,06,326 or £63,291, i.e. £2,859 less than the original estimate of £66,150.

On the next day, 19th January, 1803, there was another State procession from the new Government House to St. John's Church to celebrate the conclusion of the Peace of Amiens. A dismounted detachment of the Bodyguard lined the steps of the great stair-case on the North front—as they did on state occasions in my day, the Governor General was in his State carriage,[1] and troops lined the streets.[2]

A week later occurred the great Fête in Government House, in honour of the same event, which was probably the most magnificent entertainment ever given within its walls. The State rooms were lighted up for the first time ; a throng of 800 persons assembled for dancing, fireworks and supper ; and a minute account of the proceedings has been left to us not only by Lord Valentia, who happened to arrive in Calcutta on that very morning, but in official publications. A description of this Ball will be given in another chapter, to which it will be more germane. It furnished the concluding incident of the four years' period of construction, and the inaugural episode of more than a century of official pageantry that lay before Lord Wellesley's completed structure. The lavish expenditure on this entertainment and on others that occurred at about the same time, attracted the serious attention of the Court of Directors, as will be narrated later on.

The new building being now in working use, the Governor General issued the following Regulations to explain the manner in which its accommodation should be employed. I reproduce them here [3] because, though trivial in themselves, they illustrate the wonderful continuity of ceremonial observance—amounting almost to a

---

[1] What it was like may clearly be seen from a coloured drawing in Fraser's "Views of Calcutta," which is reproduced later in this volume.

[2] "Asiatic Annual Register," 1803, p. 69.

[3] Seton-Karr's "Selections," Vol. III, p. 124.

ritual—that prevails in India, while indicating certain of the differences that a century had brought about in social usage.

"The 24th March, 1803.

"In order to prevent difficulty and confusion in the arrangements which are become necessary for the public accommodation at the new Government House, the following Regulations are published for general information :—

" 1. A room on the basement floor is appropriated to the use of the Aide-de-Camp in waiting at the New Government House. All persons having business to transact at the Government House will be received by the Aide-de-Camp in waiting between the hours of nine and three.

" 2. All persons are desired to enter the Government House through the arches under the steps on the north side, excepting on public occasions, when the entrance will be by the great steps leading to the northern portico.

" 3. One of the Aides-de-Camp will attend at the Government House every day, notwithstanding the temporary absence of the Governor-General from Calcutta.

" 4. On Levée days, there will be two Aides-de-Camp in waiting (who will be designated) for the express purpose of receiving the cards of strangers, and of presenting strangers to the Governor-General.

" 5. All persons desirous of being presented to the Governor-General are requested to write their names and stations on a card, and to deliver the card (previous to the Levée) to one of the Aides-de-Camp in waiting.

" 6. The Levées at the Government House will, in general, be holden in the centre room of the upper floor. The Company will assemble on the marble floor, and will be conducted from thence to the Levée room as soon as the Governor-General shall be ready to receive them.

" 7. The Company will enter the house by the north-east staircase, and return by the north-west staircase.

" 8. On Levée days, the Chief Justice, Judges of the Supreme Court, Members of Council, General Officers, and Judges of the Sudder Dewanny Adawlut, will be conducted to the Levée room immediately on their arrival at the Government House.

" 9. The general entrance into the Government House on all occasions is from the *northward*; but on the Levée days, public balls, and entertainments, the southern entrance will be open to the Chief Justice, Members of Council, Judges of the Supreme Court, General Officers, Judges of the Sudder Dewanny Adawlut, the suite of the Governor-General, and their respective families, if they should choose to enter on that side of the house.

"M. SHAWE,

"NEW GOVERNMENT HOUSE,   "Private Secretary.
   "The 23rd March, 1803."

Other expenses were incurred before the first bill for the new house was made up, and these may perhaps be best described in the words of the Governor General, who reported as follows :—

" A further expense was incurred for extra works, such as gateways, an iron railing round the area, of Sicca Rupees 1,26,994-7-2-, or £15,874.

" The expense of ornamental work by Mr. Croese within the house was also an additional expense, amounting to Sicca Rupees 69,000, or £8,625.

" In order to complete the general plan for erecting a new Government House and for improving the town, as well as for concentrating the public offices, and reducing the rent of the public buildings, it was necessary to purchase several houses belonging to individuals and to purchase some ground in the vicinity of the new house.   The expense incurred on this account was Sicca Rupees 5,71,500, or £71,437.

" A further expense was incurred in prosecution of the general plan, of Rupees 27,466, or £3,433, in making two new streets in the vicinity of the new house."

The total expense would seem, according to the figures supplied by Lord Wellesley in the same Report, to have been as follows :—

	Sicca Rupees		£
For the building	7,02,320	or	87,790
For the purchase of land and houses.	5,71,500[1]	or	71,437
For the making of 2 new streets[2]	27,466	or	3,433
	13,01,286	or	£162,660

at 2s. 6d. the Sicca Rupee.

The original furnishing is generally reported to have cost Sicca Rupees 50,000, or £6,250, which must be added to the above, making a grand total of Sicca Rupees 13,51,286, or £168,910.[3]

I think, however, that the outlay on furniture must have been

[1] This land was assessed for municipal taxation, in my time, on a basis of Rupees 32,40,000, or £216,000.

[2] These must have been Government Place, outside the Northern compound of Government House, and Wellesley Place leading direct from it to Tank Square.

[3] If these official figures are correct the statements contained even in authoritative writings must be inaccurate.   Carey (" The Good Old Days of John Company ") said that the ground cost Rupees 80,000, the buildings 13 lakhs, and the furniture ½ lakh.   Hunter in the " Imperial Gazetteer " gave the same figures converted into pounds at 2s. the rupee, i.e. £8,000 + 130,000 + 5,000 = a total of £143,000, or at the then value of silver (in 1885) £175,000.   But he forgot to notice that the estimates of 1800–1804 were calculated in Sicca Rupees, the value of which was 2s. 6d.

much greater, for, as will be seen later on, the Court of Directors brought it as a point in the indictment against Lord Wellesley that in the two years 1801–2 and 1802–3 the charges for plate and furniture alone exceeded Sicca Rupees 1,60,000, or (as calculated by them) £18,560. Nor do Lord Wellesley's figures quite correspond in other particulars with those which were adduced by the Court in their subsequent arraignment of the Governor General. However, the two tables of calculations are sufficiently close to show that a total of some £170,000 must have been spent by Wellesley on the Calcutta house and grounds—a sum which would represent a third or fourth only of the cost at the present time.

I now pass to the conflict that arose between Lord Wellesley and the Court of Directors over the erection of Government House, and what they held to be the extravagant and unauthorised outlay upon it. The story is only dimly alluded to in the various Lives of Wellesley, and was obscured in the public eye by the much greater importance of the other charges brought against the 'Sultanised Englishman,' and also by the futility of censuring that which had been already triumphantly carried out. Indeed not till now has the true story ever been told, nor could it be told without access to the original documents both in India and in London. I have perused the whole of these, and I reconstruct the narrative here, partly because to the historian of Government House it possesses an interest in excess of its intrinsic importance, but still more because it represents a significant phase in the protracted struggle between the Court of Directors and their haughty representative, and enables us to realise how difficult it was for the two parties to get along.

The history of the controversy is to be found in the following sources of information :—the recorded Proceedings of the Government of India, the same Proceedings in so far as they were sent home to the India House, the correspondence between the Governor General alone or the Governor General in Council in India and the Court of Directors in England, the communications between the Chairman of the Court or the Court as a whole and the President of the Board of Control or the Board as a whole in London,[1] and finally a statement or summary of his case which must have been communi-

[1] The ensuing narrative will be more easily followed if the reader understands the almost incredible system of Government that existed at this time for the British dominions in India. It will be found fully explained in Vol. II, Chapter XI.

cated by Lord Wellesley after his return to England to the " Asiatic Annual Register," in whose pages it was published in 1807. For purposes of abbreviation I will describe this in future as his Defence.

We have seen that Wellesley, having arrived in Calcutta in May 1798, lost no time in setting to work upon a new Government House. In his Defence he states that his plans for this object were " stated in the Proceedings of the Government, under date the 24th December, 1798, and the 1st April, 1801 "—from which it might be inferred that the earlier of these Proceedings had been sent home soon after that date and had been in the hands of the Court at some time in 1799—a procedure which, if it had been followed, would undoubtedly have acquainted the Court with what was in contemplation at a period when they could have instituted enquiries or issued a prohibition had they pleased, while their failure to do so would in a measure have transferred the responsibility to them. But it is certain that a copy of these Proceedings (whatever their actual contents) was never sent to England at all. There is no trace of them in the India Office, and the Court expressly stated at a later date (in their Draft 128) that Government House had been begun in 1798 without their knowledge or previous consent. I sought to discover the missing record in India ; only to find in the MS. volume of the Proceedings for 1798, that those of 24th December, 1798, had been cut out !

In the same Draft 128, the Court wrote that :

" The first intimation which we received relative thereto was in a letter from the Governor General to our Chairman, dated the 2nd April, 1801, transmitting several statements of reductions in the Civil and Military Departments, among which was a statement tending to prove that it was cheaper to erect new Buildings (including an estimate for building a new Government House) than to repair the old buildings, or continue to rent as heretofore. The expense of building a new Government House was estimated at Sicca Rupees 579,338."

This letter, which was received in England on 12th November, 1801, is in the India Office. But there is no necessity to reproduce it here, for it deals generally with the revision of the Civil Establishment of Bengal, and contains no specific reference to Government House. The enclosures have disappeared.

This, however, is of little moment, for there can be small doubt that the statements referred to are identical with those which went home in the ordinary course with the Proceedings of the Governor

E

General in Council of 1st April, 1801—the date above referred to by Lord Wellesley.

On that day, the new building being now well advanced towards completion, the Governor General had placed before his colleagues in Calcutta a detailed vindication of his policy, both in its administrative and financial aspects. He said nothing about this in his letter to the Chairman of the Court on the following day, and it was not till 20th March, 1802, that a copy of the Proceedings of 1st April, 1801, reached the India House, their departure from Calcutta having certainly not been unduly accelerated. These documents I reproduce, because they contain the nucleus of the subsequent Defence.

" Extract from the Proceedings of His Excellency the Most Noble
   the Governor General in Council, in the Department of Reform,[1]
   under date the 1st of April, 1801.

" The execution of the plan respecting the Buildings occupied for public purposes adverted to in the Extract from the Resolutions of the Governor General in Council of the 24th December, 1798, being nearly completed, His Lordship now states the general grounds on which he adopted that Plan.

" The necessity and expediency of a new arrangement with regard to the Buildings occupied for Public purposes at the Presidency, and in the interior of the Country, will appear from the following facts and observations connected with the state of the several buildings, their fitness for the purposes to which they are applied, and the principles by which the amount of the Rent of such of the Buildings as are private property, has been regulated.

" That the apartments contained in the building occupied by the Governor General, and denominated the Government House, both with respect to their construction and accommodation were inferior to the apartments in the ordinary Houses of Individuals, exposing the health of the Governor General to the most serious injury from the effects of the Climate.

" That the Building did not furnish any accommodation for the family[2] of the Governor General, or for the Public Officers immediately attached to his person.

" That the Building did not contain any apartments suited to occasions of Public Ceremony, or for the reception of the augmented number of the Inhabit-

---

[1] Lord Wellesley would seem to have established a separate Department under this title, in connection with the revision of the Civil Establishment. But there is no record of Proceedings so designated in the India Office, and this may explain how it was that the record of 24th December, 1798, failed to come home.

[2] The word " family," as I have previously explained, was used at that time in the wider sense of " suite " or " staff," and did not merely connote relatives. Lord Wellesley had no family in the ordinary sense with him in India ; for although in 1794 he had married the French lady, Mlle. Roland, with whom he had lived for many years and who had borne him several children, and although he took out her picture by Hoppner to India and hung it in Government House, it was thought prudent not to challenge criticism by presenting her as the official head of Calcutta Society.

ants of the Capital of the British possessions in India, reducing the Governor General to the necessity of hiring buildings constructed by Individuals for places of entertainment whenever Public or other occasions required that he should assemble the principal officers and Inhabitants of the Settlement.

"That from the decayed state of the Building the Sum of Sicca Rupees 79,000 was requisite for putting it into a suitable state of repair; that the Proprietor could not with justice have been required to defray this charge, in addition to the heavy expenses which he had recently incurred for repairs and alterations and consequently that the expence of the further repairs required must have been made at the expence of Government.

"That the Amount of the Rent paid for the Building being Sicca Rupees 1,625 per Month far exceeded the value of the Building."

Here followed a number of paragraphs relating (*a*) to the Council House—the substance of which (as afterwards reproduced by Lord Wellesley in his Defence) has been given in Chapter II—and (*b*) to other official buildings.

"These considerations determined the Governor General in Council to purchase the House hitherto appropriated for a Government House, to direct that House, as well as the Council House (which was the property of the Company) to be taken down and a suitable Government House to be erected on the Site of those Buildings."

(Then followed some paragraphs dealing with the Supreme Court and other buildings.)

"His Lordship now records the accompanying General and separate Statements marked No. 1 and 2 exhibiting the cost of the Buildings erected or purchased, and the saving of expence and Reductions of rent effected under the general operation of the foregoing Plan."

"From the General Statement No. 1 it appears :—

"That the total cost of the buildings purchased and erected on account of the Company and the estimated charge of the repairs of those buildings for the unexpired part of the term of the Company's Charter amounts to Sicca Rupees 773,838.

"That the total amount of the charge of rebuilding the Council House, with the charges heretofore incurred on account of Public buildings and for the Rent of Offices which will now cease to be a charge upon the Company, amounts to Sicca Rupees 1,520,380.

"That the saving which will arise in pursuance of the plan adopted amounts to Sicca Rupees 746,542 being equal to an annual income of Sicca Rupees 74,654, which Sum with the addition of compound interest for the term of

7 years 2 mos. and 26 days will amount to a Saving of 773,739—and for the term of 13 Years to a saving of Sicca Rupees 1,830,725.

"That the permanent benefits resulting from the Plan will be as follows.

"That the whole of the buildings erected or purchased will be a clear property to the Company within the period of seven years and one quarter besides a saving in Money at the expiration of the term of 13 Years of Sicca Rupees 1,056,887.

"That instead of the expensive and inadequate buildings hitherto appropriated to public uses, the Government and all the Public Officers in the various branches of the Government will be provided with Buildings in every respect suited to the requisite purposes, either as they may be connected with the maintenance of the dignity of the Government, the accommodation and convenience of the Governor General, and of all the Public Officers at the Presidency, the concentration of the Public Officers at the Presidency, the prompt dispatch of the Public business, or the safety of the Public records of every branch of the Government.

"In consequence of the preceding arrangement, the Sums now inserted in the Book of Establishments on the account of the rent of the buildings included in the arrangements should be struck out of the Book of Establishments and in the room of those sums should be entered the Rent now paid at the reduced rates together with the Interest at 10 per cent on the Cost and Charges of the repairs of the Buildings erected or purchased by Government, but at the expiration of Seven Years and one quarter when the Expense of the buildings will have been redeemed by the savings effected the amount of such Interest should be struck out of the Book of Establishments as ceasing to be a charge on the Company.

"The principles of this Plan remain to be extended to several of the buildings in the Commercial Department and to some detached Offices. This extension of the Plan will be productive of a further saving to the Company in addition to the saving above stated.

"The Governor General annexes the separate Statement marked No. 2 to show that independently of the other branches of the General Plan respecting the Public Buildings the expense of erecting the New Government House exceeds only in the sum of Sicca Rupees 165,478 the charge which would have attended the rebuilding the Council House, and the continuance of the payment of the Rent of the former Government House, with the other consequent expenses. The necessity which would have existed of rebuilding the Council House will appear from the annexed report marked No. 3.

"It may be proper to observe that the preceding Plan does not include the buildings and ground purchased in Garden Reach, and the buildings rented in town for the purposes of the College established at Fort William. The expenses incurred on account of such ground and buildings will be a charge on the funds which may be provided for defraying the expenses of the College."

GOVERNMENT HOUSE (1820)

The Governor General in the above record alludes to (A) General Statement No. 1, (B) Statement No. 2, and (C) Report No. 3. I append these three documents. They are probably identical with the papers which he had sent without comment or explanation as enclosures to his letter to the Chairman of 2nd April, 1801.

"STATEMENT NO. 1.

"Fort William, 1st April, 1801.

"No. 6. General Statement of the saving effected in the Charge for Houses and House Rent throughout the several Departments in pursuance of the Plan of concentrating the several Public Offices and establishing the Rents in future to be paid by the Company on permanent Leases for the unexpired Term of the Company's Charter.

Estimated expense of erecting a new Government House including the purchase of the old Government House and Grounds vide separate statement . .	5.79.338 . .
Purchase of the Court House including a new Building for the Records	80.000 . .
Repairs computed at 2 per cent for 13 years .	16.000 . .
Purchase of a House and a piece of Ground from Mr. Burroughs for the Office of the Registrar of the Sudder Dewanny and Nizamut Adawlut . . .	37.500 . .
Repairs computed at $1\frac{1}{2}$ per cent for 11 years (there being none required for 2 years) equal to a present outlay of	4.000 . .
Purchase of a House from Samuel Doss Baboo for the Board of Revenue	32.000 . .
Repairs computed at $2\frac{1}{2}$ per cent for 13 years .	7.000 . .
Purchase of Grounds contiguous to the premises viz. :	
From Mr. Hampton 10.000	
From Mr. Thornhill 2.500	
From Mr. Paul 5.500	18.000 . .
Difference being a Principal equal to the annual saving effected by the pursuance of the present Plan .	7.46.542 . .
Sicca Rupees	15.20.380 . .

Charge of rebuilding the Council House and of the Rent of the Old Government House etc. *vide* separate statement . . . . 4.13.860 . .

Monthly Rents hitherto paid by the Honourable Company to be discontinued for the Supreme Court 1.400

> Record Office — do. — . . . 200
>
> Board of Revenue 600
>
> Sudder Dewanny Adawlut . . . 400
>
> Stamp Office 250
>
> Superintendent of the Public Granaries 200
>
> Judge Advocate General's Office . . 250
>
> ————
>
> 3.300

which being payable monthly is equal to an annual payment of 41,400 and to a principal of . . . 4.14.000 . .

Monthly Reductions
Rent of the Writers Buildings heretofore paid for at the rate of A. Rs. 3.800 or Sa. Rs. 3.538 now reduced to   Sa. Rs.1.520

Difference 2.018 . .

Reductions already made in the Rents of the several Revenue Judicial Cutcharies amounts to 3.500 . .

————

5.518 which

being paid monthly is equal to an annual saving of Sicca Rupees 69.252 and to a principal of . . . 6.92.520 . .

Sicca Rupees | 15.20.380 . .

"Result of the Statement.

"The above Difference is equal to an annual saving of Sa. Rs. 74.654 which at Compound Interest at 10 per cent. per annum for 7 years 2 months and 26 days will amount to 7.73.739 or nearly to the Net outlay and in 13 years will produce a saving equal to Sa. Rs. 18.30.725 exceeding the net outlay of [1] Sa. Rs. 10.56.887."

[1] A mistake for " by."

"STATEMENT NO. 2.

"Fort William, 1st April, 1801.

"No. 7.   Separate Statement of the Expense of Erecting a New Government House including the Purchase of the Old Government House and Grounds compared with the Charges of Rebuilding the Council House and of the rents and repairs heretofore paid for the old Government House for a period of 13 years being nearly the unexpired term of the Company's Charter.

Purchase of the Old Government House and Ground	90.000	. .
Estimated expense of erecting a New Government House Drains Platforms etc. etc.	4.75.038	. .
Repairs computed at 1 per cent for 11 years (there being none required for the two first years) equal to a present outlay of	39.300	. .
Deduct	6.04.338	. .
Value of the materials of the Old Government House and Council House .	25.000	. .
Sicca Rupees	5.79.338	. .

Estimated expense of rebuilding the Council House	1.20.000	
Repairs computed at 1 per cent for 11 years as per Contra	9.920	
Monthly Rent heretofore paid by the Honble. Company for the Government House 1.625 which being payable monthly is equal to an annual[1] payment of 20.394 and to a principal of	2.03.940	
Ordinary Repairs of the Government House hitherto defrayed by the Company about 3.000 Rupees per annum equal to a principal of	30.000	
Annual Expense of fitting up apartments at the theatre for the public Entertainments 5000 rupees equal to	50.000	
	4.13.860	
Difference being the Extra Expense of building the new Government House	1.65.478	
Sicca Rupees	5.79.338	

[1] The text says *amount*, which is an obvious error.

"N.B. The sum of 79.000 Sa. Rs. the estimated amount of the expenditure requisite for putting the Old Government House and Offices into a suitable state of Repair over and above the ordinary repairs is omitted in this statement because it might be supposed that if that sum had been defrayed by the Company, a correspondent reduction might have been effected in the monthly rent of 1.625 Sa. Rs. the proprietor however of the Old Government House would not have been able to disburse the sum of 79.000 Sa. Rs. without receiving compensation by an equivalent increase of the Rent and the charge must ultimately have fallen on the Company. If this sum be added to this side of account, the Balance would stand as follows :—

Amount of the Charges for rebuilding the Council House etc. as above 4.13.860
Add extra repairs required for the Old Government House . 79.000

Deduct 4.92.860
Net expense of erecting etc. the New Government House per Contra 5.79.338
Difference being the actual Extra Expense of building the New Government House " 86.478

"REPORT NO. 3.

"Fort William, 1st April, 1801.

"To D. Campbell Esq.
"Sub Secretary.

"Sir,

"In reply to your letter of the 31st ultimo we beg leave to submit our report of the particulars of work required in repairing the Council House vizt.

"To remove old Terraces of the Centre Building, and to renew them both to the Roof and Story, and rebuild the Ballustrade. To take down the old Walls of the Western Staircase to rebuild them, and make a new principal staircase. To renew the two small staircases in Teak wood. To rebuild the outer wall (much cracked) to the Eastern Wing. To renew one third of the Beams to the Roof and Story and entirely the Burgars. To take up the lower floors, and to flew them in many parts of the Building; as also of the Western Wing, and to repair the rest. To take off the old Plaister inside and out, and to renew the whole throughout the Building. To renew one third of the Windows and frames, make several new Doors, and repair all the others. To make proper Drains round the Building. To paint the Windows Doors and Sashes. Also the Beams throughout the Building three times with the best Europe Oil and Colour—To remove all the old Materials and rubbish.   To complete the above Repairs the Expenses will amount to Sicca Rupees 43,243.

"We beg leave to observe in laying out so large a sum the Building will derive no other benefit than what may arise from replacing with new materials such old and defective parts of the Work as appear to be in a state of decay. That even with such repairs as may tend to render the Building more habitable and secure, according to the above Statement, It would prove in our opinion an unwise, and an unprofitable expenditure to the Public inconsistent with our Idea to recommend, because the Building being in general very bad is deserving of no such Charge ; would always be defective, and liable in future to the Expence of other Repairs.

"We are &ca.

"Signed C. Wyatt Capt. Engr.

„   Edward Tiretta

Civil Archt.

"CALCUTTA
the 18th September,
1798."

If, as appears certain, these enclosures were identical with those that reached the India House in November 1801, or even if they did not reach it till March 1802, the question may be asked why did not the Court at once take action upon them.   The answer I think is twofold.   First, before even the earlier of those dates, the Court must have known pretty well, from private communications with Calcutta, that matters had gone too far to render a veto practicable.   Secondly, they had already, three months earlier, issued orders which, as it were by anticipation, covered the very infraction of rules that had occurred, and, if any degree of suspension were now possible, would effect it before any fresh instructions or reprimand could reach Calcutta. These orders represent the next stage in the narrative.   They were issued in the Military Department on 26th August, 1801, and they were concerned primarily with the increase in the cost of military buildings in Bengal, to which was appended a paragraph imposing an absolute limit of 1 lac in any one year's expenditure on civil buildings. I print the letter.

"Military Department.

"Our Governor General in Council at Fort William in Bengal.

"We notice with concern the great Increase in the expense of buildings and Fortifications under Bengal in 1799–1800, and as estimated for 1800–1801, compared with the expense of the two preceding years[1] it is true, part of this

| [1] 1797–8, | 308,000 | 1799–1800 | 1183,000 |
| 1798–9, | 662,000 | 1800–1 estimated | 1247,000 |

increase is occasioned by Repairs to the Forts in the Viziers Dominions under the engagements with him in 1798, but as it is absolutely necessary to confine these charges within the most economical bounds, we positively direct that no new and expensive buildings either civil or Military be commenced on any account whatever, until the reasons for proposing to erect the same are laid before us, and the measure has had our previous concurrence, and for the present we direct that not more in any one year shall be laid out upon buildings in the Civil or Judicial Departments or in the purchase of Lands for that purpose than One Lack of Current Rupees ; and on Military Buildings or Works not more than four Lacks of Current Rupees.   " We are

" Your affectionate friends
" D. Scott.

" London   " Charles Mills
    26 August 1801 "   &c &c &c

This letter reached Calcutta in February 1802. But the Court made it one of the chief items of complaint in their subsequent draft 128 that though these orders were communicated upon arrival from the Military to the Judicial Department, they were never replied to or even acknowledged, and that, in despite of them, the advances made in 1802–3 on account of the new Government House alone, amounted to Sicca Rupees 202,887, and for the purchase of Houses and Grounds on the same account, to Rs. 125,000, or a total of Rs. 327,887. Lord Wellesley's subsequent reply to this charge in his Defence, that

" this order certainly cannot be considered to apply to buildings which had already been commenced, and were in a state of progress, nor is it reasonable to suppose that it could be intended to prevent the Government from making the necessary repairs to decayed buildings, or even from rebuilding public offices or houses which were in a state of ruin "—

strikes me, apart from its posthumous character, as being more ingenious than convincing.

A long interval now elapsed, the Court being either conscious of their impotence, or absorbed in larger controversies with their Governor General. Meanwhile the latter had not merely completed his palace, but had held in it the series of costly entertainments which were also at a later date to bring him into collision with his employers. He was therefore master of the position, and could afford to snap his fingers at enquiry or censure.

Early in 1804 Captain Wyatt returned to England, and was the bearer of the following letter from the Governor General in Council to the Court :—

" Honble. Sirs,

" Captain Charles Wyatt of the Corps of Engineers on the Establishment of Bengal being on the eve of his departure for England, the Governor General in Council has entrusted to the care of that Officer, for the purpose of being submitted to your Honourable Court, the Plan, Section and Elevation of the new Government House lately erected in Calcutta.

" The Plan of the Government House having been furnished by Captain Wyatt and the Work having been completed under his immediate Superintendence and Direction, he will be enabled to afford any information which may be required by your Honourable Court in explanation of the drawings now transmitted to you.

" The Zeal, Diligence, professional Ability and integrity manifested by Captain Wyatt during a course of long and useful service in India have established a just claim on the approbation of this Government. At the period of Captain Wyatt's resignation of the situation of Superintendent of Public Works, the Governor General in Council considered it to be proper in justice to Captain Wyatt to state on the public records his sense of Captain Wyatt's distinguished merits. A copy of the Minute entered on the proceedings of Government on that occasion is annexed to this letter, and the Governor General in Council recommends Captain Wyatt to the favourable notice of your Honorable Court as an officer from whose faithful and able Services for many years the interests of the Honorable Company have derived considerable advantage,

" We have the honour to be

Honble. Sirs,

" Your most faithful Humble Servants

" (Signed) Wellesley

G. H. Barlow.

" Fort William   G. Udny.
    the 27th February 1804."

Captain Wyatt announced his arrival in a letter which was read at the Court Meeting on 17th October, 1804 ; but there is no further reference to the matter in the Court Minutes, nor can any trace of the plan and elevation be found in the India Office. That the latter were delivered is evident from a paragraph in the later Draft 128. The letter itself was noticed in a General Despatch from the Court of 10th April, 1805, saying that the matter would be dealt with in a separate communication. This no doubt was the celebrated Draft No. 128, which had already been referred to the Board of Control, and to which I now turn.

The tension between the Court and the Governor General, over the entire field of policy—his wars, his treaties and alliances, his appointments, his sublime indifference to orders from home, quite apart from the minor question of Government House—had for long been growing to a point at which an explosion was inevitable. In fact it is clear that the Court would gladly have dispensed with Wellesley's services, were it not that he received the constant and loyal backing of Pitt, his intimate friend and the all-powerful head of the Ministry, and of Castlereagh, President of the Board of Control. Moreover whenever the news of some fresh war or arrogation of political autonomy on the part of the Governor General reached England to inflame the already exasperated sensibilities of the Court, with it came the consciousness that the little Proconsul was probably the only man to carry the matter to a successful conclusion ; while if a message of wrath went out to India, its arrival was as a rule discounted by some resounding victory, which enabled the Governor General to treat it with scornful indifference. If this situation was one of rather futile stale-mate, first on one side and then on the other, it at least reveals the amazing fatuity of the system by which India was then governed from England.

Early in 1805, the feelings of the Court, after prolonged incubation, found vent in a draft Despatch, covering the entire ground of controversy, which under the rules they were bound to submit to the Board of Control. I shall reproduce here the introductory paragraphs of this draft (known as No. 128) in its original form, and also those relating directly to Government House. But in order that the progress of events may be correctly apprehended, I will give in advance a brief synopsis of its earlier official history, as recorded in the original papers at the India Office.

A practice had grown up by which the Chairman of the Court sent informally in advance to the President of the Board, a draft which was about to come up officially from the Court. The first draft of No. 128, thus marked as a Pre-Com. (i.e. previous communication) is docketed as having been received by the President in February or March 1805, and returned to the Chairman as unaltered,

" His Lordship (*i.e.* Lord Castlereagh) not caring to go into the matter as arranged." The paragraphs relating to Government House were not in this draft, which stopped at paragraph 67, paragraphs 68–80 being left blank, to be filled in later. The Court on receiving this curt intimation of the obvious disapproval of the President as representing His Majesty's Government, removed a few of the more offensive phrases or sentences, inserted paragraphs 68–80, to make their case complete, and submitted the draft officially to the Board on 4th April. This was how it ran :—

"Draft Despatch No. 128.

" In our Political Dispatch of 28 November 1804, after animadverting on the conduct of our Governor General Marquis Wellesley in omitting to inform us of the Orders he had issued for commencing hostilities against the Maratta Chieftain Jeswunt Row Holkar, an omission contrary to obvious propriety, as well as the positive injunctions of an Act of Parliament, and productive of serious inconveniences at home, we intimated an intention of delivering, on a future occasion, our Sentiments on other measures of his Lordship's administration which had made a deep impression on our minds. We now proceed to perform that intention. On several occasions we have found ourselves called upon to bestow our warmest commendation on the Measures of Marquis Wellesley : and that we have embraced those occasions with pleasure may be evinced by the testimonies given him of our approbation which have not been exceeded by those conferred on the most illustrious of his predecessors. It has been with the sincerest regret that we have seen other proceedings of His Lordships which it was impossible for us to contemplate with satisfaction. Our free opinions upon those measures have been long witheld, partly from reluctance to convey censure, and partly in the hope that single acts, as they for a time appeared, of an exceptionable nature, would not occur again. We still retain all the consideration for the talents of Marquis Wellesley to which they are justly entitled, and are still willing to bestow our praise upon every measure of his Government which has been in our judgement calculated for the public good. But after deliberately reviewing the course of his proceedings for some Years past, there appears in it such a series of deviations from the Constitution established by law for the Government of British India and from the usages of our Service, such frequent instances of disregard in Affairs both of greater and inferior moment to all other Authorities, and of continued assumptions of new authority by the Governor General himself, that the character of our Indian Government has in his hands undergone an essential change. It has in fact been turned into a (pure and)[1] simple despotism; the powers of the Supreme Council have been completely absorbed ; the subordinate Governments have been reduced nearly to the condition of Provinces of the Bengal Presi-

[1] Omitted in Second Draft.

dency ; the authority of the Court of Directors has, in many instances, been disregarded (and in some astonishingly insulted, even that of the Board of Control has been overlooked);[1] informations of the most important and necessary kind have been witheld from this Country ; very great irregularities and defects have taken place in recording important Transactions ; instead of that economy in public expenditure which the spirit of the Constitution of British India as well as the constant tenor of our Instructions has enjoined ; there has been, in many instances, a needless profusion, which has contributed to swell the Company's Debt, now increased to an enormous amount . . . . . ."

Then followed a number of paragraphs upon Foreign Relations and Wars, accusing Lord Wellesley of " alarming infractions of the Constitution," and a series of charges about appointments, neglect to consult the Council in the subordinate Presidencies, and usurpation of powers belonging to them, contempt for his own Council, disobedience to the orders of the Court, failure to send home accounts, etc. Next we come to paragraph 21, which marshalled a long list of alleged acts of insubordination, subsection 15 of this paragraph bringing us directly to Government House.

" In continuing to make advances on account of buildings &c beyond the bounds prescribed in the Court's letter in the Military Department of the 28th August, 1801, which limited the Disbursements for Buildings and for the purchase of lands for that purpose, in the Public and Judicial Department to the sum of one lac of Rupees per annum. Notwithstanding the positive and distinct line prescribed by that letter, which was received in Bengal in February 1802, it appears that the advances made in 1802–3 on account of the new Government House alone, amounted to Sicca Rupees 202,887, and for the purchase of Houses and Grounds on the same account, to Rs. 125,000, making together the sum of Rs. 327,887. We must here remark that although the before mentioned orders limiting the expence in the Judicial Department were communicated from the Military Department to that Department, they have not been replied to, or even the receipt thereof acknowledged although orders of the same date and by the same conveyance, and in the same Department were regularly replied to under date the 17th April, 1802.

" 22. We have much reason further to complain of the defective state of the information respecting the New Government House, a work of unexampled extent and magnificence, and which was undertaken without any previous or regular communication to us of such a design, of its necessity or the scale of its expence. Although this work was begun in June 1798 and appears to have been carried on, at an enormous cost, the first intimation which we received relative thereto, was in a letter from the Governor General to our Chairman dated the 2nd April, 1801, transmitting several statements &c of reductions

---

[1] Omitted in Second Draft.

in the Civil and Military Departments, among which was a statement tending to prove that it was cheaper to erect new Buildings (including an estimate for building a New Government House) than to repair the old Buildings or continue to rent as heretofore.   The expence of building a new Government House was estimated at Sicca Rupees 579,838, whereas it appears that the advances for the Building alone, exceed that calculation by nearly three lacs of Rupees, and including the purchase of Ground, by above seven lacs and a half of Rupees, making an expenditure of Rupees 1,338,879 or £167,359 upon a Building begun in 1798 without our knowledge and previous consent, and without any information being communicated to us respecting the progress of the building, and the expence attending it until the Work was completed, when the plan and elevation were transmitted and referred to us in a letter from the Governor General in Council dated 27th February, 1804.   Our being kept so long uninformed with respect to the expenditure of so large a sum as upwards of thirteen lacs of Rs. or £167,000 forms a striking contrast to the information contained in your Dispatches from time to time, respecting trifling expenditures, particularly in the 64th Paragraph of your Military letter of the 28 February 1803, by which we are acquainted that you had authorised the sum of (97) ninety seven Rupees (13) thirteen Annas to be disbursed in the repair of the temporary Military Buildings at Captain Gunge."

With paragraph 23 the schedule of acts of alleged disobedience and neglect came temporarily to an end ; and paragraph 24 was consecrated to the following rebuke :

" 24. We have been led to the foregoing painful recital of some of the principal instances in which the orders of the Court of Directors have either been evaded or disobeyed, for the purpose of impressing upon the minds of our Governor General and our Council the necessity of a due submission to our orders in future; as well for the sake of the example which such a conduct on the part of the Supreme government in India is likely to produce in the minds of the Subordinate Governments, and in the minds of our servants in General, who might thereby be taught to imbibe sentiments of insubordination dangerous to the existence of the Company's authority in India as for the sake of conveying to you our determined resolution to resent any future instance of similar disobedience to the plain and positive orders of the Court of Directors on the part of any of our Servants in an exemplary manner."

Then followed many more specific charges of irregularity, and of action by the Governor General in independence of the Council or of the Court, until we come to the further paragraphs 68–80 relating to Government House and other subjects, which had not been included in the first draft.   They appeared under the heading " Increase of Expenses."

"68. Notwithstanding our frequent inculcations of economy in the public expenditure, and the revision of Establishments . . . we have observed with very great concern a growing increase in the charges of carrying on your Government ; the expenses of the General Branch brought to account in 1802–3, the last we have yet had an opportunity to examine far exceed those of any preceding year " . . . .

"71. The expenses we have been put to in building the new Government House and for the purchase of furniture &ca for the same, fall completely within the scope of these observations. The Governor General in his Minute of the 1st of April 1801, on the subject of this new edifice has referred to two statements calculated to shew that a considerable saving would accrue from the measure proposed by him of building a new Government House and Offices for the public service, but in order to prove the weakness of arguments founded on such Hypothesis it is only necessary to observe that the nett expense of building the new Government House and purchasing the old House and ground is estimated in the second of these statements at Sicca Rupees 540,000 or £62,600,[1] whereas it appears by the Dead Stock accounts that Sicca Rupees 855,000 or £99,000 had been advanced for these purposes to the 31st January 1804 ; and by the first of these statements the expense of building the Government House and of purchasing Houses and Grounds for new Offices, *including a calculation for repairs*, is given at Sicca Rupees 774,000 or £89,784 nearly, but the actual advances by the Dead Stock Accounts above mentioned amount to upwards of Sicca Rupees 1,320,000 or £153,120 *exclusive of any calculation for repairs* ; this exposition will sufficiently shew the fallacy of Estimates of the nature referred to by the Governor General on this subject.

"72. The sum charged for Plate, Furniture &ca for the new Government House in 1801–2 and 1802–3 exceeds Sicca Rupees 160,000 or £18,560."

Paragraphs 73–75 related to the expenditure incurred in connection with Barrackpore (to be noticed in Chapter X), the Governor General's tours, and his lavish entertainments in Calcutta (*vide* Chapter IX) They concluded with the following lecture :

"76. It has always been our desire that the dignity of the office of our Governor General should be maintained with becoming state, suitable to the genius of the National character, and to the peculiar constitution of the Governing Power. But we think it unnecessary and inexpedient that he should in his Houses, his Attendants, his Establishments, give in to the style of Asiatic pomp and display. Nothing of this kind is requisite for the support of the British authority in the East, which was acquired and has been preserved by other means, and we think the indulgence of such a taste would have an unfavorable influence upon the British character in that quarter. If these observations

[1] The figures are given in the Statement referred to and already printed here, as Sicca Rupees 5.79.338 ; but it is clear that in order to arrive at the total of 540,000 the Court deducted the Sicca Rupees 39,300 computed by Lord Wellesley as the cost of repairs for 11 years. The Court also adopts a slightly different rate of exchange from the Governor General, who calculated a Sicca Rupee at 2s. 6d.

are in a political view just, they apply also with particular force in the state in which our finances have been for some years past wherein the necessity has been evident of the utmost practicable retrenchment in every article of ordinary and accustomed charge, and so much more of avoiding expenditures new and superfluous, either in kind or degree, as most of these on which we are now animadverting must be acknowledged to be."

The Draft meandered along through many more similar charges and rebukes, which we need not follow here, because they are not germane to our present subject.   More pertinent is it to relate the fate that attended the entire pronouncement.

On 22nd April, 1805, the Board replied with ominous brevity that "they had perused the Court's Draft No. 128, but that they must defer for the present taking it into their further consideration till they receive from the India House the documents upon which it is founded."   They added a few sentences, however, of dissent from a particular contention of the Court (not relevant to this discussion) but of concurrence in the "importance of maintaining the control at all times in its full vigour of the Government at home."   It does not seem necessary to reproduce this letter.

On 9th May, 1805, the Court, snatching as much consolation from the last phrase as they could, replied as follows :—

" My Lords and Gentlemen,

" We have received Mr. Holford's letter of 22nd ultimo, and conformably to the requisition contained in it, now enclose a list of references to all the documents which substantiate the matters contained in our Draft No. 128. Many of those documents, as will appear by the list, are already in your possession, the rest, consisting of Eight Collections Nos. 1 to 8 we have now the honour to transmit.   With respect to the Letter itself, which is supported by these documents, we wrote it after much serious consideration under a deep sense of the importance and necessity of asserting and reverting to the principles of the Constitution established by Law for the Government of British India, and with a thorough conviction that our view of that Constitution both with respect to internal Government and foreign policy was consonant to the intention of the Legislature and the sense in which the Court has understood the Law ever since it was passed.

" We are happy to learn that your right Honorable Board concur with us in thinking it necessary to recall the Government General to the constitutional mode of transacting the public business, and take the liberty respectfully to express our opinion of the importance of transmitting orders to that effect as speedily as possible.   " We have etc.,

                                                      " W. Ramsay."

F

Among the documents enclosed by the Court with this reply was one entitled " Expenditure for Buildings etc. and Government House." It contained the following :

" Statement of Dead Stock of Fort William, 31st January 1804.
Advances for the new Government House

	Sa. Rupees
In 1798–99	225,000
1799–1800	105,000
1800–01	140,900
1801–02	90,092
1802–03	202,887
1803–04	108,000
Purchase of Houses	871,879

		Sa. Rupees
From	Mr. Ken	80,000
,,	W. Burroughs	37,500
,,	Samuel Doss	32,000
,,	Captain Thornhill	2,500
,,	Paul Derozario	5,500
,,	Lt. Thos. Anbury	3,500
,,	Wm. Dring	5,000
,,	H. and R. Abbott, agents to the marriage settlement of Mrs. Shaw	15,000
,,	Campbell and Radcliffe	32,000
,,	Wm. Fairlie	60,000
,,	Colvin	13,500
,,	Mr. Palling, Exr of the estate of Dr. Allen	2,500
,,	Alexander & Cotton, attornies to Mr. Harding	25,000
,,	Cockerell, Trail & Co, attornies to the Exrs of the estate of the late Mrs. Powney	28,000
,,	Wm. Fairlie, agent to Mr. Larkin	50,000
,,	J. Dashwood, agent to Mr. Auriol	10,000
,,	Cockerell, Trail, Palmer & Co, agents to Mr. Evelyn	35,000
,,	B. Turner	30,000
		467,000[1]
	Sa. Rs.	13,38,879
		£167,359 "

---

[1] I have compared this list with the actual Title Deeds of Government House, Calcutta, which were deposited in the Office of the Comptroller General in my time, and a list of which is printed at the end of this chapter. About one half of the items correspond. But the Court's list is remarkable for containing no mention of the purchase for Rupees 1.07.733 of the property belonging to Nawab Dilawar Jung on which the former Government House stood. Perhaps they had not got the figures.

After five months' consideration the Board replied in language which, while much of it is not directly relevant to the subject of Government House, it seems desirable to quote in full. They ended by cancelling Draft No. 128 and substituting another of their own—as their statutory powers gave them the right to do.

" Whitehall,

" Sir,   " 19th October, 1805.

" 1. The Board in pursuance of an intimation to that effect contained in their Secretary's letter of 22nd April last having resumed the consideration of Draft No. 128 proposed by the Court to be forwarded to Bengal, direct me to transmit to the Court the following observations.

" 2. The Courts Draft may be considered, as dividing itself into two parts, 1st Remarks on the mode in which the Government has latterly been conducted and 2ndly Observations on a great variety of the measures which have been carried into effect during the period of Marquis Wellesley's administration.

" 3. With respect to the latter, the Board see no occasion to depart from the usual course of delivering their sentiments upon these several points, namely in the course of replying to the different letters which have relation to these subjects.

" 4. The compass of a single despatch is very insufficient to the fair examination of such an extent and variety of matter, nor do they see for what purpose of practical utility this review is, at the present moment, brought forward, as no measure whatever, either has been, or is now proposed to be founded upon it, whilst it appears to the Board very injuriously and unjustly to reflect upon the British Councils in India for a series of years past.

" 5. The Board in their letter above alluded to have expressed their early dissent from the construction put by the Court on the 33rd of the King, section 42, and their application of that construction to the transactions abroad.   With respect to the precise grounds on which the sentiments of the Board on the several important political measures in question differ from those which the Court appear to have adopted, it would be impossible for the Board satisfactorily to explain them without entering at very great length into the detail of each question respectively, which the Board feel to be altogether unnecessary at the present moment.   1st Because no specific measure is proposed for their consideration and 2ndly Because such directions as have appeared to the Board expedient in the present state of affairs have already been transmitted to India, either from the Court itself or through their secret committee.

" 6. The Board concurring in opinion with the Court that an obvious departure has latterly taken place in the mode of conducting the Public business abroad, which cannot be justified according to the principles of the Government, as by law established, have thought it expedient to recall the attention of the Company's servants to the leading irregularities, which have occurred in sufficient detail, to guard against their repetition in future.   But the Board in the mode of doing it, are desirous of avoiding everything which might bear the appearance of general censure and they feel assured from the terms, in which the Court have expressed themselves, with respect to Marquis Wellesley's services, at the outset of the Draft as well as upon many other occasions, that it cannot be their wish that such an impression should be created.

"7. The Board for the reasons stated have found it most convenient to cancel Draft 128 and to convey their sentiments in that herewith returned, which they desire may be transmitted to India, and which in substance they apprehend will not be found to differ materially with respect to those points on which it treats, from the opinions which have been expressed by the Court of Directors. "I have etc.

"George Holford."

It is not necessary here to reproduce the substituted Draft, because while it recalled the Governor General in language of dignified rebuke, but without vehemence or asperity, to a proper conception of his constitutional position in the "established system of Indian government" in relation both to his own Council, and the Presidency Governments and to the Government at home—it made no reference to Government House, either deeming that the matter was of relatively inferior importance, or that it would involve an undue examination of detail, or that it was too late.

To this letter and Draft the Court replied on 6th November, 1805, in a long letter, very ably defending their attitude towards the Governor General, and vindicating the main groundwork of their rejected Draft.   They made no further reference to Government House.

On 30th November, 1805, the correspondence closed with a courteous rejoinder from the Board, declining to reconsider their position.

So the duel ended—certainly not in the triumph of the Governor General, who had experienced a severe rebuke at the hands of his political friends, nor altogether in the discomfiture of the Court of Directors, who found the main principles for which they had fought conceded by the Government; but in the relegation to the background of the many minor subjects, such as the expenditure on Government buildings in India, with which their all-embracing anger had tempted the Court to deal.

Eight months later the Court secured a belated revenge; for on 23rd July, 1806, they succeeded in introducing into a lengthy despatch to Calcutta a few paragraphs which contained in sublimated form their long suppressed sentiments about the expenditure on the Government Houses at Calcutta and Barrackpore.   This however was very much a *brutum fulmen*, for in the meantime Lord Wellesley had returned to England and was immersed in politics there, Lord Cornwallis had succeeded him in India and had died, and Sir George Barlow, who had, it is true, been a colleague of Lord Wellesley on his Council, but was not at all likely to reproduce his foibles or errors, was Acting Governor General in India, pending the appointment of a successor.

I append the paragraphs of this Despatch which relate to Calcutta ; those which deal with Barrackpore will be noticed in a later chapter.

Extract from a Despatch from the Court to Bengal, July 23, 1806.

" 39. In our Despatch in this Department under date the 10th April 1805, we expressed our intention of communicating our sentiments on the building of the new Government House at Calcutta in a separate Despatch ; circumstances however having occurred to prevent us from so doing, we shall now make such observations as the subject at present requires.

" 40. In the first place we have very much to complain of the defective state of information in which we were kept respecting the construction of this Building, a work commenced in June 1798, and proceeded in at an enormous expense.   The first intimation we received upon the subject was in a Letter from our Governor General to the Chairman dated 2nd April 1801, submitting statements tending to prove that it was cheaper to erect new Buildings than to repair the old &c.   The estimated expense of the New Government House was stated at Sa. Rs. 5,79,838, but the advances alone for the Building exceeded that sum by nearly 3 Lacs of Rupees and including the purchase of Grounds &c. by above 7½ Lacs of Rupees, making an expenditure of Rs. 13,38,879 or £167,359 upon a Building commenced without our knowledge and previous consent, nor had we any intimation of its progress until the Work was completed, when the plan and elevation were transmitted and referred to in your Public Advices of the 27th February 1804, thereby precluding us from expressing our sentiments upon the subject until we had no alternative but to submit to the large expenditure which had been incurred, notwithstanding our repeated Orders to confine the expense of Buildings within the most economical bounds and not to commence new and expensive Buildings without our previous sanction."

The question suggests itself—how was it that even this modified censure received the sanction of a Board that had shown itself so averse from dealing with the subject of Lord Wellesley's building megalomania at all ? I think that the answer must lie in the political circumstances at home.   Wellesley's chief friend Pitt had died in January 1806, and in February Sir Gilbert Elliot (afterwards the first Lord

Minto), who at this stage was no admirer of Wellesley, had become President of the Board of Control in the Ministry of all the Talents. It is true that he was succeeded on 15th July, 1806, by Thomas Grenville, but the despatch had probably been sanctioned by Elliot before quitting office. It was left to him a little later as Governor General to carry out the views of the Court, at any rate as regards Barrackpore.

Such is the true and detailed history of Lord Wellesley's peccadilloes as regards Government House, Calcutta. It cannot I think be disputed that he acted, and intended to act, without sanction, either because he feared opposition at home, or because he intended to establish an autocracy in matters which he regarded as in the main of local concern. It is also clear that he sent as little information as he could and as tardily as he could.[1] That he escaped from coming to grief was the consequence partly of political conditions in England, but still more of the fact that it took the best part of a year for information to reach London and for the reply to come back to Bengal. No such circumstances we may be sure will attend the building of the successor to Wellesley's Government House, which has for years been taking shape at Delhi, although it will involve a total expenditure to which Wellesley's extravagance was a bagatelle.

That Wellesley regarded his conduct as requiring defence is however evident from the action which he took in publishing a sustained Defence in the columns of the " Asiatic Annual Register " for 1807. He had evidently been supplied by some friendly hand with a copy of the cancelled Draft No. 128, and this he proceeded to answer *seriatim* and not without effect. I will not reproduce here even those portions of his reply which relate exclusively to the Calcutta house, because they are of enormous length, and because all the salient portions have already been quoted either in the documents previously cited, or in the text of this narrative. There however the full and complete rejoinder of the injured Proconsul is to be found, though, so far as I am aware, it has never attracted the notice of any historian.

The situation is not inaptly summarized in the doggerel of " Tom Raw the Griffin " (written in 1824 by Sir C. D'Oyly), which often sheds a quite illuminating light upon the opinion of contemporaneous Calcutta.

[1] In his Defence Lord Wellesley claimed that " all his proceedings relative to Government House had been regularly submitted, at different periods of time, to the notice and control of the Court of Directors." Here again some elasticity of interpretation seems to be required.

GOVERNMENT HOUSE, FROM CHOWRINGHI (1820)

" And further yet that noble edifice,
   The seat of Government and Wellesley's pride,
Type of the brains that fill that noble head of his,
   And the high horse he loved so well to ride.
'Twas built against the British powers allied
   When o'er the dams and banks of Leadenhall
His grand magnificence poured forth its tide.
   Directors' tears cemented each fair wall,
And joint stock sighs but firmer knit each rising hall."

Whatever the opinion in England, there can be little doubt that public sentiment in Calcutta and the voice of contemporary criticism on the whole condoned the Governor General and admired his stately creation.   It was regarded as a worthy symbol of British Government and as a structure noble in appearance and style.   Nothing is so open to attack as architecture, and no one is so ready to apply it as the amateur.   Here every tyro considers himself an expert, and the building has not yet been raised by man which commends itself to every observer.   The new Government House met with its fair share of local criticism—some of it not undeserved—but the general consensus was flattering to Captain Wyatt, and must have been consoling to the Marquis.

Lord Valentia, who had witnessed the inaugural ceremony, wrote of it :—

" The Esplanade leaves a grand opening, on the edge of which is placed the new Government House erected by Lord Wellesley, a noble structure, although not without faults in the architecture ; and, upon the whole, not unworthy of its destination.   The sums expended upon it have been considered as extravagant by those who carry European ideas and European economy into Asia, but they ought to remember that India is a country of splendour, of extravagance and of outward appearances ; that the Head of a mighty Empire ought to conform himself to the prejudices of the country he rules over ; and that the British, in particular, ought to emulate the splendid works of the Princes of the House of Timour, lest it should be supposed that we merit the reproach which our great rivals, the French, have ever cast upon us, of being alone influenced by a sordid mercantile spirit.   In short, I wish India to be ruled from a palace, not from a counting-house ; with the ideas of a Prince, not with those of a retail-dealer in muslins and indigo." [1]

The concluding sentence of the above extract has commonly— and even by such an authority as Sir W. Hunter in the " Imperial Gazetteer "—been attributed to Wellesley himself ; and even if it was not

---

[1] " Voyages and Travels in India," etc., Vol. I, p. 235.

borrowed from a Despatch or State paper of the Governor General, one cannot help suspecting that the noble Lord, whose style was on a lower rhetorical plane, must have annexed it in conversation with his resplendent host.

"Naufragus," publishing his work in 1827, but writing somewhat earlier, said :—

"Tassit pointed out to me the Government House, built by the Marquis of Wellesley, at an amazing expense, and worthy of the princely city of Calcutta. It is situated on the western side of the Esplanade, and is a most august and beautiful fabric, from whatever point it is viewed." [1]

Bishop Heber was rather more critical :—

"The Government House has narrowly missed being a noble structure. It consists of two semi-circular galleries, placed back to back, uniting in the centre in a large hall, and connecting four splendid suites of apartments. The columns are however in a paltry style, and instead of having, as it might have had, two noble storeys and a basement,[2] it has three storeys, all too low, and is too much pierced with windows on every side." [3]

Miss Emma Roberts, who was in Calcutta in 1835, and upon whose gossipy narrative I shall draw freely in ensuing chapters, did not agree with the Bishop :—

"Bishop Heber, in speaking of the Viceregal Palace of Calcutta, says that it has narrowly missed being a noble structure; persons of less refined, or as some would call it less fastidious taste, do not concur in this censure, or admit that the architectural blunders of which the critic complains have had an injurious effect upon the appearance of the building. It is altogether, whatever may be the fault of its details, a splendid pile ; and, standing isolated on the Calcutta side of the large open plain, which forms so magnificent a quadrangle opposite Chowringee, it is seen to the greatest advantage from every point, being sufficiently connected with the city to show that it belongs to it, yet unencumbered and not shut out by any of the adjacent buildings.

"Somewhat of effect was probably sacrificed to convenience and the accommodation necessary for the establishment of the Governor General; but the great objection to it as an Asiatic residence, which does not appear to have struck the elegant and accurate commentator, is the want of colonnades and porticos. The principal entrances are approached by noble flights of steps, but these, being without shelter, are never used except upon State occasions, when a native Durbar is held, and the nobles of Hindostan come in all their

---

[1] "Adventures of Naufragus," p. 34.
[2] I.e. the Kedleston plan of the central block.
[3] "Narrative of a Journey in India," etc., Vol. I, p. 24.

barbaric pomp to pay their respects at the Viceregal Court—a circumstance of rare occurrence in the present day.[1] The carriages of the European visitants drive under these steps and the company enter through the lower regions."

In one sentence of the above passage the lively authoress draws attention to a feature of Lord Wellesley's palace, as it then appeared, that differentiates it materially from the building as we see it now. In the early years of the 18th century it stood up, straight and stark from the Maidan, surrounded or sheltered by no gardens, and obscured from no spectator, near or distant, by the vestige of a tree.   The soldiers from their barracks in Fort William could note every window and doorway in its glittering southern façade ; a man standing on the site of the present Cathedral could have seen it scarcely less clearly. In all the pictures of the time it stands up solitary and imposing—like a huge wedding cake on a bare table cloth—and the big gateways in the railing of the compound lift their heads like four isolated sentinels on each side of it.   Now the building is wholly screened off from the Maidan by the trees in the garden, above which the dome and parapet alone emerge, and the gateways are so embowered in foliage that I had to cut it away to prevent the ferocious imitation lions on the summit from being lost to view.

In almost every critique of the period censure is passed upon the small and poky staircases at the four corners of the main block.   Tom Raw (Sir C. D'Oyly) is particularly sarcastic at their expense :—

> " In such a palace one might have expected
> A splendid staircase, as at home we find
> In noble edifices well erected,
> And made in spacious turns and sweeps to wind.
> But here, forsooth, there's nothing of the kind,
> It certainly a strange and very rare case is,
> One must suppose the architect was blind,
> When there was so much room, and lots of spare places,
> To build four little dingy miserable staircases." [2]

Certainly from the point of view of architectural dignity the absence of a great internal staircase is a defect, and is one of the respects in which the plan differs conspicuously from that of Kedleston. This blemish was pointed out to Lord Wellesley after the building was completed, and he is said to have been willing to correct it ; but the

---

[1] The allusion was to the modest régime of Lord W. Bentinck.
[2] " Tom Raw the Griffin," p. 69. 1828.

suggestion was vetoed by the architect. I am not sure from the standpoint of convenience that the latter was not right ; for a great staircase, involving in all probability the sacrifice of the existing four, might have led to an inconvenient clashing of the rival streams of guests on the occasion of State functions ; whereas visitors are now brought up one staircase and dismissed down another with tolerable ease, three at least of the staircases being always available for this purpose.

This synopsis of the criticism of an earlier day may be concluded by the verdict of a more competent authority. Fergusson, who knew India well, thus described Government House, laying stress, it will be noted, on the condition to which I have called attention :

" The Government House at Calcutta is the principal edifice erected by the English in India during the first period indicated above. The idea of the design was copied from Kedleston and was a singularly happy one for the purpose. It consists of four detached portions appropriated to the private apartments, and joined by semi-circular galleries to the central mass containing the State-rooms of the Palace, an arrangement combining convenience with perfect ventilation, and capable of being treated with very considerable architectural effect ; all which has been fairly taken advantage of. The principal defect (as it now stands) is that of being too low ; but it must be borne in mind that when erected, it stood alone, and the tall houses around, which dwarf it now, were all erected since. Its effect is also marred by the solecism of the order running through two storeys, while standing on a low basement. If this might be tolerated in the centre, under the dome, it was inexcusable in the wings, where it throws an air of falsity and straining after effect over what otherwise would be a very truthful design ; but, taken altogether there are few modern palaces of its class either more appropriate in design, or more effective in their architectural arrangement and play of light and shade, than this residence of the Governor General of India." [1]

To this I may add that when in 1902 I had the pleasure of entertaining there the Officers of a German and an Austrian Man of War, who had come up the Hugli after a prolonged cruise in many parts of the world, they were lost in admiration at the scale and appointments of a structure which they said greatly transcended the palaces of many kings. Sixty years earlier the famous Dost Mohammed, when a refugee in Calcutta in the time of Lord Auckland, had expressed similar sentiments when he asked if there was really in Europe a larger house than Government House.

[1] " History of Modern Styles of Architecture," pp. 471-2. 1873.

Appendix to Chapter III

List of the Title Deeds of Government House, Calcutta, deposited in the Office of the Comptroller-General.

Document No.

372	Title deeds of the Government House purchased from Nabab Dillawar Jung with his receipt for the old mortgage deeds.
373	Title deeds of the Court-House and Bond of Indemnity of Cockerell, Trail and Company relating to them.
374	Title deeds of two houses purchased from Mr. William Burroughs.
375	Title deeds of a house purchased from Samul Dass to the north of the Government House.
379	Title deeds of a house purchased from Captain Thornhill that was the property of Mrs. Pennitz.
384	Deed of release from Mr. Hickey to the Hon'ble Company of the house purchased from Mr. Burroughs.
408	Title deeds, &c., of a house bought from executors of Colonel Hampton and Lieutenant Thomas Hampton.
460	Bill of sale of a house bought of Manik Doss, 20th February 1771.
461	Certificate of Robert Dobinson as auctioneer of the Hon'ble Company.
462	Letter of Attorney, Mr. H. Norris to T. S. Hancock.
463	Release of a mortgage bond, 1st January 1776.
464	Bill of sale of a upper-roomed house, 1st January 1776.
465	Extract from the will of Mrs. Mary Barclay.
466	Lawrence Pecachy, executor to William Larkins' lease for a year.
467	Release, 19th June 1787.
468	Peter Gilbrith to William Larkins, an assignment.
469 470 471 472	Pottahs granted to William Larkins.
474	Thomas Gibson, Administrator of Michael Collings, deceased, to Peter Gilbrith.
475	Lease for a year, dated 18th May 1803.
476	Release, dated 19th May 1803.
	[Documents Nos. 460–76 are deeds of the house bought from the Executors of William Larkins.]
480	Deeds of a house, &c., purchased from William Fairlie, formerly the property of Allan McPherson.
481	Deeds of a house, &c., purchased from A. Colvin, the executor of Isaak Eaton.
482	Deeds of a house, &c., purchased from Mr. Robert Campbell and Colonel Macfarlane, late the property of Captain Robert Macfarlane.

Document No.

483   Conditional and Indemnity Bond from Cockerell, Trail and Company's
       house with the deeds of a house purchased from them belonging to
       Mrs. Catherine Powney.

       Also release in fee of a messuage and piece of land from Geo. Powney
       and others to the United Company with letters from the Sub-
       Treasurer to the Company's Attorney and the Advocate-General's
       opinion, &c.

577   Deeds executed in Europe by Mr. William Harding and others con-
       cerned to convey his house to Company.

CHAPTER IV

GOVERNMENT HOUSE

Exterior, Grounds, and Garden

" Mark well her bulwarks, set up her houses, that ye may tell them that come after."

Psalm xlviii, 13.

I WILL now give a fuller description of the new Government House—to which however this will be the last time that I shall apply that epithet—and of the various changes which more than a century of time, and a long succession of occupants, have wrought in its appearance and contents. For this purpose, I shall utilise much curious information that has never before been made public, but has lain hidden in official or often in private hands. A good deal of this it has been difficult to procure, partly because it has been strewn about in so many different and often unsuspected quarters, still more because those who are tenants of a place for only a short time are apt to be capricious in their changes and short in their recollection. Indeed one has only to pause a moment in order to realise that the history of such a building must be as obscure as it is unique. Government House, Calcutta, has always been a sort of nomad camp, albeit invested with the dignity and stability of a permanent habitation. For at least seven and frequently eight months of each year it remained, while it was the residence of the Viceroy, unoccupied and closed ; and I used sometimes to picture to myself the possibility of its being usurped during that period by colonies of unauthorised and unsuspected denizens. Then suddenly in the month of December it leaped into life, and a feverish activity converted it into the place of residence and daily work of hundreds of human beings, and the scene of entertainment and amusement for thousands—for all of which purposes great and continuous exertion and a constant outlay were required. At the end of March it relapsed again into solitude and slumber. In each year the persons and staff who occupied and administered it were little by little changing. Then every four or five years came a complete transformation. Practically the whole of the personnel—except the native servants—was swept away. A new Viceroy and his family, with a new Private Secretary, Military Secretary and Staff, very likely with new ideas as to functions, entertainment and life, appeared upon the scene. He knew nothing save by hearsay of the doings of his predecessors ; their records were soon buried in oblivion ; for a short period he and his wife imprinted their own tastes in furniture, decoration or landscape-gardening upon the scene ; and then they too disappeared, and in a distant land forgot the greater part of what they had done. Even the visitors who passed through and recorded their fugitive impressions in works of travel—valuable as their testimony sometimes is—are more apt to retail gossip than to provide the material for history. In this kaleidoscope of incessant change it has not been easy to trace the successive phases or to find out who was the agent responsible for particular effects. Sometimes a single detail has involved protracted research or correspondence with persons scattered in different parts of the world. I shall divide this part of my subject into two chapters, dealing respectively with the surroundings and exterior of the house, and with its interior and contents.

When the architect handed over the completed mansion to Lord Wellesley, it was in main essentials the same outside as it is now —with one conspicuous difference. I have spoken previously of the sharp emergence of the new fabric on the South side a century and a quarter ago from the treeless levels of the Maidan. But these conditions prevailed, though to a less extent, on every one of its faces. Now the extensive compound is so thickly fringed with trees that it is entirely screened off from the town, and you come upon it suddenly, and cannot see it until you are at the gates. This has been the creation almost entirely of the last fifty years. Until about 1870, there was scarcely a tree or plant in the enclosure, and engravings or photographs before that date reveal a framework of sward, as nude except for a few flower beds as the glacis of a fort.[1] I have always wondered why, in a climate where verdure can be conjured up with the rapidity of Jonah's gourd, it never occurred to a long succession of Governors General to carry out a definite scheme of planting the compound

[1] The engraving of Government House in Lord Canning's time (*vide* " Two Noble Lives," Vol. II, p. 57) shows a few shrubs and plants in the Southern garden; and Lady Canning more than once wrote with enthusiasm of the beautiful flowers in the flower beds. But how little the planting amounted to, is shown by her statement (Vol. II, p. 189) that from her room she could see the British soldiers " drawn up like a red wall," and the native regiment in white, on the rampart of Fort William, firing the *feu de joie* on the Queen's Birthday in 1857.

until Lords Mayo, Northbrook, and Lytton appeared upon the scene. But so it was.

As to the area of the grounds, it is large. Sir W. Hunter, writing in the "Imperial Gazetteer" in 1885, gave it as eight acres. But this figure was very wide of the mark. Before Lord Wellesley commenced operations the ground occupied by the old Government House and Council House together—both of which were taken for the purpose—amounted, as worked out to scale from Baillie's and Upjohn's maps, to over twenty *bighas*. Considerable purchases were then made of surrounding land, and when we come to Simm's survey of 1850, we find the area of Government House and compound given as more than seventy-five *bighas*. Later surveys return the area as over eighty *bighas* or rather more than twenty-six acres, and upon these figures the present municipal assessment for taxes is based.[1]

The four great external gateways consisting of masonry arches, surmounted by sculptured lions and sphinxes (the lions on the main or central arch, the sphinxes on the lower side arches), were a part of the original design, and are frequently mentioned in the official announcements of Lord Wellesley's time. When the house was illuminated in honour of the numerous Peaces that were concluded in that period, these were decorated with lamps and transparencies. It appears that when the gates were first erected the lions and sphinxes were not placed upon them, but were soon after added by the skill of a local carver and decorator named Wollaston who was a sort of handy-man for all such jobs. The first sphinxes were made of clay and the lions of wood; but there seems to have been difficulty in securing animals of suitable appearance and proportions, for the accounts in the first ten years after the completion of the house testify to frequent experiments. Eventually, in 1814, the four beasts were all made of teak wood, but these have since disappeared, and the images that adorn the summits of the gateways are now made of brick coated with cement and painted. A contemporary skit, to which and to the notes appended to it, we are indebted for many amusing details about the Government House of the first quarter of the last century,[2] and which I have

---

[1] In my time the annual assessment for house and grounds was Rs. 185,000, and for outlying quarters Rs. 27,000, or a total of over £14,000 p.a.

[2] "Tom Raw the Griffin: A burlesque poem describing the adventures of a Cadet in the East India Company's service." By a civilian officer of the East India Establishment. London, 1828. (He was Sir Charles D'Oyly.)

more than once quoted, says that originally the sphinxes had plaster breasts which were cut off by order of an A.D.C. who thought that Lord Wellesley might be shocked by their exuberance. I fancy that this alludes to the big sphinxes at the bottom of the great Northern staircase rather than to the creatures who are banished to the more sequestered altitude of the gates.

The iron railing running round the Northern compound and also the iron railing, now creeper-covered, on either side of the great exterior staircase, as well as the shabby iron gates leading into Wellesley Place (as they were in my time), were of the same date as the house. I was so much struck by the meanness of all the iron gates, which would have discredited a workhouse, that I obtained sanction for an entirely new set, and procured designs from the best iron-workers in England. But these plans were cut short by my resignation, and were not pursued by my immediate successor. It was reserved for the second Lord Hardinge to remedy the deficiency ; and the visit of the present King and Queen to Calcutta in 1911 was made the excuse for providing the North and South Gateways with handsome wrought-iron gates, containing the Royal Cypher in the centre, which were executed and sent out from England at a cost of about £2,000. New gate pillars of Surajpur stone were erected at the same time.

The compound on the North side of Government House remains much as it was in 1803, with certain exceptions. In 1843 Lord Ellenborough set up on a platform in front of the great staircase a huge iron gun, mounted on a winged dragon with red glass eyes and tremendous scaled convolutions of the tail ending in a forked point. Around the platform were planted upright in the ground ten other guns with embossed Chinese inscriptions. The main cannon bore on its platform the following inscription :—

" Edward Lord Ellenborough, Governor General of India in Council, erected this trophy of guns taken from the Chinese, in commemoration of the peace dictated under the walls of Nankin by the Naval and Military Forces of England and India under the command of Vice Admiral Sir William Parker and of Lieutenant General Sir Hugh Gough " (1842).

At first it was contemplated to erect over this gun a marble pavilion copied from some Moghul original at Agra. But this atrocity was fortunately not perpetrated, and the gun stood out in the open.

The same Governor General also placed two other brass cannon

CHINESE GUN IN FRONT OF GOVERNMENT HOUSE

BRASS CANNON CAPTURED IN AFGHANISTAN

in front of the wings on the North façade. One of these was very heavily embossed and bore the figures of two dogs, to serve as handles, upon the top. It has the inscription on the base, " Ghuznee 6th September, Cabul 16th September, 1842 "; in other words it commemorated the successes of Nott and Pollock in the second Afghan War. The second was also embossed with a Moghul pattern, and had upon its exterior two pairs of very heavy brass rings. It bore the inscription on its base : " Meeanee 17th February, Hyderabad 20th March, 1843," and was set up in honour of the victories of Sir Charles Napier and the annexation of Sind.

Large as Government House appears to be, it possessed singularly poor accommodation for guests, and every Christmas-time a regular camp of well appointed tents covered the lawn fronting the main entrance. The screen of trees, however, running round the interior of the railing is of modern creation, and as it grew up, sufficed to shelter a range of low buildings used as cowshed, plant-houses and carpenters' shops. Lord Minto executed a further improvement, for whereas the kitchens in my time were in Government Place North, at a distance of very nearly two hundred yards from the house, to which every dish had to be carried in green wooden boxes rather like a sedan, he expelled the cowshed from the North-West corner of the compound and erected a *pukka* kitchen building in its place.

On the East side of the house the space of ground enclosed, so to speak, between the two projecting wings, was utilised by Lord Dufferin in 1881 for the construction of an open air tennis court (with asphalt floor and wooden walls). At an earlier date there was a platform there, on which the Viceroy's Band used to play during entertainments. A corresponding structure on the West side was employed for menial service.

When we come to the South face of the house, with its umbrageous garden projecting far into the Maidan, it is not easy to determine the exact date at which this was enclosed. Before Government House was built, Esplanade Row ran in a continuous line East and West without a break from the river to Chowringhi. The interruption of it by Government House Garden was probably synchronous with the building of the house ; but for years the present garden remained a bare enclosure, surrounded first with a wooden paling and afterwards with a plastered balustrade, erected in 1823, and open ditch

G

(still in existence). The various illustrations of Calcutta between 1800 and 1825 do not all agree as to its precise features ; and we may conjecture that some of them were sketched on the spot, and filled in by the artist afterwards.

One feature however has remained unaltered from then to my time, though afterwards removed by Lord Minto, namely the white posts and iron chains that border the broad gravel drive leading to the South entrance of the house, between the South-east and South-west gates. The posts were originally of wood. As early as December 1808 we read of the chains being so loosely fixed that they were stolen by the natives and had to be replaced. Stone posts were substituted in 1823. An illustration in Mrs. Graham's book (1810) depicts a circular grass plot, surrounded by posts and rails, on the spot fronting the Southern door where a big gun now stands. In 1818 we hear of Lord Hastings importing fine sparkling gravel all the way from Bayswater to lay on the walks of Government House ; and an Indian white gravel has been discovered since my day that is now brought by rail and laid down. It was not till 1844 that the iron gate was erected leading from the garden directly on to the Maidan, opposite the site now occupied by the statue of Lord Lawrence. His statue and that of Lord Hastings are the only effigies that could be seen from any part of Government House, the one facing directly down the main avenue leading to the Southern doorway, the other in a similar relation to the Northern entrance.[1]

The space of ground outside the Southern façade is sprinkled with no fewer than eleven relics of successful warfare, each on its white plastered platform.

The first two of these, placed outside the curving corridors of the house, were brass cannon, mounted on wooden gun-carriages. The muzzles and also the hubs of the wheels were shaped in the form of a tiger's head, and at the end of the spokes of each wheel were brass tiger's paws. They bore the inscription " Seringapatam, 4th May 1799," and were placed there by Lord Wellesley.

In the centre stood a large plain brass cannon, mounted on a plain gun carriage, with the names inscribed on the platform, " Moodkee December 18th 1845, Subraon February 10th 1846, Ferozeshur

---

[1] The statue of Lord Hastings by Flaxman, which stood in a portico in front of the Dalhousie Institute, has now been transferred to the Victoria Memorial Hall.

DUTCH GUN IN GOVERNMENT HOUSE GARDEN

BURMESE GUN IN GOVERNMENT HOUSE GARDEN

December 21st and 22nd 1845." This was the contribution of Sir Henry afterwards Viscount Hardinge, and commemorated the triumphs of the first Sikh War. The gun itself was known as Futteh Jung and was captured at Aliwal. The cannon balls belonging to it rested in receptacles on the base.

In front of this cannon were two small brass mortars, with the labels, " Mandalay, Burma 1885–1886." The brasswork of these mortars bore the inscription " Compagnie des Indes De France. Fait par Gor à Paris 1751 "—showing that they had had a varied career before they were captured from King Theebaw by Lord Dufferin.

There were two other Burmese captures, one a brass cannon with finely chased handles and a coat of arms stamped upon the barrel, underneath which appeared the letters A. G. F. ; the other was a plain brass gun. Both were inscribed " Mandalay, Burma 1885–1886," and had their complement of cannon balls on the platform.

On the edge of the grass lawn of the Garden stood two even more interesting trophies. One of these inscribed " Dutch Gun at Cabul 1879 "—a spoil from Lord Roberts' campaign—was a small brass gun, with the representation of a ship (man-of-war) in full sail upon it, and the inscription below.

ASSUERUS · KOSTER · ME · FECIT
AMSTELREDAMI · 1630

and the monogram of the Dutch East India Company V.G.C.

The other gun of this pair was a small brass cannon, captured at Seringapatam in 1789, and testifying its French origin by a heavily embossed coat of arms with the inscription

A · DOUAY · PAR · BERENGER
4 · 7 · 77

Finally, in close proximity to the flower beds, were two big iron cannon, one of immense length, each with two pairs of iron rings, and mounted on old iron stands. These bore the inscription " Mandalay, Burma 1885–1886."

To this collection I contributed a Boer gun brought back from the South African War in 1904. India had despatched a large force of European troops as well as of native non-combatants to this campaign, and was also represented by the European Volunteer Contingent raised by Colonel D. M. Lumsden, and known as Lumsden's Horse, whom I had the honour, as Honorary Colonel, to despatch to the War in 1900, and to welcome back again in 1901. This gun however was afterwards removed.

The Western side of Government House looking towards Council House Street is seldom seen, because neither business nor entertainment moves in that quarter. The enclosure and railings were completed here in a leisurely fashion, and were not finished until 1825.

The Southern garden, now so pretty with its great expanse of *dhoub* grass, backed by leafy walks and winding ponds, only began to assume its present form under the fostering care of Lady Mayo and Lady Lytton. A photograph (included in this Volume) shows what it was like when the former began to plant. Other Governors General or their ladies had tried their hand, but all in vain. There is rather a pathetic passage in one of the letters of Miss Emily Eden, sister of Lord Auckland, dated 14th April, 1841, in which she says :

" Lady Amherst made a magnificent garden round the house, which stands in the centre of what we call a huge compound. Lady William Bentinck said flowers were very unwholesome, and had everything rooted out the first week. I never thought of restoring it till last year, and now it is all done very economically, and only on one side of the house, and at a considerable distance. I am just finishing two little fish-ponds."[1]

I am afraid that Miss Eden's horticultural embellishments went the way of their predecessors—such are the vicissitudes of a nomad occupation and of Viceregal life. When, however, the final attempt was made, in the two reigns to which I have referred, Lady Mayo began the planting, Lord Lytton constructed the ornamental water and rustic bridge, as well as the raised mound, at the Southern extremity of the garden, and in the two years 1877–8 and 1878–9 we

---

[1] " Miss Eden's Letters " (ed. V. Dickinson), 1919, p. 340.

GOVERNMENT HOUSE, BEFORE 1870

GOVERNMENT HOUSE GARDEN, BEFORE 1870

find an allotment of over Rs. 11,000 for these purposes. I deepened the ponds which had become silted up, but made few other alterations.

Once a year this garden was thrown open to Calcutta society for the State Garden Party, which was attended by between 1500 and 2000 persons, European and Indian, but, like all garden parties, was a somewhat depressing function. Later on this entertainment was sometimes given in the evening. At that hour great flying foxes or bats used to lurch from tree to tree (they have since been scared away) ; towards midnight jackals emerged from the drains and howled in the shrubberies, and stinking civet cats would clamber up the pillars or pipes to the roof of Government House. There they liked to linger, sometimes descending at night and even entering the bedrooms on the Southern side, in surreptitious search of food or drink. We shot several of these horrid creatures creeping along the frieze under the parapet in the moonlight, and their successors have since been trapped and extirpated. In the day time the garden used to contribute to the beauty, though not to the peacefulness, of the scene with clouds of green parroquets which would fly shrieking past the windows and settle upon the cornice of the house. The dense belt of bamboos, palms, and other tropical verdure that had grown up all round the garden served another purpose besides that of a screen ; for it sufficed to shelter a regular colony of native *malis* or gardeners, of whom there were between 30 and 40 living in mat-huts in the compound completely hidden from view.

Except for the State functions that took place there, I do not know that Government House Garden was ever associated with any memorable incidents. Its increasing seclusion as the vegetation grew up, rendered it more and more available to the occupants of the house. But I used to conjure up the picture of Lord Canning, harassed and alone, tramping round and round its gravel pathways—then all too exposed—in the dark hours of the Mutiny, the sole form of exercise that he permitted himself at that fateful time. Ten years later, Sir John Lawrence, who but for the Mutiny would never have found himself in Government House, sought a different and less anxious solace in the garden, for he was so fond of playing croquet there, (often to the interested delight of a large crowd of spectators in the street), that he would even continue the game by lamplight after the short twilight had vanished. Somewhere " among the flowers " in the garden Lord Dalhousie buried his favourite Arab " Maharaja " in 1853.

Passing from the garden to the exterior of the house, the main difference that Lord Wellesley would notice, were he to come to life again now, would be changes for which I happened to be largely responsible. I broke the monotonous level of the parapet, unrelieved by a single ornament, by placing upon it classical urns at regular intervals. These are a familiar feature of classical houses of similar design in England, and I procured a number of drawings from Chatsworth and other places, experimenting with different shapes and sizes in brick and plaster. It would scarcely be believed by anyone looking at them from below that these vases are over six feet in height. Another change during the past century has been the number of projecting green wooden sunshades or *jhilmils* fixed on to many of the windows looking towards the sun.

Some mystery attaches to the gigantic coats of arms standing up against the sky on the parapets of the four wings. It was always intended that there should be four of these, two representing the Royal Arms, and two the Arms of the Company. An illustration in Mrs. Graham's " Journal " (1810) represents all four in position. But I am doubtful whether the two on the Northern front were ever erected. The " Bengal Gazetteer " of 1841 says :

" The wings on the southern side are surmounted by the Royal Arms. Those on the northern side are ornamented by the Honourable Company's, *but none are at present visible.*"

This may mean either that the arms were not there, or that the shields had been erected without the arms. I incline to the former view, which is supported by drawings and engravings. Anyhow there were no arms on the Northern wings when I arrived ; whereas the records showed that those on the South had been renewed in 1853. They were however of so portentous a description, both the lion and the unicorn transcending all bounds even of oriental imagination, that I decided to erect new ones on each wing. These were constructed in cast-iron by Messrs. Macfarlane of Glasgow. At the same time I filled the empty tympanum of the pediment on the North front, which had remained unadorned for a century, with a cast-iron representation of the Royal Arms, the cost of the five being, as I remember, £1,300, and the weight 100 tons [1]

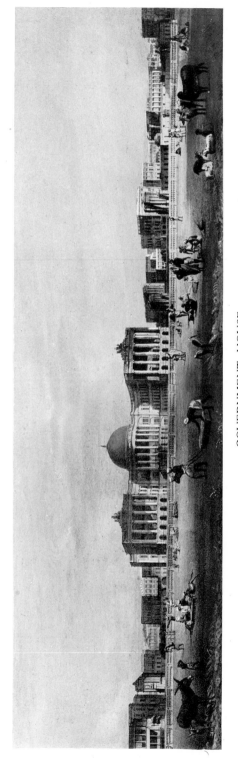

GOVERNMENT HOUSE

From the drawing by W. Wood, 1833.

I also painted the exterior of the house white, instead of a dirty umber or yellow—which had been the colour favoured before my time. Every year, with its new coat of distemper, the building would emerge in December spotless and ravishingly cool. I was never in Calcutta during the monsoon ; but I believe that the appearance which it then presented, stained and mildewed by the drip of the summer rains, was the reverse of inviting.

One feature of the exterior has been the subject of many vicissitudes and of infinite jest. This is the dome erected over the projecting portico or verandah on the southern side. When the house was first built, the dome was not there, but it was soon added (in deference I think to the Paine drawing of Kedleston) to increase the apparent elevation, at a cost (it was made of wood) of Sicca Rupees 30,000 or £3,750 ! In those days it had neither figure nor flagstaff on the top, and Mrs. Graham's picture (1810) depicted it with a low rim. In the official description of the fete that was held on 2nd December, 1814, in honour of the general Peace, when Government House was illuminated, we are told that " the dome in the centre rose like a pyramid of flame." From an early date this unhappy protuberance seems to have been the butt of the local wits ; and the facetious Tom Raw (1824) thus reflected the popular opinion, while incidentally revealing the very practical purpose to which the dome was turned :

> " One word about the dome—'tis so superior
> In every way to domes of brick or stone.
> It covers nought below ! but ripens sherry or
> Madeira[1]—a wood box, perched up alone,
> To aid proportion and for dumpiness to atone."

In 1824 the offending object being reported as over-heavy as well as hideous, was taken down and replaced by another at the cost of Rs. 36,700. Visitors to Calcutta will remember the colossal marble statue of Lord Cornwallis formerly hidden away on the ground floor of the Town Hall, and now in the Victoria Memorial Hall on the Maidan. The wags of 1824 suggested that the disconsolate statue should be shifted to the summit of the new dome. However, a figure was substituted of a mighty female holding a spear and a shield, of whom it was disputed whether she was Britannia or Minerva ; and she may be seen in W. Wood's and Sir Charles D'Oyly's published drawings

---

[1] The popular beverages of those times. *Vide* Lord Valentia and other authorities.

of a few years later.   No sooner had she been put up than Government
House was struck by lightning, and the spear was altered so as to
prevent a renewal of the celestial anger.   In 1829 both dome and
figure were so enfeebled that a Committee was appointed to report
upon their condition.   They were again patched up ; but the hand
of Providence was not to be denied, and in 1838 either or both were
again struck by lightning and considerably damaged.   Lord Dalhousie
ended the long and unsuccessful warfare with supernal powers by
taking down both the dome and the figure, and erecting a new iron
dome (without Britannia) at a cost of Rs. 13,420 or £1,340 in 1852.

At the same time the pedestal of the dome was raised in order to
give it a less squat appearance, and its exterior was painted a golden
bronze.

While I was in India, there were persons still living in Calcutta
who declared that they remembered Government House without a
dome at all.   The explanation of this apparent impossibility was only
forthcoming when Lord Dalhousie's Private Correspondence was
published some years later, and I read in it, under the date 18th
September, 1852 :

" There was a great dome on this house, which was taken down last year
to prevent it tumbling down.   They now propose to put up the new one ;
it will take three months, and the house will not be habitable while the work
is going on."

It is clear therefore that there *was* an interval of at least a year
in which the building was domeless.   To complete the history, in
1862 a flagstaff was erected in place of the figure (and has remained
there ever since), and it was reserved for the first Lord Elgin in 1863–4
to add a coronal and gallery to finish off the summit.   Since then the
dome has ceased to provoke either the ridicule of man or the wrath
of heaven.   No one has again thought of making it the cellar of Government House ; but in my time it provided a useful receptacle for
the storage of empty trunks.   As an architectural feature it redeems
the monotony of a skyline too aggressively horizontal.   But it has
no structural justification, since it is not visible from within, and is
merely laid down like a dish-cover on the flat roof.

Another external difference between the Government House of
the present and that of an earlier day is the disappearance of the
great cranes, known as adjutants, which throughout the first half of

GOVERNMENT HOUSE (1903)

GOVERNMENT HOUSE, SOUTH FRONT (1903)

the last century and as late as 1870—in fact until a modern system of drainage was instituted—used to frequent Calcutta, and were fond of taking their stand on the gateways and parapets of Government House. They were the unpaid scavengers of the city, in the days when all refuse was thrown into open drains, and human corpses used to be tossed into the Hugli, even from the jails and hospitals, to float up and down with the tide. In one of Fraser's drawings, there are as many as sixteen of these birds standing on the parapet of Government House, not counting those perched on the gates or circling in the air. Every year they went away in the breeding season for three months to the Sunderbunds and then returned, like crossing sweepers, each to his appointed pitch. Many of them bore collars put on by the householders whom they patronised and befriended ; and there was one bird in particular, that was said in 1868 to have mounted guard at Government House for thirty years.

If so, he may have been one of the regiment which Miss Emily Eden had described so amusingly in her first year at Calcutta (1836) :

" It charms me when I see one great adjutant kick another off the roof of Government House. They are nearly 6 feet high, and sometimes there are 150 on the roof, where they each have their own place ; and if one takes the place of the other, the rightful owner simply kicks him down." [1]

Elsewhere the lively lady tells the story of an adjutant which, evidently not content with swallowing the live cats, rats and crows that were the ordinary food of its kind, was found to be so heavy that it could not fly. It was accordingly captured and killed, and upon being cut open was found to have swallowed a baby whole.[2] This reminds me of the story of the bear (or was it an ostrich?) in the London Zoo, which died prematurely, and on being opened was found to contain in its stomach a copy of the " Daily Telegraph."

In two respects I was able to add to the external amenities of Government House. Large as was the building and extensive the compound, both were quite unequal to accommodating the enormous number of persons, menial and otherwise, who were required for its service. Calcutta society had swollen in my day to such dimensions, the crowd of cold weather visitors was so great, the mass of work of every description was so overwhelming, that the necessary instruments

[1] " Letters from India," Vol. I, p. 188.
[2] *Ibid.*, Vol. II, p. 90.

for coping with this triple burden could not be compressed within the available space. I have said nothing so far about the policies, nor the servants and attendants' quarters at Government House. All of these were perforce located outside. Little by little premises had been acquired, though in the most haphazard way, mainly in the network of old-fashioned streets between Government Place and Dalhousie Square. Here were the quarters of the Private Secretary, or the Military Secretary, presuming either to be a married man, constructed by the second Lord Elgin, the Viceroy's stables and coach houses, the residences of the steward, chef, and native servants, the stables and quarters of the Bodyguard, the Private Secretary's Office and Press, the Dispensary and Kitchen.

How many of the guests from the outside who sat down to a dinner of 100 knew that every particle of food had been cooked at a distance of nearly 200 yards from the house, and been transported thither as I have before remarked, in *dhoolies* or boxes carried on poles on the shoulders of men? But this was far from the greatest of the discomforts or inconveniences. The Viceroy's Band had to be accommodated half a mile away in the Fort, in constant danger of eviction by the Military authorities, who wanted the quarters. So contracted was the space in the stableyard, that every time the big carriages were used, they had to be dragged out by coolies into the compound of Government House and the horses harnessed to them in front of the main entrance. These and other anomalies induced me in 1905 to take steps, under the terms of the Land Acquisition Act, for the purchase of a larger area outside the compound on the North. I did not profit by these operations, but my successor did, and there now confront Government House on that side a handsome and commodious range of buildings, in which all the principal servants of Government House were quartered and which are now at the disposal of the Governor of Bengal.

Further, the growth of the city right up to the gates of Government House, accompanied by much of the squalor and a good deal of the careless irregularity of an oriental town, had resulted in a setting to the seat of government which was neither dignified nor orderly. Accordingly I drew a parallelogram bounded on the North and South by Dalhousie Square and the Esplanade, and on the East and West by Old Court House Street and Council Street, and within this space I provided for the proper paving and lighting of the principal

EAST GATEWAY TO GOVERNMENT HOUSE (1904)

streets at the cost of Government instead of the Municipality. Proceeding a little further and regarding Dalhousie Square—the Tank Square and Park of old Calcutta—as a spot of historical sanctity as well as natural charm, I laid out the ground afresh, squared the famous Lal Dighi, or Red Tank, surrounded it with a pillared balustrade and a beautiful garden, swept away the unsightly sheds and public conveniences, and converted it into an open-air resort for the public and a Valhalla for the Bengal Government. Thither were transferred the statues of Sir Ashley Eden (previously placed on the site of the Holwell Pillar) and Sir Stewart Bayley (from outside the South-west gate of Government House), and there the equestrian figures of Sir John Woodburn and Sir Andrew Fraser were afterwards set up. I felt that a loving memory required this attention, and that the heart and centre of the Calcutta of our forefathers ought to be made a worthy antechamber to the sacred associations of the neighbouring Fort and the newly recovered and demarcated site of the Black Hole.

On the other or South-eastern exterior side of the Government House Compound, I sought to render a like service to the plot of open ground, seamed by untidy paths and scattered with rubbish, that extended from Esplanade Row East to the Ochterlony Monument and included the Dharamtolla Tank. I filled up the tank, and converted the entire area into an exquisite garden. Subsequent photographs have shown me that I have not entirely escaped the fate of my predecessors. The site has not indeed relapsed into a wilderness, but my garden planning lost a good deal of the symmetry and completeness which I designed.

I only mention these undertakings here, because they were parts of an organised policy, directed not only to preserving and beautifying Government House itself, but to rendering seemly its immediate surroundings and approaches (to which nobody in recent years seemed to have devoted even a passing thought), and thus enabling Calcutta, a city that aroused my warmest affection, to vindicate the proud title which destiny at that time seemed to have placed within her grasp, of Queen of the Eastern Seas.

There is one respect in which Government House, while gaining in seclusion, owing to the luxuriant growth of timber in the compound, has suffered in tranquillity, owing to the advance of the city right up to and even beyond its gates. Almost to the end

of the 19th century, it stood apart from the business quarters of the
city, and was relatively free from its din. Now the low buildings
in Old Court House Street, with which I was familiar, have been
replaced by towering structures, and electric tramcars scream along
the streets. The Governor of Bengal finds himself working in
conditions far less peaceful than the Governor General or Viceroy
of India in earlier times. Fortunately on one side he is safe. For
Calcutta regards with a jealousy, like that of the most passionate of
lovers for the most beautiful of mistresses, the open and inviolate
expanse of the Maidan.

CHAPTER V

GOVERNMENT HOUSE

INTERIOR AND CONTENTS

Full of great rooms and small the palace stood
All various.—TENNYSON, " Palace of Art."

GOVERNMENT HOUSE consists, as has been seen, of a
Central Block connected by corridors with four wings or
pavilions, which are almost in the nature of detached houses.
The Central Block is devoted entirely to purposes of entertainment and
State. Taking the wings in turn as we enter by the main or Northern
entrance, that on the North-east contained the Council Chamber,
and rooms for the Staff, the family, or guests ; the North-west wing
was usually reserved for guests ; the South-east wing contained the
drawing-room and private rooms ; the South-west wing was always
occupied by the Governor General and his wife. Postponing for the
moment the ground floor or basement of the whole mansion, which
was almost exclusively absorbed by offices and Staff, and assuming
that we are entering by the great exterior stairway and passing through
the portico to the State rooms on the first floor, I will first deal with
the apartments in the centre of the mansion.

THE CENTRAL BLOCK

As I shall show in subsequent chapters the outdoor staircase, whose
white steps glitter so fiercely in the sun, unshaded by the two solitary
palms that rise one on either side of it[1] has been the scene of many
imposing and some moving events. Each new Governor General
(with few exceptions) ascended those steps to the assumption
of his great office—all was then novelty, brave hopes, and high
aspirations. Down them, a few years later, he walked with feelings,
very often how different, into the cold dissecting-chamber of history.
Great monarchs, famous commanders, illustrious statesmen, all have

---

[1] These were planted in or about 1870.

93

been received upon those stairs. If their stones could speak, what a tale they might tell.

The main floor of the central building to which they lead, is divided into three apartments, shaped like the letter H laid upon its side, or like the letter T with its head duplicated at the base. Thus : I. The first of these rooms was used in my time as the Breakfast room and Luncheon room. Like the two others it is paved with grey marble[1] and its walls and pillars are *chunammed* or painted white.

I shall give presently a list of the principal Government House pictures as they existed in my day ; but as they have since been dispersed, it will be of no use to describe them minutely, as they were then hung in every apartment and passage. Here up to 1912 were the portraits of Sir John Shore (afterwards Lord Teignmouth), Governor General 1793–8, Sir Charles Metcalfe, Acting Governor General 1835–6, Lord Ellenborough, Governor General 1842–4, Lord Dalhousie, Governor General 1848–56.

But the most conspicuous feature in this apartment was the white marble statue by John Bacon junr., of the builder of the house, Richard Colley, second Earl of Mornington and first Marquis Wellesley, Governor General 1798–1805, which stood on a marble pedestal on the right hand side between the pillars that separated the centre of the room from the westerly extension. The inscription upon the pedestal states, in gilded letters, that the statue was

" Erected by the British inhabitants of Bengal in testimony of their high sense of the wisdom, energy, and rectitude of his administration."

As far back as 14th and 21st February, 1802, at two meetings of the British inhabitants of Calcutta, it was resolved to present an address to the Governor General " on the happy restoration of peace to the continent of India " by the close of the Mahratta campaign, and to erect a marble statue of His Excellency at Calcutta " as a lasting memorial of the sense which the British inhabitants of the Settlement entertain of his public services." On 28th February the Address and Resolution with regard to the statue were presented to Lord Wellesley at Government House ; and after acknowledging the former at considerable length, he made a second speech referring to the gift of the statue,

[1] The whole of the original consignment of this marble came from China, and a store of it was kept in the godown of Government House. When I wanted to reproduce it in some other apartments I found that it could be procured equally easily and much more cheaply in India.

in the course of which he said, in phrases that seem nowadays rather pompous and out of date :—

" I accept the high and extraordinary testimony of approbation which you have been pleased to confer upon me with the deepest sense of its value.

The just object of public honours is not to adorn a favoured character, nor to extol individual reputation, nor to transmit an esteemed name with lustre to posterity ; but to commemorate public services and to perpetuate public principles.

The conscious sense of the motives, objects and result of my endeavours to serve my country in this arduous station inspires me with an unfeigned solicitude that the principles which I revere should be preserved for the security of the interests now entrusted to my charge, and destined hereafter to engage my lasting and affectionate attachment.

May then the memorial, by which you are pleased to distinguish my services, remind you of the source from which they proceeded, and of the ends to which they were directed ; and confirm, in this flourishing and prosperous Settlement, the principles of public virtue, and maxims of public order, and a due respect for just and honest Government." [1]

John Bacon junr., the sculptor of the statue, which is characterised by equal simplicity, dignity, and beauty, was also the author of the colossal monument to Lord Cornwallis, referred to in the last chapter. It was originally intended to place both effigies in the new Town Hall, then in contemplation, and at a public meeting held on 21st February, 1804, to further the project, the Resolution that was passed stated as its double object " the convenience of the Settlement and the reception of the statues of the Marquess Wellesley and the Marquess Cornwallis."

But for some reason or other, perhaps owing to the controversies that raged around Lord Wellesley upon his return to England, and that threatened his public disgrace, the execution or, at any rate, the despatch of his Calcutta statue was delayed, and it was not till 1824 that it reached India during the time of Lord Amherst, when the Town Hall site was abandoned, and the figure was set up by the wish of the Directors in the North Entrance Hall of Government House.

When the Victoria Memorial Hall collection, destined to be the

[1] " Wellesley Despatches " (ed. Montgomery Martin), Vol. III, pp. 579–86, and "Asiatic General Register " 1807, paras. 81–7. On the same occasion Lord Wellesley was asked to convey to the Commander-in-Chief, General Lake, the resolution of the British inhabitants of Calcutta to present to him a sword of the value of £1,500, and to Major General Wellesley (the younger brother of the Governor General, afterwards Duke of Wellington) a sword of the value of £1,000 ; in recognition of their services to the East India Company and their country.

National Portrait Gallery of India, was first formed in 1905, I transferred this statue, already the property of the people of Bengal, to that collection, then housed temporarily in the Museum. From thence it was taken back to Government House by my successor, when the collection was temporarily broken up in 1906. But the object of the original donors has since been fulfilled ; seeing that both the Bacon statues, that of Cornwallis and that of Wellesley, have since been placed, as I desired that they should be, in the Victoria Memorial Hall.

On the opposite side of the Hall to Wellesley once stood the marble statue by Sir John Steell R.S.A. of another and even greater Governor General, James Andrew Broun Ramsay, tenth Earl and first Marquis of Dalhousie, Governor General 1848–1856. This statue also has had its vicissitudes. Originally erected in honour of Lord Dalhousie by public subscription on his retirement from India,[1] it was first placed, in default of any other suitable site, in Government House ; but when the Dalhousie Institute was founded out of the proceeds of the Dalhousie Testimonial Fund and other funds in 1865–6, as " a monumental edifice to contain within its walls statues and busts of great men," and was tacked on to the back of the open loggia or portico that had been built to enshrine Flaxman's statue of Lord Hastings at the end of Wellesley Place [2]—Sir John Lawrence, then Viceroy, surrendered the statue to the Hall or Valhalla that was henceforward to bear Dalhousie's name, and it was transferred thither from Government House in August 1870. There it stood until 1905, when, the Dalhousie Institute having entirely changed its character in the interim, and become, instead of a Hall of Fame, a place of public entertainment, with library and reading rooms attached, this statue and a number of other statues and busts were formally made over by the Council of the Institute to the Victoria Memorial Trustees, and were placed by me in the Collection in the Museum. Lord Dalhousie's statue was afterwards removed temporarily to Government House, but when the Victoria Memorial Hall was completed, it found its ultimate and proper destination in the Gallery of Sculptures there.

[1] Lord Dalhousie gave sittings for this statue to Sir John Steell in Edinburgh in Sept. and Oct. 1857. A plaster replica was added to the National Portrait Gallery in Edinburgh by purchase in 1886.
[2] For an illustration of this statue and portico before the Dalhousie Institute was erected, *vide* Sir Charles D'Oyly's " Views of Calcutta and its Environs," London, 1848.

The Marble Hall

From this apartment we pass into the Marble Hall or principal State room of Government House.

This hall, which consists of a central nave separated by pillars from side aisles—on the model of a Roman atrium—has always been the State Dining Room[1] of Government House, accommodating for this purpose about 120 persons. Like the other State rooms on this floor it is paved with grey marble and the coffered ceiling is gilded and painted white. The defect of the room is the want of height; but on great occasions, when laid out for an official Dinner, or for the Supper at a State Ball, with a show of plate along the sides, and with the scores of native servants in their scarlet uniforms, moving about against the background of dazzling white, it presents a striking appearance. The first Lord Minto, upon his arrival in 1807, not unfairly described it in a letter home as " this noble and magnificent marble hall." It is not however to be mentioned in the same breath with the Marble Hall at Kedleston, which ascends through two storeys to the roof and is supported by magnificent fluted columns of solid alabaster.

By the white pillars of the Calcutta Hall hangs a tale. When erected by Lord Wellesley they were covered with the exquisite *chunam* or plaster, said to have been made of burnt shells, for which India has long been famous, and which when polished took a surface, as Mrs. Maria Graham said in 1810, like " Parian marble,"[2] or perhaps more like burnished ivory. In the passage of time the *chunam* decayed and the pillars were painted,[3] and when Lord Mayo came to India in 1809, I have the authority of his brother and Military Secretary, the late Major Edward Bourke, for saying that " those beautiful columns in the big hall were painted black and all the teak doors white." Lord Mayo at once set to work to redress this outrage : *chunam* workers were brought up from Madras, then the home of the art, and the whole of the pillars on this and on the upper floor were renovated. At the same time the handsome teak doors, throughout the building,

[1] In earlier days when the Governor General was sometimes in residence at Calcutta in the hot weather, we hear of the marble hall having been occasionally used as a sitting room or reception room, *e.g.*, by Lady William Bentinck and the Misses Eden.

[2] " Journal of a Residence in India," 1812, p. 137.

[3] Lord Dalhousie's Committee reported in 1852 that " the walls and even the pillars are covered with common whitewash. In its bare rafters and whitened walls the House resembles a common *cutcherry*."

H

which had apparently been covered over with white paint since the beginning, and were found to be encrusted with innumerable layers, were scraped clean and polished and gilded as they have been ever since.

Again in my time I found that the *chunam* had perished, big pieces had been chipped out and filled in with ordinary plaster, the surface had been defaced by constant rubbing and by many scratches and bruises, and the pillars would not stand the test of more than a cursory inspection. But I found that the art of *chunam* had so entirely decayed that only in Madras and Jaipur could any workmen be found who still practised it. Accordingly I had small parties of the best artificers summoned from both places, and I set one party to work upon one set of pillars and the other upon another, watching their labours as they proceeded, and intending to give the order to the winner of the competition. The result however was so thoroughly unsatisfactory, the new surface in both cases being gritty, dirty and destitute of the wonderful high polish of the old work, and withal so costly, the estimate for the pillars on the two floors being Rs. 30,000 or £2,000—that I did not feel justified in pursuing the experiment, and ordered the pillars to be simply painted with enamel paint. No one in my day detected the difference. But with the passage of time and the accumulation of dirt the result proved disappointing. Another coat of *chunam* was applied to the pillars in 1920. But the modern cement is not comparable with the old.

When the Marble Hall was built by Lord Wellesley, the ceiling, as well as that of the Ball Room above, was painted on canvas by a local artist named Creuse, whose bill for the decorations of Government House amounted to the substantial total of Sicca Rupees 69,000, or £8,625. His taste seems to have been florid rather than refined ; for the amusing Tom Raw tells us, with better humour than scansion, that the ceilings were

> "adorned with Gods in many a string,
>   In imitation of basso-relievo-ing."

from which we may conclude that the artist had tried to represent classical figures and deities, in the style of painting, perhaps in *grisaille*, that was so popular in those times. However he did not allow for the white ants of Calcutta, and in a few years' time his deities and his

THE MARBLE HALL, GOVERNMENT HOUSE

canvas had alike disappeared. The latter however was renewed, and the ceiling was still of canvas in the days of Lord Canning. It was not till Sir John Lawrence came in 1865 that the present coffered wooden ceiling was substituted for it. I believe that the present designs in white and gold were the work of Mr. H. M. Locke, formerly Principal of the Calcutta School of Art. I shall speak of the chandeliers when we ascend to the Ball Room.

Along the East and West walls of the aisles of the Marble Hall are ranged the more than life-size marble busts of the Twelve Caesars, replicas of a series not infrequently met with in the adornment of palaces and princely mansions during the classical revival of the 18th century. A better illustration of the difficulty of writing history in the case of such a building as the Calcutta Government House, with its constant change of tenants and break of tradition, could not be given than the case of these effigies. When any ornament of importance in Government House has been unaccounted for, the custom has been to say that it was seized from a French ship by a British ship in the wars at the end of the 18th century. I conclude that something of value was once so acquired ; but as tradition has told the same tale both of the pictures of Louis XV and his Queen (to be mentioned presently), which were captured on land at Chandernagore, and of the glass lustres, which were brought from Claude Martin's palace at Lucknow, I was always suspicious of the legend with regard to the Caesars. Even if it were well founded, the authorities did not agree as to the circumstances or the date of capture ; for whereas Lord Dalhousie's Committee of 1853 said that the Caesars were " sent out, we understand, by the Dutch Government for the adornment of their Government House in Java, but taken by us at sea "—a legend which is somewhat discounted by the attribution of the pictures of Louis XV and Marie Leczinska in the next sentence to the same source—other writers declare that the fateful ship was taking the Roman Emperors as a present either from the French King to the Nizam of Hyderabad or from Napoleon to Tippu Sultan. Whether a European Sovereign would have been likely to offer such a gift to an oriental potentate who can never even have heard of the Caesars is, I think, a little doubtful, although Napoleon was capable of it. If they came from the Dutch Government House at Java, it would be natural to suppose that they were brought to Calcutta by the first Lord Minto, when he went to Java and took over the Govern-

ment on behalf of the East India Company in 1811. But there is
no mention of them in his published correspondence. Neither do I
know of any authority for the statement in Mr. Cotton's " Calcutta
Old and New " (p. 124) that the Caesars " were at one time among
the ornaments of the Court House Assembly Room (in the Old Court
House) and accompanied the pictures of Louis XV and his Queen
to Government House "—a story which if well authenticated would
suggest that they were also a portion of the spoil of the capture of
Chandernagore by Watson and Clive in 1757. I am inclined to
suggest the more prosaic explanation that just as the busts of the
Twelve Caesars (of corresponding size) are placed along the walls of
the basement Hall at Kedleston, so did the architect of Government
House, Calcutta, in taking my home as his model, think fit to reproduce
them in the palace that he was designing there. The series of Caesars,
whether in marble or in plaster, was a very familiar feature of the
Palladian architecture of the 18th century.

After looking down for a century upon the revels of the Marble
Hall, the Caesars still in my day reposed upon the most hideous painted
wooden pedestals, out of all proportion to the size of the busts. I
procured examples of the best Indian marbles, and had a new set of
pedestals fashioned from the handsomest of these to a superior scale
and design.

The big East and West verandahs of the Marble Hall are ordinarily
used for domestic service ; but I found the South corner of the former,
when fitted up and screened off, a very cool and convenient lounge
for coffee and cigarettes after lunch. These verandahs were not a
part of the original building but were added afterwards.

During its century of Viceregal use, the Marble Hall was sometimes used for other purposes than those of official entertainment.
Here more than once the Viceroy received loyal or congratulatory
Addresses, and here, on occasions that attracted a large gathering, the
Legislative Council of the Governor General sometimes sat. Perhaps
the most famous of these meetings was that at which the so-called
Ilbert Bill, that convulsed the European population of India during
the Viceroyalty of Lord Ripon, was discussed in January 1884. The
following account of the proceedings, never previously published, was
given to me while in India by an eye-witness :

" The audience, which was a mixed one, consisted of English merchants and officials, with their wives, many of the leading Natives of Calcutta, the representatives of the Press, and the Nizam of Hyderabad, then a lad of 18 (who in the following February was invested by Lord Ripon with full powers at Hyderabad). The Viceroy sat at the head of the Council Table with his back to the Throne Room, all the curtains of which were drawn. Perhaps it was one of the most trying positions in which a Viceroy was ever placed ; for popular feeling, which ran very high on the Bill, was almost entirely against him. But no one who saw him could fail to have been struck by his attitude, which was throughout calm and dignified, and the speech in which he addressed the Council at the close of the second day's debate was probably the best he delivered in India. Mr. (afterwards Sir Griffith) Evans opened this day's debate and had not proceeded far with his speech when he was interrupted by cheers. The Viceroy promptly called the assembly to order ; he explained that the Council Room was not a place of public meeting, that his wish was to give the public as far as possible the opportunity of listening to the debate on a measure which excited popular interest, but that, if any further demonstration took place, he would have the Hall cleared."

The Throne Room

Through the hanging curtains at the upper end of the Marble Hall we pass into the long room or upper branch of the **I**, which, during the last half of the 19th century, was known and used as the Throne Room. Before that date the Throne was placed and the Levées were held in the upstairs Ball Room, and the apartment we are discussing was employed for many other purposes. We read in Wellesley's Dispatches [1] that "His Excellency the Visitor took his seat at the west end of this room" on the occasion of the Public Disputation of the Students of the College of Fort William on 29th March, 1803, and that on the next day he conferred the prizes, diplomas and degrees, and delivered a speech in the same place.

When Lord Dalhousie became Governor General, this room was used as the Dining Room for small parties, and he complained bitterly of having "to go through the dining room to get at the drawing room" (in the South-east wing). One of his changes therefore was to convert the then Drawing Room into a sitting room for Lady Dalhousie ; while he furnished the Southern portion of the Marble Hall as a drawing room. An outlay of Rs. 34,800 was sanctioned for this purpose ; and as a Drawing Room it was used by Lady Canning, who described it as provided with handsome red damask furniture, but was always lamenting its drawbacks as a passage room. It was only

[1] Vol. III, p. 64.

converted into the Throne Room after her time, either by Lord Elgin or Sir John Lawrence.

While I was in India this apartment served many purposes, for all of which it was far from badly adapted. It was primarily the Throne Room where Durbars were held, Princes received, and Addresses presented, and where the Levées and Drawing-rooms took place. But it was also the Dining Room on all ordinary occasions, *i.e.* for parties of not more than fifty, and on the occasion of larger banquets, the meeting room in which the guests were assembled in a row all round the room, before the Viceroy and his wife came in for the introductions that preceded the entry into the Marble Hall for dinner. I further found the West end of this room where Lord Wellesley had discoursed, occupied by a billiard table, which I removed from these incongruous surroundings to Barrackpore. The walls of the Throne Room were for the first time hung with silk by Lord Lytton, who imported a blue damask from Paris for the purpose : they were re-hung in Lord Lansdowne's time with green silk, and by myself with rose silk, and have since been again re-hung in 1918. Neither material nor colour will last for more than fifteen years in the Calcutta climate.

Since the room was converted into a Throne Room—the Throne being placed with its back to the Southern wall (where one of the windows was closed and barred for the purpose) so that it faced straight down the Marble Hall, and its occupant could, when the curtains separating it from the latter were drawn aside, be seen from the top of the great external Northern staircase—the Throne canopy has undergone similar changes. In Lord Mayo's time, it was a heavy structure, erected, I believe, by Sir John Lawrence when the Throne Room was changed, and was upholstered in dark velvet, with the Royal Arms embroidered at the back. This very old fashioned and cumbersome erection was superseded by another, scarcely less fearfully and wonderfully made, and upholstered in the taste of a suburban drawing room in pale green. This also having become dilapidated, I took a good deal of pains in replacing it by a more dignified erection, and obtained permission to have a reproduction made of the beautiful canopy in the Royal Palace at Munich—the handsomest that I knew. A photograph of this canopy, as set up at Calcutta, is included in this book. When Delhi was made the Capital, the then Viceroy, Lord Hardinge, ordered a sale by auction of the less important furniture of Government House

CANOPY IN THE THRONE ROOM, GOVERNMENT HOUSE

—a proceeding which excited much adverse comment—and directed the more conspicuous articles to be despatched forthwith to Delhi or to Simla, with small regard to their ultimate use or destruction. Eleven years later I enquired what had become of this canopy. No one was aware of its existence ; until at length after prolonged search the remains of it were discovered in rags and tatters in a godown or storehouse at Simla, where for over a decade they had been permitted to rot into irretrievable decay.

On ordinary occasions there stands, or stood, beneath the canopy a small, rather low, gilded seat of oriental pattern, with cushions of crimson velvet, on which (or on one of the silver State chairs) the Viceroy took his seat when he received Princes or Deputations, and in front of which stood a small footstool of similar design. This was always reported to be the Throne of Tippu Sultan, and to have been brought by Lord Wellesley to Calcutta after the Mysore campaign. But it was exceedingly unlike a throne in the ordinary sense of the word, and I could find no one to tell me anything else about it. It contained large brass rings fixed to the base which showed that it had once been strapped or attached to something else.

Furthermore, I knew the tradition that Tippu's Throne was adorned or supported by great gold tiger heads, and I had seen in the Royal Collection at Windsor one of these tiger heads, together with other emblems said to belong to it.

There are several passages relating to the real throne in the correspondence of Lord Wellesley. In a letter of 20th January, 1800, to the Court of Directors, describing the objects captured at Seringapatam which he was sending home to the King he wrote :—

" The golden tiger's head (which formed the footstool of Tippoo Sultaun's throne) I hope will be placed in St. George's Hall in Windsor Castle, as a noble trophy of the triumph of the British Arms in the East. It would have given me pleasure to have been able to send the whole throne entire to England, but the indiscreet zeal of the prize agents of the army had broken that proud monument of the Sultaun's arrogance into fragments before I had been apprized even of the existence of any such trophy." [1]

Forty years later, when he was an old man of eighty, Lord Wellesley penned this fuller description of the throne :—

[1] Despatches etc. of the Marquis Wellesley (ed. Montgomery Martin), Vol. V, p. 402. The Editor added that the tiger's head and bird of royalty which stood on the top of Tippoo's throne are now (1846) preserved at Windsor, and were frequently placed on the royal table on occasions of State during the reign of William IV.

" The Throne of the Sultan of Mysore was of an octangular form, the canopy being in the form of an umbrella; it was surmounted by a representation of the Uma (or species of eagle) which is now deposited in Windsor Castle; the figure of the bird is composed of pure plates of gold closely inlaid with precious stones with a collar of pearl, and pearls at the eyes and suspended from the beak, and the tail spread and ornamented with pearl and precious stones; the edges of the canopy were fringed with the richest pearl ; it was supported by eight pillars, the capitals of which were in the form of the head of a royal tiger, enriched with precious stones; the whole was covered with plates of pure gold; the octangular pavilion rested on the back of a royal tiger couchant ; this figure also was covered with plates of pure gold; and the eyes, tusks, and claws were of rock crystal; the head and paws of the figure are in Windsor Castle; the head is covered with inscriptions in the Persian character."

As a matter of fact, though the Uma had been presented to George III, the tiger's head had been kept by the Court of Directors and deposited in the Museum at the India Office, where it remained till Lord Wellesley himself, happening to be Lord Steward of the Household, suggested that it should be presented to William IV. This was done, and the King, who was delighted, gave a great dinner to the Directors and others in honour of the gift. There is an illustration of the original throne in the Victoria Memorial Hall Collection. In none of these passages however is there any mention of the Calcutta seat, or anything to indicate what part, if any, it played in Tippu's establishment ; and I could only conclude that it must have been a seat used by Tippu on elephant-back on other occasions, or that it was made to be lifted on staves. This seat, of which I give an illustration,[1] is still in the Throne Room, but has been replaced under the canopy by a fourlegged sofa with silver lion-arms that is said to have belonged to Warren Hastings, and was brought here from Belvedere.

On State occasions, such as the Levée, the Drawing-room, or official Durbars, there were substituted for this seat one or both of the great silver chairs of State. As no one in Calcutta seemed to be aware of the origin or history of these pieces of furniture, I took the trouble to ascertain it.

There were two such chairs in my time, and I append an illustration of them as they then were. Both were said to have been made in the Viceroyalty of Lord Northbrook by Messrs. Hamilton of Calcutta.

---

[1] There is a gold-plated throne or seat very similar to it in the Indian Collection at the Victoria and Albert Museum in London, which is of the date 1800 and belonged to Runjit Singh.

STATE SEAT OF TIPPU SULTAN IN GOVERNMENT HOUSE

The larger chair with lion-arms, the Star of India chased on the back and an Imperial Crown rising from a lotus-flower at the top, was made for the Viceroy, and has so been used ever since. But I am inclined to think that it was at least ten years older than Lord Northbrook's time ; for in an account of a great Durbar held by the earlier Lord Elgin at Agra in February 1863, I read that he was " seated on a massive gold (*sic*) throne, with crimson velvet cushions and two lions of the same precious metal forming the arms."

Anyhow the smaller chair, with the Prince of Wales' Feathers at the back, was made for the then Prince of Wales (afterwards King Edward VII) when he visited India in 1875–6, and was used by him throughout his tour. Both chairs were upholstered in crimson velvet. At the Drawing-rooms they were placed on the dais behind the Viceroy and his wife. They were used at the Delhi Durbar of 1903 by the Duke of Connaught and myself. When however the present King and Queen visited India for the Coronation Durbar of 1911, certain alterations were made in both chairs. It was felt that the symbolical Imperial Crown on its lotus flower would not provide a very suitable background for the seated figure of the King wearing the real Imperial Crown. Equally was there no reason why the Prince of Wales' Feathers should adorn the seat of the Queen. Accordingly both of these emblems were removed, and a chased and embossed crown was further substituted for the Star of India on the back of the Royal Chair. Both chairs were gilded at the same time, and the crimson velvet upholstery was covered with rich embroidery in gold. A facsimile pair of chairs was also cast in silver at the Calcutta Mint, since there were occasions on which a duplicate set was required by Their Majesties. I publish a photograph of the chairs as altered.

In the Throne Room the Levées were held in my time by the Viceroy, the crowd entering by one of the open doorways from the Marble Hall, which was divided into pens or enclosures for the occasion, and passing out at the other. The annual Drawing-room was also held by the Viceroy and his wife in the same place. On these occasions the soldiers of the Bodyguard formed a semicircular ring or *cheval de frise*, between the two doors immediately facing the Throne, each touching the other, and remaining absolutely immovable during a performance that sometimes lasted an hour and a half. Occasionally however the strain proved too great, and a stalwart trooper, dizzy with standing in the extreme heat, would fall with a resounding crash to the ground. I found this room carpeted, but discovering that there was the same beautiful polished marble flooring underneath, I removed the carpet, and the floor remained bare during my time.

Here, before the Throne, was enacted, forty years ago, the saddest ceremony that this room can ever have witnessed. On 8th February, 1872, Lord Mayo, who during his three years of office had by his charm of manner and his noble bearing won in a peculiar degree the esteem of the Indian Princes and the confidence of the public, was stabbed to death by the hand of a Pathan convict at Port Blair in the Andaman Islands.[1] Ten days later his body reached Calcutta, and lay for two days on 19th and 20th February in State in the Throne Room, a procession of sorrowing friends and admirers passing before the coffin. Then the body was carried down the Marble Hall on to the great staircase, where an impressive funeral service was performed by the Bishop of Calcutta before a vast crowd, after which it was conveyed by a man-of-war to Ireland for interment.

The Throne Room was hung, when I arrived in India, with the oil paintings of George III and Queen Charlotte; Louis XV, King of France, and Queen Marie Leczinska; Lord Wellesley, Governor General 1798–1805, Lord Hastings, Governor General 1813–1823, Mr. John Adam, Acting Governor General January–August, 1823, and Lord Amherst, Governor General 1823 to 1828. Changes were subsequently made to admit of hanging the State Portraits of King Edward VII, by Sir Luke Fildes, and Queen Alexandra, which were sent out in 1904. All of these, with the exception of King Edward and Queen Alexandra, have now been taken away.

Of the above pictures I will only allude to the portraits of the French King and his Polish Queen, of which, when I came to India, I read the following in the official Catalogue, published only a few years before :—

" It is said that these pictures were captured at sea in a vessel bound to

---

[1] The Jemadar or head of the Native attendants who was attached to me while in India had been present with Lord Mayo when he was struck down and described to me the incident. The assassin, who was serving a life sentence, had no grudge against the Viceroy, but only against the Indian Government, and he killed the former because accident had thrown in his path a victim of greater eminence than any upon whom he had long hoped and plotted to wreak his revenge. While in India I heard on unquestioned authority a curious story of a famous native astrologist who, in a distant part of India, was asked as a proof of his skill to cast a horoscope on that very night. He did so, and having worked out the calculations replied, "The King of Delhi is dead to-day." None of those present understood, and he declined to explain, this oracular utterance. Not till five days later, there being no telegraph to the Andamans, did the news of the assassination of the Viceroy reach India.

STATE CHAIRS, BEFORE 1911

STATE CHAIRS, AFTER 1911

Mauritius. An exactly similar picture to that of the Queen is in the Louvre, painted in 1747, and signed on the thickness of the table ' Carle van Loo,' when the Queen was 44 years of age."

I was never however a warm believer in the man-of-war theory, which was expected in my opinion to serve too many masters : and it was accordingly with no surprise, that in the course of my studies I came across the following passage in the writings of the Dutch Admiral Stavorinus, whom I have previously quoted, and who came to Calcutta from Chinsura in 1769. Describing his visit to the Old Court House at Calcutta (where St. Andrew's Church now stands), he wrote :—

" In one of these rooms are hung up the portraits of the King of France and the late Queen, as large as life, which were brought by the English from Chandernagore when they took that place." [1] (23rd March, 1757.)

There can be no question that the reference is to these pictures, which must have continued to hang in the Old Court House till its demolition in 1792, and were then removed to the precursor of the present Government House.

The marble-paved verandah on the Southern exterior façade of Government House, behind the Throne, was originally laid with Chunar stone. But marble was substituted for this in the time of Lord Ripon, and occasionally on hot nights in March it formed an agreeable place for dinner. I recall a pleasant dinner there with Lord Kitchener and Sir Ian Hamilton, fresh from Manchuria and the Russo-Japanese war. In Lord Wellesley's time his guests used to assemble in this place to see the fireworks on the Esplanade.

We will now ascend to the upper floor by the interior staircase at the South-east end of the main block. This staircase was hung with pictures in my time, of which the most remarkable were R. Home's picture of the Duke of Wellington, and a picture of Fath Ali, Shah of Persia 1798–1834. The latter with its ambrosial beard, covering a foot and a half of canvas, must have been brought to India by one of the Indian Missions that were despatched to the Persian Court in the early years of the 18th century.

On the upper floor the shape of the big rooms is identical with that which we have been examining below. The central room over the

[1] I subsequently discovered that this reference had been unearthed by H. F. Rainey in his " Historical and Topographical Sketch of Calcutta," Calcutta, 1876. But no one had paid any attention to it, and the error is repeated in guide books to this day.

Marble Hall was the Ball Room, the Southern Ante-room was a Drawing Room used as such on the occasion of large dinner parties, the Northern Ante-room was used for the buffet at Balls. All have teak floors and handsome teak doors.

LARGE DRAWING ROOM

The Southern room, above the Throne Room, was entirely devoid of any furniture until the middle of the last century. Lord Dalhousie in 1852 rather plaintively remarked of it :—

" The South room at the end of the ball room should be furnished with ottomans, sofas, etc., of which it is entirely bare, and a couple of good mirrors, one at each end, would be an improvement, and not add materially to the expense."

Lord Dalhousie probably did not know, what I never discovered until a further volume of the Letters of Miss Emily Eden (the sister of Lord Auckland) was published in 1919, namely that there had been mirrors here which were hung by Lord Wellesley, but that as they had lost all their quicksilver Miss Eden decided to sell them in 1841. Greatly surprised, she obtained £400 for them at auction, and with this sum she set about gilding the Ball Room adjoining.[1]

It was not however till Lady Mayo's time that this room was at all adequately furnished. A Royal visit lends a tremendous and highly esteemed fillip to the furniture of Government Houses in all parts of the world, just as a Viceroy's visit is a godsend, in this respect at any rate, to Lieutenant Governors, Residents, and other officials in India. The Duke of Edinburgh's impending visit to Calcutta in 1870–1 applied the spur in this case, and the Louis XVI gilt furniture was ordered from Paris for the purpose. The silk upholstery was pink in those days, but both the walls and the furniture were afterwards covered with yellow damask, which I renewed. Whether Lord Dalhousie's modest desire for a couple of good looking-glasses was gratified in his day, I do not know : it was reserved for Lord Dufferin to hang here some resplendent mirrors from the palace of King Theebaw at Mandalay.

THE BALL ROOM

The central Ball Room is almost the most interesting apartment in the house, for it was the scene of the first great revels held in Govern-

[1] " Miss Eden's Letters " (ed. V. Dickinson), 1919, p. 340.

UPPER DRAWING-ROOM, GOVERNMENT HOUSE

ment House after its opening in 1803, it has been used for the same purpose ever since, and it was for more than fifty years the Throne Room
in which Durbars, Levées and Receptions were held by the earlier
Governors General. Up the centre, on the occasion of the State
Balls, has walked in stately procession every Governor General from
Lord Wellesley to the second Lord Hardinge; and every figure,
male and female, who has been famous in the Calcutta Society of the
18th century, has trod a measure upon its floor. A good many of
these sprang to life again for a single night, when on 26th January,
1903, I gave a Fancy Dress Ball in this room, in which the costumes
worn were those of Lord Wellesley's celebrated Ball in the same place,
exactly 100 years before.

When State Balls were held in my day, a modest dais was erected
in the open archway at the Southern end of the Ball Room on which
were placed a few gilt chairs: and in front of these were danced the
State Lancers with which the Ball opened. But a century ago, a
much more imposing ceremonial was observed. There, for instance,
Lord Wellesley on State occasions took his seat under a State Canopy,
which had been made at a cost of Sicca Rupees 6,550 or £820 by the
versatile Wollaston (architect of the lions and sphinxes on the Gates)
and was repaired for Lord Hastings at a cost of £500 13 years later.[1]
In front of the Governor General, on either side, a semicircle of chairs
was placed for the Members of Council, the Chief Justice, and Judges
of the Supreme Court; and when this august assemblage was seated,
the dance began. From the same Throne and place Wellesley would
hold Durbars and Investitures, and listen to the prize speeches and
dissertations of the leading students in his short-lived College of Fort
William.[2] This practice was continued by the first Lord Minto,
and Mrs. Maria Graham was present on one of these interesting
occasions:

" At stated seasons general examinations take place at the College, and public
disputations are held by the students in Persian, Hindustani and Bengalee,
in the Government House in presence of the Governor General, who usually
makes a speech on the occasion, setting forth the advantages of the College,

[1] In Lord W. Bentinck's time, according to Miss Emma Roberts, who was very severe upon the
social delinquencies, as she regarded them, of that Governor General and his wife, " the Throne, never
particularly superb, is now getting shabby ; a canopy of crimson damask, surmounted by a crown and
supported upon gilt pillars, is raised over a seat of crimson and gold."—" Scenes and Characteristics
of Hindostan," Vol. III, p. 74.
[2] On one occasion, as has been stated, this function was held in the present Throne Room.

the anxiety he feels for its success, the liberality of the Company with respect to it, and the College at Hertford,[1] blaming the slothful in general but commending the diligent by name, and medals are distributed to such as have distinguished themselves."[2]

How well one knows the sort of thing ! I can only congratulate myself that to my many duites this was not added. Of the Ball Room and its incidents I shall have something more to say in a later chapter about Ceremonies and Entertainments at Government House.

The most conspicuous feature of this upper range of rooms (and in a scarcely inferior degree of the State rooms that have been described on the first floor) is the immense number of glass lustres or chandeliers by which they are or were lighted, originally with wax candles, and later with electric light. Miss Emma Roberts in 1835 wrote that

"handsome sofas of blue satin damask are placed between the pillars, and floods of light are shed through the whole range from a profusion of cut glass chandeliers and lustres."

Here too tradition had been unable to tear itself away from the obsession of the all-conquering man-of-war ; and this belief I found firmly established when I came to India. And yet, had any one taken the trouble to read the story of Lord Valentia, who attended the Ball of 26th January, 1803, he would have learned the historical fact, viz.: that the original chandeliers and mirrors were purchased at the sale of the effects of that curious personage General Claude Martin, which was held at Lucknow on 15th October, 1801, after his death in September 1800, at his fantastic palace of Constantia, now known as La Martinière.[3]

There they had been seen and described by Sir John Shore, when as Governor General he paid a visit to Lucknow and stayed with General Martin in February 1797. In his diary on the 26th of that month he wrote—in a passage which seems to have escaped notice :

" The two rooms containing the company, consisting of somewhat more than forty ladies and gentlemen, were covered with glasses, pictures and prints ; in short you could see no walls three feet from the floor. He had a pair of glasses ten feet in length and proportionately wide, and

---

[1] *I.e.* Haileybury College.
[2] " Journal of a Residence in India," p. 138.
[3] The "Calcutta Gazette" of December 1800 and throughout 1801 frequently advertised the impending sale of the General's effects, including the lustres and girandoles.

BALL ROOM, GOVERNMENT HOUSE

estimated his glasses and lustres only in the said two rooms at 40,000 Rupees or £4,500."[1]

Twenty years later Bishop Heber repeated the story,[2] which also appears in W. Hamilton's "Description of Hindustan" (1820). I have read elsewhere that the British Resident at Lucknow purchased them at a very low figure, the King of Oudh declining to run up the price against him. That this is the true genesis of the original chandeliers I entertain no sort of doubt. During the succeeding century they were frequently added to or repaired, usually by the firm of Osler and Co., in London. It was possible however to distinguish between the old and the new lustres; and I re-hung the entire collection in the various apartments, where they had been jumbled up in the most incongruous fashion. The greater part of them have now been taken away to Delhi.

The furniture in these upstairs rooms and also in the verandahs of the Ball Room, which were used as sitting out rooms during a Ball, was the least creditable part of the equipment of Government House, and I was able to order a new Empire suite with a view to the visit of the Prince and Princess of Wales (now King George and Queen Mary) in 1905.

Having completed the survey of the Central Block, we will next visit the wings, commencing with the North-east wing, in which was the Council Chamber, the meeting-place for more than a century of the Executive and later also of the Legislative Council of the Governor General. The corridor leading to this wing, and the adjoining staircase were hung with the portraits of several Governors General and Viceroys—Lord William Bentinck 1828–1834, Lord Auckland 1836–1842, Lord Canning 1856–1862, Sir John Lawrence 1864–1869, Lord Mayo 1869–1872, Lord Northbrook 1872–1876, Lord Ripon 1880–1884, Lord Dufferin 1884–1888, Lord Lansdowne 1888–1894, the second Lord Elgin 1894–1899. Truth compels me to add that many of these pictures were exceedingly poor. That of Sir John Lawrence was painted some time after he had returned to England, and did not present the least likeness to the appearance he wore in India, his chin being covered with a long beard. The picture of Lord Canning was deplorable, that of Lord Mayo no better, the

---

[1] "Memoirs of Lord Teignmouth," Vol. I, p. 409. These must have been the mirrors subsequently sold by Miss Eden.
[2] "Narrative of a Journey in India," Vol. I, p. 383.

portrait of Lord Ripon could not possibly be described as a work of art. Some of these pictures were painted by artists who had never seen their subject, others were bad copies of poor originals. Later a more generous and scientific system prevailed ; and to every retiring Viceroy the India Office addressed a formal invitation to sit for his portrait and select the artist at a fee of £500. In this way the later paintings attained a much higher level of merit, and were in any case originals. When the Capital was moved in 1912, and I realised that the paintings were destined to disappear, I resolved that Calcutta should not be without the portraits of the Viceroys and Governors General who had ruled there, and I procured for the Victoria Memorial Hall, partly by gift and partly by purchase, a far finer series than had ever adorned the walls of Government House.

The Council Chamber is preceded by a small Waiting-room in which the Secretaries to Government awaited their summons. On the occasion of meetings either of the Executive or the Legislative Council, the Members assembled in the corridor before the arrival of the Viceroy, who, after shaking hands with each, entered the room and took his seat at the head of the table. Behind him on the Southern wall hung the famous picture of Warren Hastings with the motto inscribed above it, which suggested the well-known passage in Macaulay:

" A person small and emaciated, yet deriving dignity from a carriage which indicated habitual self-possession and self-respect, a high and intellectual forehead, a brow pensive but not gloomy, a mouth of inflexible decision, a face pale and worn but serene, on which was written as legibly as under [over] the picture in the Council Chamber at Calcutta, *Mens æqua in arduis*—such was the aspect of the great Proconsul."

The original portrait has passed through many vicissitudes. It was painted by A. W. Devis, but at what period or where is not absolutely certain. Devis was born in 1763 and he can therefore only have been 22 years of age when Hastings left Bengal. Devis is not known to have resided or painted in India before the year 1791 ; and the picture of Hastings, which we hear of as in existence in Calcutta in 1784, and as in the hands of his friends, must therefore have been a portrait by some other artist. We may presume that Devis painted his own portrait of Hastings from such earlier picture or from such details as were given him on the spot. The portrait became the property of William Larkins, a close friend of Hastings, who was Accountant General in

WARREN HASTINGS

From the painting by A. W. Devis, in the Council Room, Calcutta.

Bengal and was placed by the latter in charge of his financial interests after his departure. When Larkins himself left India in 1793, he transferred the portrait of Hastings to Charles Chapman, a civil servant who had at one time acted as Private Secretary to Hastings, and was devoted to him. In the following year Chapman also went home, and the picture then passed to Samuel Turner, who had been an A.D.C. to Hastings, and whom the latter had sent on the well-known expedition to Tibet. Turner hung it in the upper floor of Hastings House, and when his time came to go, restored it to Chapman, who offered it to the Indian Government, by whom it was hung in the old Government House (Buckingham House), opposite the portrait of Cornwallis. When Lord Wellesley built his new palace, and placed the Council Chamber in the South-east wing, he hung the portrait of his great predecessor there, but in what exact position is not known. At a later date Sir J. Lawrence's fine picture of John Adam, who officiated as Governor General in the three months' interval between Lord Hastings and Lord Amherst, occupied for a while the place behind the President's chair ; but by Macaulay's time (Lord William Bentinck) the picture had acquired or had resumed its central position, and there it remained until the year 1885, when, having been sent to England to be cleaned, it was kept by the Secretary of State and deposited in the National Portrait Gallery in London, a very inferior copy being sent out in 1887 in its place.[1] No doubt the view was taken that so interesting and valuable a picture would be better looked after at home.

Being convinced that there was no ground, subject to reasonable care, for this belief, my colleagues and I in 1905 successfully urged the Secretary of State to return to us this picture, which had been paid for by the Government of India, and had already for a hundred years withstood, with little or no injury, the shocks of the Calcutta climate. When it came out again in 1905, it was replaced in its old position. At the same time I procured a new and worthier copy of it for the Victoria Memorial Hall. After I had left, this copy was, by an inexplicable error, presented to the Calcutta Corporation, who declined to give it up. It is now in the Town Hall. The original painting by Devis was afterwards removed to Viceregal Lodge, Delhi, where it now hangs. The copy by Miss J. Hawkins, that hung in the

---

[1] At the same time the Devis original, which was first mezzotinted in 1794, was engraved by C. J. Tomkins in London. The engraving, however, is not very successful.

I

Council Chamber when I arrived in Calcutta, has gone back to its old place. The Devis original has I believe since suffered from unskilful treatment in India. The picture represents Hastings as a middle-aged, almost a prematurely aged, man (he was 52 when he left India), bald and shrunken, very unlike the well-to-do cavalier who was painted in England by Stubbs a few years later. In the background in a niche in the wall is depicted a marble bust of Clive. It should be added that the portraits of Hastings in middle life vary considerably according to whether they present him covered or uncovered. He became very bald at an early age : and accordingly, when painted without a hat, he looked prematurely old.

The remaining pictures then hanging in the Council Room were those of Lord Clive, Governor 1758–1760 and 1765–1767, by Sir N. Dance ; Lord Cornwallis, Governor General 1786–1793 and 1805, by A. W. Devis ; Lord Wellesley, Governor General 1798–1805, by R. Home ; the first Lord Minto, Governor General 1807–1813, by G. Chinnery ; Lord Hardinge, Governor General 1844–1848 (a copy from the original by Sir F. Grant in the National Portrait Gallery, London); the first Lord Elgin, Viceroy 1862–1863, also a copy from Sir F. Grant. The majority of these pictures have since been transferred to Delhi.

As to the Council Room itself, it served very well for the meetings of the Executive Council, at which more than ten persons were never in the room at the same time.   But it was barely large enough for the meetings of the Legislative Council—consisting at that time of 20 members—and for the reporters and the public as well. The latter were accommodated in chairs at the North end of the chamber, or wherever space could be found. But there was no room for more than a sprinkling, and whenever a larger gathering was expected we met in the Throne Room instead. These conditions were greatly aggravated when the enlarged Council, over sixty in number, first met in the time of my successor, the later Lord Minto, and a most unsightly and inconvenient arrangement had to be made by which a gallery for reporters was constructed over the President's head. Such a makeshift could not have subsisted much longer, and a new Council Chamber must have been provided even had the move to Delhi not been made. Such indeed was the experience of Lord Carmichael, the first Governor of Bengal under the new system.

Before the institution of the enlarged Council, the speeches were delivered, or rather, as a rule, read by the speakers seated at the table, and in the month of March, when the heat was sometimes very great, the performance of a long-winded orator was the excuse for a justifiable slumber. I cannot say that the room was at all suited for the purposes of the Legislative Council; nor indeed was it ever constructed for such a purpose, the idea of a deliberative body in which representatives, both Indian and European, of all parts of India should take part, being half a century later in origin than the erection of Government House. Of all the apartments in the latter, Council Room had, I suspected, changed least since 1800; and apart from ordinary repairs, and the occasional shifting of pictures, I could not ascertain that any money had been spent upon it, except when in 1886 the windows and doorways were fitted with some rather sombre crimson curtains.

It was in this Council Chamber that each new Viceroy was " sworn in," although no swearing took place in my time, and all that I had to do was to listen to the warrant of my appointment being read by the Home Secretary, a ceremony that did not occupy five minutes. I shall allude to this ceremony in Chapter XI.

A curious episode is recorded in certain of the Bengal Public Proceedings in the India Office, in which the names of the two artists R. Home and T. Hickey, who were painting in India circ. 1800, are involved, and which shows that it was the original intention to put painted ceilings in the Council Room and on the three principal staircases of Government House. In these papers for 14th August, 1806, is entered a letter from Mr. R. Home, stating that in March 1803 he received orders to paint ceilings for the three staircases of Government House and for the Council Room at a price of Rs. 8,500 (4,000 for the Council Room and 1,500 for each staircase). Since then he had spent on the work Rs. 6,029, and had been given an advance of 2,500. He now asked instructions as to completing them. If it were decided to put up no more ceilings in Government House, he was willing to bear the loss of his time and trouble, but he would be out of pocket by Rs. 3,529. He suggested, therefore, that " Government should allow him to keep the 16 portraits of natives painted by Mr. Hickey at Madras, and which was (sic) sent to him about twelve months ago by Captain Sydenham to get framed for the Government House. . . . Mr. Hickey's prices were 50 pagodas a head, which at 325 Sicca Rupees to pagodas 100 was 2,600.[1] The materials of the ceilings he would take, to make up the deficiency."

It was ordered that Mr. Home be informed that it is not considered to be expedient to authorise the expense of furnishing the ceilings which he was instructed to prepare for the Government House ; he would, however, be reimbursed the Sicca Rupees 3,529 he had spent over and above the advance already made ; and also the cost of framing the sixteen portraits of the late Tippoo Sultaun's family, on the due delivery of those pictures.

Whether the painted ceilings were ever actually erected is left in doubt by the above narrative—probably not—for I have never found a reference to them in any other quarter.

I now pass to the North-west wing, containing the principal guest chambers. These were so badly arranged, an immense amount of space being sacrificed to one or two rooms of unnecessary size, while the remainder was divided up by wooden partitions into old-fashioned bathrooms and sweepers' staircases,[2] that in 1905, before the anticipated visit of the Prince and Princess of Wales, I drew a plan for the reconstruction of the two floors which added considerably both to the accommodation and to convenience. The pictures and objects in this wing and in the corridor leading to it are, or rather were, not of sufficient interest to be mentioned here.

Passing to the Southern wings, that upon the South-east has for years contained on the first floor and still contains a smaller Drawing Room, used on ordinary occasions by the family or visitors or by a party of moderate size after dinner. This is the room, the use of which as a general Drawing Room excited Lord Dalhousie's anger, because the way to it lay through the Dining Room (*i.e.* the present Throne Room), and which he accordingly converted into a boudoir for Lady Dalhousie. As such it was also used by Lady Canning, who endeavoured for the first time to furnish it adequately. When King Edward VII came to India as Prince of Wales in 1876, this suite of rooms was prepared and furnished for him and a special bathroom was constructed for his convenience. In those days and later the central room of this suite was known as the Pink Drawing Room,

---

[1] *i.e.*, about £325.

[2] In Lord Dalhousie's time this wing was given over to the Private Secretary, Military Secretary, and Aides-de-Camp—hence the small accommodation for guests of which he complained.

owing to the colour of the wash upon the walls ; the ceilings also were simply distempered in white. Lady Dufferin used this room as her boudoir. In the second Lord Elgin's time this apartment was for the first time hung with green silk, and became known as the Green Drawing Room. I made considerable alterations here, sweeping away the nest of little rooms that had been constructed when this floor was used for sleeping purposes, and providing out of the available space, with little structural alteration, a billiard room, an ante-room, and a room in which the Band could play after dinner, while leaving the main Drawing Room in the centre untouched. In this way we could, with the aid of the verandah, accommodate in this suite any party up to thirty after dinner, without the necessity of moving to the desert spaces on the upper floor of the Central Block. On the wall of this room the second Lord Elgin had rescued from obscurity and exposed to view the remains of a magnificent china dinner service (of Worcester manufacture) bearing upon each article the arms of the old East India Company. No doubt this splendid service was once in daily use in Government House, and had suffered accordingly. It was fortunate that the few surviving relics were preserved before these too had vanished. They have since been removed. A portrait of Queen Victoria by Angeli was a conspicuous feature in this apartment. I need say nothing of the guest rooms above, except that in one of them, during my first season in Calcutta, my subsequent colleague Mr. Winston Churchill, who was very nearly being a member of my staff, immured himself for hours daily, writing his book on the Omdurman Campaign.

Passing to the South-west wing, we come to that part of the house which had for a hundred years been consecrated to the official and domestic use of the Governor General ; though it had on occasions been surrendered to illustrious visitors, as it was to the present King and Queen when they visited Calcutta in 1905–6. The big room on the first floor looking on to the garden,[1] was throughout that time the work room of the Governor General, except during the short time for which it was surrendered by Lord Mayo to his Private Secretary, the Viceroy preferring to do his work in the smaller but cooler apartment adjoining, with a Northerly outlook. The other and more

[1] An iron spiral staircase by which he could slip out unobserved from the verandah to the garden was made by Lord Ripon.

convenient arrangement has suited every other occupant ; for on one side of the Viceroy was the A.D.C. in waiting, and a waiting room for visitors, and on the other side his Private Secretary, Assistant Private Secretary and Typist.[1]   A century earlier the needs were somewhat different, for Lord Wellesley had a Political as well as a Private Secretary, and at that time there were accommodated in Government House, presumably on the ground floor, half a dozen of the most promising young civilians from the newly founded College of Fort William, who took down and copied the Governor General's Dispatches, and generally filled the place now occupied by stenographers and type-writing machines.

Probably the big room, with the verandah on the South, has witnessed discussions as agitated and decisions as heavily charged with fate as any private apartment in the wide circumference of the British Empire.   Here Wellesley must have dictated many a haughty reply to the exasperating censures of the Directors in London ; here Lord William Bentinck threshed out with Macaulay the new scheme of Western education which has revolutionised India, and had more momentous consequences than any decision of Indian policy during the past century ; here Lord Auckland bent his head over the agonising news from Kabul ; here Lord Dalhousie penned those masterly Minutes which have been the model and the despair of his successors ; here Canning sat, surrounded by piles of boxes which he was too unbusiness-like to open, declining to believe in the Mutiny until the storm was upon him, or to disband his own Bodyguard though the danger was at his gates, but inflexible in his policy of mercy, while almost within hearing excited crowds of his fellow countrymen in the Town Hall were clamouring for his recall ; here John Lawrence worked in a costume as untidy as when he was a Deputy Commissioner on the frontier ; here Lord Dufferin turned his polished phrases ; and here Lords Lansdowne and Roberts planned the strategy of another Afghan campaign.

In one respect fashion had changed before my time.   I suspect that Lord Wellesley was usually in his chair at 6 a.m.   Now European hours, together with European habits, European dress, European food and drink, and European games, have overrun India.   If I may

[1] The wooden partition dividing these rooms was erected by Sir George Colley, the ill-fated Military and Private Secretary to Lord Lytton, who was afterwards killed at Majuba Hill.

GREEN DRAWING-ROOM, GOVERNMENT HOUSE

speak for myself, I was seldom in that chair before 10 a.m., but once there I rarely left it, with the exception of an hour or two for meals, or a public function or a private drive, until 2 a.m. the following morning, or sometimes later. Among the many interviews that I recall in that room, it will perhaps be harmless to mention one. I recollect a petty chief from the North-West Frontier who had come down for the first time to Calcutta, and whom the Foreign Secretary had implored me to relieve of some of the wind that was said with good reason to be in his head. I must have succeeded in this operation, for his native attendant remarked to one of my Staff, as his master went away, that he had left the presence of the Viceroy " sweated and surprised."

The upper floor of this wing contained the bedrooms of the Viceroy and his family—and here I furnished a very pretty sitting room for my wife (to save the ten league march to the South-east wing) which was afterwards occupied by the present Queen. Another necessary innovation for which I was responsible was the introduction of an electric lift into this wing, which was useful both for domestic purposes and also for any visitor incapacitated from climbing the great stairs.

The Basement

I may dismiss the ground floor or Basement in a few sentences, for it has been the subject of so many changes that a consecutive history would be impossible even were it not insignificant. Most visitors however to Government House have some knowledge of it, for the general entrance on the North front is by the door leading into the Basement hall under the main steps. Miss Emma Roberts in 1835 was very sarcastic as to these dispositions, which prevailed then as now :

" The effect upon a stranger, who has not been previously made acquainted with the cause of the arrangement, is very singular. It is scarcely possible for a lively imagination to escape the notion that, instead of being the guest of a palace, he is on the point of being conducted to some hideous dungeon as a prisoner of State. The hall, which opens upon the dark cloister formed by the arch of the steps above, is large, low, and dimly lighted, completely realizing the *beau idéal* of the interior of the Inquisition. A good deal of rubbish of various kinds, piled confusedly and put out of the way behind rows of pillars, traversing the length of the hall, favours the supposition that it is a place of punishment ; for in their shapeless obscurity, these fire-engines, or printing-presses, or whatever they may be, have very much the appearance of instruments of torture.

"Upon the floor, the spectator, who has imbibed the apprehension that he has been entrapped into some pandemonium of horror, may see the dead bodies of the victims to a tyrannical Government thickly strewed around—human forms apparently wrapped in winding-sheets, and stretched out without sense or motion upon the bare pavement add to the ghastly effect of the scene. These are the palanquin-bearers, who, wrapped up from head to foot in long coarse cloths, are enjoying the sweets of repose, little dreaming of the appalling spectacle they present to unaccustomed eyes. Many dusky figures move about with noiseless tread ; and, were it not for one redeeming circumstance, the whole panorama would be calculated to inspire horror and alarm. In the midst of these dreary catacombs gay parties of visitors, ladies in ball-dresses, and gentlemen in full uniform, are passing along, not in the least discomposed by appearances so familiar to them, even when there is the additional agremen of a fog, which in the cold season usually casts a mystic veil over these subterraneous apartments." [1]

Palanquins and their bearers have long ago disappeared, though the dusky figures still move about, and on occasions the gentlemen in uniform are seen. Whether the private Printing Press was located there in Lord W. Bentinck's time I do not know; but it flitted about from place to place in the basement until it was finally turned out, with the Private Secretary's Office, in the time of Lord Ripon, to find a new home first at Loudoun's Buildings, then at 1, Larkins' Lane, and finally at 6, Council House Street, its last home. Similarly, the Military Secretary's Office, which used to be in the basement of the North-west wing, was, in my time, in the South-east. In these mysterious regions crowds of minor officials and babus performed the ministerial work of Government House, and dispensed the invitations, the programmes, the bills of fare and what not. Here the Comptroller of the Household and the A.D.C.s managed the affairs of an establishment numbering, all told, many hundred persons. On the ground floor of the North-east wing the smoking and billiard room of the A.D.C.s was a universally popular resort. I was not responsible for any great change here except for paving the central basement hall (under the Marble Hall) with the same grey marble as elsewhere. The furniture here was the oldest in Government House, and had, I suspected, descended from floor to floor with succeeding generations.

The reader who has accompanied me so far through the principal

[1] " Scenes and Characteristics of Hindostan," Vol. III, p. 72.

rooms will perhaps have wondered what was the general stamp and quality of the furniture and equipment in them. The increasing standard of comfort, the greater resources of Government, the superior provision of Calcutta shops, and the more frequent visits of illustrious guests, had made a great difference in recent years; and when I left Government House it was probably the best appointed Government House in the Empire. But it was not always so, and the records of earlier Governors General, particularly in the first half of the 18th century, tell a tale of almost pitiful parsimony on the part of the Company and of indignant complaint from its most powerful servants

This deficiency applied equally to furniture and to table equipment, such as china, cutlery and plate. As early as 1766, Lord Clive's plate, upon his final departure for England, was purchased by the Company for the use of the Governor. What afterwards became of it I do not know, for we find Lord Wellesley in 1806 saying in his reply to the strictures of the Court, that—

"The whole of the furniture and plate for the new Government House was purchased in small quantities and at various times during a period of six years[1] (*i.e.*, while the new house was being built)."

But it must soon have deteriorated or disappeared, for in 1824 a report was made that the condition of the porcelain, glass, silver and cutlery was deplorable. Governors General in those days were constantly absent for months at a time, in marches to distant parts of India, and although their place in Government House both at Calcutta or at Barrackpore was usually taken by the senior Member of Council who acted with the title of Vice President of the Council and Deputy Governor, we may imagine that the deficiencies of Government House either escaped notice under this arrangement or were regarded as relatively immaterial.

Lord William Bentinck in 1828 requested the sanction of the Court to a renewal of the furniture, plate, mirrors, etc., and asked to be allowed to spend Rs. 2,000 annually on the purchase of furniture. The Court returned no reply to this communication; but Rs. 30,000 were given to the Private Secretary between 1828 and 1830 for the purpose. It was reserved for Lord Dalhousie to adopt more strenuous measures.

From the very moment of his arrival he complained bitterly, in

[1] Miscellany in the "Asiatic Annual Register," 1807, p. 66.

letters to his intimate friend Sir George Couper, of the nakedness of the land. He had not been a week in Calcutta when he wrote :

" I find the house superb, the furniture disgraceful ; an A.D.C.'s bed absolutely broke down to the ground with him the other day from sheer age ; the plate and table equipage very poor. I can't afford to spend money in plate." [1]

Three years later (18th August, 1851) we find him writing with pardonable pride, but with equal indignation, to the same correspondent :

" From the hour I landed I have husbanded the Company's money as I never did my own at the poorest. Though the Government Houses at Calcutta and Barrackpore are furnished as no servant of the Company at the Presidency would endure his own, and though urged, I may say, by the whole community to render them fitting the residences of the head of the Government, I have refused to this moment to do so. I do not believe that in nearly four years I have expended Rs. 20,000 on all the appurtenances of furniture, etc. which are allowed me. I have ordered no plate, no ornaments, no china— nay, in camp last year the service was actually made up with blue delft soupplates of which I was myself ashamed."

At length, in 1852, the patience of the Governor General finally broke down, and having decided to act, he proceeded with characteristic precision, to appoint a Committee of Enquiry, to write a Memorandum with his own pen, and to address the Court of Directors. The Committee, consisting of J. A. Dorin (then Financial Secretary) and J. P. Grant, both of whom were afterwards members of Lord Canning's Council, while the second became Lieutenant Governor of Bengal, reported, in language which must have delighted their Chief, that the furniture of Government House was " so very old and mean as to be a public discredit," that it was " offensively incongruous," and that the older parts of it " would not be received into the worst room of any hotel in Calcutta intended for the reception of ladies and gentlemen." Lord Dalhousie sent home this Report, with the reasoned Memorandum from which I have occasionally quoted, seeking the sanction of the Court to the necessary expenditure. This was given in gracious terms in a reply dated 2nd February, 1853 : and Lord Dalhousie, who was most businesslike and economical, set to work to satisfy the more pressing needs, procuring the requisite articles, partly from a local firm named Shearwood, whose prices he described

[1] " Private Letters of Lord Dalhousie " (ed. J. G. Baird), p. 20.

as "enormous," partly from England. He concluded his final Memorandum with the words :

" Some of the furniture in this house which is in daily use, has been so used for fifty years since 1803 ; I expect Messrs. Shearwood's furniture to be such as shall survive till the Governor General of 1903 can say the like of it, when that time shall come."

I happened to be the successor in question, and I conclude that the greater part of the mahogany furniture (for which Lord Dalhousie expressed a preference) was the result of this Napoleonic commission to Messrs. Shearwood fifty years before. If so I am glad to say that on the whole it had creditably survived the test.

Lord and Lady Canning were the first to profit by Lord Dalhousie's outlay. But that it had not, in their opinion, satisfied the deficiency is shown by Lady Canning's frequent complaint of the " waste white rooms of Government House " and her remark, " The rooms were as bare as the Gallery at Buckingham Palace. Not a book had ever been seen in this house before." Little by little however the gaps were filled, and a higher level, both of dignity and comfort, maintained. In 1863, gas, which had been brought into Calcutta while the Mutiny was proceeding, in 1857,[1] was introduced into Government House ; in 1872 electric bells, in 1882 a hot and cold water supply, in 1899, my first year, electric light, in 1900 electric fans, superseding the old hand-pulled punkahs, although I left these in the Marble Hall and Reception Rooms, preferring the measured sweep of their old-fashioned fans to the hideous anachronism of the revolving blades (they have all gone now) ; in 1905 modern fixed baths, in place of the old green-painted wooden tubs.

In one respect the equipment of Government House struck me as defective, even in my time. I have spoken of the early purchase of plate, and of its subsequent disappearance. I found an ample supply of table cutlery, and of silver candelabra, of an ugly pattern with elephants. But there was no ornamental plate for the table or side-boards, and each Viceroy had to bring out his plate of this description from England, if he possessed any, in order to hide the nakedness of the land.[2] Similarly there was hardly a table ornament or knick-

[1] The first gas-lamp was lit in Calcutta on July 5, 1857.
[2] Ali Baba (G. Aberigh-Mackay) in his well-known skit " Twenty One Days in India," written in the time of Lord Lytton (1876–1880), wrote of " the tons of gold and silver plate that once belonged to John Company, Bahadur, as still reposing on the groaning board of the great ornamental " (*i.e.* the Viceroy). But this was pure imagination, and not even the smallest and flimsiest of sideboards could have groaned under the Government plate that existed in my time.

knack in Government House, and the reception rooms, great and small, were entirely dependent for their appearance upon the contributions made by the taste or resources of their successive official occupants.

Thus the interior history of Government House has been traced from the date of its foundation to the present day. In its reduced circumstances I fear that it has been despoiled of the majority of the contents which I have described, and of much of its former splendour. But even if these have departed, the ghosts of the past can never entirely desert the halls and passages where so much of brilliancy and moment has been enacted, and there is the greater reason for writing the story before it is altogether forgotten.

I have more than once alluded to the pictures on the walls, and although the major part of the collection has now been dispersed, it seems advisable to state briefly the circumstances in which it was brought together, and to give some account of the principal paintings that hung in Government House, while it was still the residence of the Governor General. A good deal of the information which I have collected is new, and appears in no other publication.

The oldest paintings were undoubtedly those of Louis XV and his Queen, which, as I have previously explained, passed into the hands of the Company as spoil of war in 1757. Next came the life-size portraits of George III and Queen Charlotte, copies of the well-known originals by Allan Ramsay, which were painted at the time of their Coronation in 1761, and distributed among British Embassies and Government Houses abroad. Doubtless they were hung in the earlier Government House. The oldest portraits of Governors General were those of Clive,[1] Warren Hastings,[2] and Cornwallis,[3] acquired towards the end of the 18th century and hung in the predecessor of the present house.[4]

Lord Wellesley, intent upon glorifying the Mysore Campaign quite

---

[1] This picture is similar to a painting by Nathaniel Dance in the possession of Lord Powis (not to be confused with the three-quarter-length picture, also belonging to Lord Powis and mentioned on page 4 of the Official Catalogue 1898). Whether the Calcutta portrait was a replica by Dance, or a copy by some other artist, is not known.

[2] The story of this picture has been told on p. 112–114.

[3] This picture was painted by A. W. Devis when residing in Calcutta in 1793, and was bought by public subscription for Rs. 20,000, or at the then rate of exchange £2,166 10s., and was originally hung in the Levée Room of the old Government House by request of the donors.

[4] In a letter of 13th September, 1797, Sir John Shore (afterwards Lord Teignmouth) when Governor General wrote : " I have now the portraits of Lord Clive, Mr. Hastings and Lord Cornwallis in the Government House, and if I could have procured a copy of Mr. Cartier, he should have been added to the list." " Memoirs of Lord Teignmouth," by his son (1843), Vol. I, p. 437. Mr. John Cartier was the predecessor of Warren Hastings as Governor of Bengal, 1769–1771.

as much as upon furnishing Government House, applied in the same letter to the Court of Directors with which he sent home the fragments of Tippu's throne (20th January, 1800) for full-length portraits of the Chairmen and Deputy Chairmen, who had presided during the period of preparations for the war and its continuance—namely Mr. Bosanquet, Sir Stephen Lushington, and Mr. Inglis ; and also of Lord Teignmouth, Mr. Dundas, and Mr. Pitt for the same purpose. Wellesley added that he had already applied to Lord Clive (Governor of Madras), Generals Harris, Stuart and Baird, for their respective portraits.[1] None of these persons would seem to have responded to this subtle form of flattery ; nor is any answer of the Court on record.

A little later, in January 1804, we find a sum of Sicca Rupees 2,050 paid to the artist R. Home for the renovation of the modest collection of paintings then in Government House.

The next pictures to be acquired were those of Lord Wellesley himself[2] and his brother, afterwards Duke of Wellington,[3] both of which were hanging in Government House before the former left India. Then followed the portraits of Lord Minto[4] and Lord Hastings,[5] all of which were in Government House before 1816, when we find a record of their restoration.

After this date the records are dumb, until we come to the well-known Minute of Lord Dalhousie dated 15th February, 1856, from which we may infer that the portrait of John Adam, Acting Governor General in 1823, by Sir Thomas Lawrence, had been the sole purchase made

[1] "Despatches, etc." (ed. Montgomery Martin), Vol. V, p. 403.

[2] There were two portraits of Lord Wellesley, both by Robert Home, one of which hung in the Council Chamber and was evidently painted in commemoration of the defeat of Tippu, the Tiger of Mysore, since there are carved and gilded tigers' heads below the frame. This appeared to be the picture which was voted by the City of Calcutta, to whom accordingly it belongs. The other picture appeared from a Bengal letter to the Court of Directors of 24th July, 1832, to have been brought to Calcutta from the Government House at Singapore, where it must have been hung at the time when the Straits Settlements were under the Governor General of India. The church in the background of the picture having been identified as that of St. Mary, Madras, the portrait was probably painted there. The former of these portraits has been reproduced as a Frontispiece to this Volume.

[3] This picture was painted in 1804 by R. Home, and was purchased from him by the Government of India in 1805 for Rs. 2,000.

[4] Painted by George Chinnery, who spent many years in India and other parts of the East. The original of one of these portraits was presented by Lord Minto to the Town Council of Hawick and the picture in Government House was a reproduction. The second picture, subscribed for by the people of Calcutta, and therefore presumably belonging to them, disappeared from India in some inexplicable fashion, was discovered in a Scotch country house in 1924, and was repurchased by me for the Victoria Memorial Hall, where it now hangs.

[5] Also the work of G. Chinnery. For many years this picture was erroneously supposed to represent Sir Eyre Coote, and was so labelled. A second picture of Lord Hastings in Government House was a later copy, by T. Hayes, of the original by Samuel Lane in the Oriental Club in London, and was ordered because Lord Canning's Government were not satisfied with the earlier and smaller picture.

in the preceding 30 years.   As this Minute is of great interest, I will transcribe it in full :

" When walking through the Council Chamber and the stately apartments of this palace which Lord Wellesley built for the Governor General of India, I have often been struck by the poor array of the portraits of public men which its walls display, and have wondered at the contrast which it has thus been long allowed to present to other great mansions of a similar class.

" 2. It might be expected that the resemblance of at least each one of the line of Governors General would have been found within the Government House ; but there are in fact very few of them there ; and those who are to be seen appear to have been unequally and strangely selected.   Warren Hastings is there and my Lord Wellesley, and the Marquis Cornwallis ; but far the greater number are absent.   Half an acre is covered by a likeness of Mr. John Adam ; but Lord Hastings is thrust away over a doorway in kitcat, and not a square inch of canvas has been allotted to Sir Charles Metcalfe or to Lord William Bentinck.

" 3. I think that this is a great deficiency, and that it ought to be repaired by placing the portrait of every Governor General on the walls, either of the Council Chamber, or of some other apartment in the Government House.

" 4. No difficulty would be found in carrying the proposal into execution ; for copies of the portraits of Lord Teignmouth and of Lord Amherst, and of the others which are wanting, could, no doubt, be readily obtained with the consent of their families.

" 5. It would be attended with no heavy expense ; for while the copies should be made by none but eminent hands, the cost of such copies is inconsiderable.

" 6. I feel confident that the Hon'ble Court would approve of my proposal that past deficiencies should be made good, and that the line of portraits should be continued hereafter, and always by the hands of artists of reputation at Home.

" 7. If the Hon'ble Court should be unwilling to undertake the task of obtaining the portraits which are missing, the Government of India could easily make its own arrangements for the purpose.

" 8. It would be mere affectation in me to be deterred from making this suggestion by a recollection of the trifling personal interest in the matter which a captious critic might attribute to me."

This suggestion went home, with the support of Lord Dalhousie's colleagues, and was accepted by the Court, who asked for a list of the missing subjects.   Upon this being received they intimated that measures had been taken to supply the portraits with the exception of those persons who had only held the office of Governor General *ad interim*.   Lord Dalhousie was then asked to sit for his own portrait, which he agreed to do, and did after his return to Scotland.

In his correspondence with his Indian physician, Dr. Alexander Grant, we find him, in the autumn of 1857, sitting simultaneously in Edinburgh for his picture to Sir John Watson Gordon, P.R.S.A., who had already painted him ten years before (a portrait which is now in the National Portrait Gallery in London), and for his statue—mentioned on page 96 of this book—by Sir John Steell.[1]

The Court however were more valiant in promise than in performance: for sixteen years later, when the matter was taken up again it was found that the only gaps anterior to Lord Dalhousie that had been filled in the interval were Sir John Shore (Lord Teignmouth),[2] Sir C. Metcalfe (Lord Metcalfe),[3] Lord Auckland,[4] and Lord Ellenborough;[5] while as regards Lord Dalhousie's successors, the intervention of the Board of Control—who in sanctioning the provision of the portrait of Lord Dalhousie had suggested that in future each Governor General might be left, if he liked, to present his own portrait, painted at his own expense—had effectually choked off any later additions to the series.

It was the lamented death of Lord Mayo that again called the attention of the Government of India to the subject, and a despatch was sent to the Secretary of State in March 1872 asking for a portrait of the late Viceroy. A little later, on 2nd May, 1872, another despatch was issued, pointing out that, exclusive of Lord Mayo,[6] there were still six deficiencies among substantive and two among acting Governors General, and proposing to set aside a yearly sum of Rs. 3,000 until they were supplied. The India Office again signified acquiescence and promised support.

However, when Lord Northbrook, who was a real lover of the arts, appeared upon the scene, and found that only a bad portrait of Lord Mayo had been received, while none of the remainder

[1] *Vide* " Alexander Grant, Physician and Friend," pp. 122–3.

[2] Painted by John Hayes from an original, said to be by Devis, in the possession of the family at Crossways, Oxford.

[3] A copy by John Hayes of an original by F. R. Say in the Oriental Club, London.

[4] This was a bad picture (artist unknown, but probably John Hayes) and was replaced at a later date by another painting by A. Stuart Wortley.

[5] Painted by John Hayes.

[6] It is strange that among the deficiencies noted in 1872 should have been the Marquis of Hastings, for not only had Lord Dalhousie mentioned a kitcat picture of him as being there in 1856 (the explanation is that some foolish person had labelled this portrait Sir Eyre Coote in the interim, an error which was not detected for many years) but the full-length portrait copied in 1857 by J. Hayes from the picture by S. Lane in the Oriental Club in London, should have been sent out to India too, but apparently had not.

had even been ordered, he set himself energetically to terminate the scandal; and it was mainly owing to his personal influence and exertions that the gaps were filled and the collection practically completed.[1]

At a later date, in 1879, the Government of India represented that four acting Governors General were still missing;[2] but the Secretary of State, rightly I think, declined to provide them.

Subsequent Viceroys have been invited to sit for their pictures on their return to England; and these have, one by one, taken their place on the walls of Government House.[3]

A catalogue was almost as late in making its appearance as were the majority of the pictures. Colonel Earle, Military Secretary to Lord Northbrook, began to make notes as a basis in 1875; but when in 1886 Lord Dufferin enquired for a catalogue, all that could be furnished was a list, giving no details and in some cases not even the names of the painters. In 1887 Mr. (afterwards Sir George) Scharf, Director of the National Gallery, made some notes on certain pictures that had been sent home to England to be cleaned. These were handed over to the Public Works Department in India, for similar notes to be prepared on the remaining pictures that had been left behind. But so unsatisfactory was the result that the second Lord Elgin in 1894 ordered the preparation of a proper catalogue, and entrusted the task to Mr. Jobbins, then Superintendent of the School of Art, Calcutta. He died before its completion, but his notes were taken over by Colonel A. G. Durand, Military Secretary to Lord Elgin, who finally brought out a volume in 1897 entitled " A Descriptive List of Pictures at Government House, Calcutta." This was

---

[1] Mr. G. F. Clarke was the copyist now employed, and in addition to the portrait of Lord Mayo he supplied the portraits of Lord Amherst (from an original by Sir T. Lawrence), Lord Hardinge (from the original by Sir F. Grant, now in the National Portrait Gallery in London), and the first Lord Elgin (also after Sir F. Grant). The picture of Lord W. Bentinck was copied from an original at Welbeck; that of Lord Canning, a very poor work of art representing him with the little beard which he wore during his last year in India, was a copy executed by a marine painter named Mornewick; the portrait of Sir John Lawrence, also depicted with a beard which no one in India ever saw, was the work of Val Prinsep, R.A. Sir John Macpherson and Sir George Barlow were not represented.

[2] The number was much larger, for there are no pictures of Sir Alured Clarke (1798), W. B. Bayley (1828), W. B. Bird (1844), Sir Robert Napier (afterwards Lord Napier of Magdala) 1863, Sir W. Denison (1863–4), Mr. J. (afterwards Sir J.) Strachey (1872), Lord Napier of Merchistoun (1872), Lord Ampthill (1904). Some of these officials only held office—and that by the accident of circumstances—for a few days. Thus Mr. John Adam (1823) and Sir C. (afterwards Lord) Metcalfe are the only two acting Governors General whose portraits had actually been admitted to Government House.

[3] Lord Northbrook, by W. W. Ouless, R.A.; Lord Lytton, copy of original by Sir J. Millais; Lord Ripon, by E. J. Poynter, R.A.; Lord Dufferin, copy of original by F. Holl, R.A.; Lord Lansdowne, by F. Holl, R.A., and H. G. Riviere; Lord Elgin and Lord Curzon, both by Sir G. Reid; Lord Minto, by P. de Laszlo.

an immeasurable advance upon anything that had preceded it ; but the work still contained many inaccuracies and was not available to the public.

In addition to the pictures just mentioned, there were in Government House two paintings of Queen Victoria, one a full-length picture in her Coronation Robes by Sir George Hayter (1862),[1] the other by Von Angeli, both duplicates of originals in England ; the State Pictures of King Edward VII and Queen Alexandra, sent out in 1905 ; a portrait of the Duke of Clarence, and portraits of Lady William Bentinck,[2] Lord Halifax, better known as Sir C. Wood, first Secretary of State for India (1859–1866), and Lord Beaconsfield (presented by Lord Lytton), the four last named being all copies. There were also a number of pictures of varying merit but some historical interest, representing Native Princes and gentlemen, and occasionally Indian scenes, the origin of which was not in all cases known. The most important of these was the collection known as the Mysore series, being in the main portraits of members of the Mysore family, painted at Seringapatam or Vellore in 1800–1 by Thomas Hickey, an artist resident in Madras, who received for the series of sixteen paintings the sum of £325. These must have been acquired by Lord Wellesley, who was himself painted by Hickey. They appear to have been hung by him in Government House, but to have been moved at a later date to Barrackpore, and there they remained until they were brought back to the Calcutta Government House by Lord Dufferin in 1885. They are now in Belvedere. Thither also have been removed from Government House the portraits of Sir John Shore (Lord Teignmouth), Lord Cornwallis, the first Lord Minto, and Sir C. Metcalfe, although why these have been spared from the general deportation to Delhi I do not know.

Now that the majority of the collection has disappeared,[3] Government House, Calcutta, has to look to the Victoria Memorial Hall for

---

[1] For this the artist was paid 200 guineas.

[2] This picture, the copy of an original at Welbeck, was presented by Lady Ossington, the niece of Lord W. Bentinck, through Lord Northbrook in 1875. It is the only portrait of the wife of a Governor General in Government House. It is interesting however to recall that Hoppner's beautiful picture of Lady Mornington (who did not accompany her husband to India) and her two sons, was sent out to India in the year in which it was painted, 1798, and was hung by Lord Wellesley in the new Government House (as soon as the latter was finished), where it remained until his departure from India.

[3] Copies of the portraits of the following rulers were however ordered for Government House—Lords Wellesley, Amherst, Hardinge, Canning, Elgin, Lawrence, Mayo, Lansdowne. Why this particular selection was made has not transpired.

J

a full pictorial record of the great figures who have lived and laboured in her midst ; and there I am glad to think that the orders and purchases and gifts for which I have been in the main responsible since I returned to England, have provided her with a collection not inferior to any that existed on the walls of Government House and in some respects more representative and interesting. Further, the Victoria Memorial Collection contains many originals of considerable value.

CHAPTER VI

THE INDIAN HOUSES OF WARREN HASTINGS

"Let us now praise famous men, and our fathers that begat us."—Ecclesiasticus, Ch. xliv, 1.

O Thou that sendest out the man
To rule by land and sea,
Strong mother of a Lion-line,
Be proved by this strong son of thine
Who took his right from thee.—Rudyard Kipling.

WHEN I went to India as Viceroy, one of the objects that interested me greatly was the commemoration of the houses in which great or famous men had lived and worked, and maybe in some cases died. In London and elsewhere I had seen the same purpose successfully accomplished by the placing of tablets or medallions, with a simple inscription, on the front of buildings that had been similarly tenanted ; and I felt that in India, where the human cycles succeed each other so rapidly and records are so soon effaced, there was the more need to call attention to these witnesses of the past, before they perished altogether or were forgotten, in order that the new generation might thus be reminded of those who had laboured in the same field before them. I drew no distinction between European and Indian, desiring to imbue the native mind with the same spirit of reverence that should be the property of all. Accordingly I addressed all the Local Governments, and the principal Native States as well, seeking for information as to the places in their respective areas which might be worthy of commemoration.

When I had received and studied their replies, and completed the necessary examination of the evidence tendered, I published lists of the buildings selected with the reasons for commemorating them, and prefixed to the lists the following Government Resolution, dated 29th January, 1904 :

" About three years ago the Government of India were led to consider the methods that might most advantageously be adopted for the preservation of historical relics and of interesting sites or buildings in India, and for the perpetuation of the surviving records of a past that is every day tending to disappear more and more from the public recollection.

" Among the objects that commended themselves to their notice from this point of view was the commemoration of the houses or dwellings which are notable for their historical associations, or in which distinguished public men, whether European or Indian, have resided at different portions of their careers. A good many of these are still standing, and are pointed out with certainty to the student or traveller. The antecedents and identity of others are already becoming matters of uncertainty; and authentic history is beginning to pass, in some cases into tradition, in others into legend. It seemed desirable, before this process has attained further dimensions, to arrest and crystallise as far as possible the definite knowledge that is still forthcoming of the former residences of men who have left an enduring mark upon the civil and military administration or upon the moral and intellectual development of India.

" 2. In England the Society of Arts has for some time past interested itself in a similar undertaking, by placing upon the façade of houses in London and elsewhere a circular terracotta medallion with a simple inscription on its face, recording the fact that this or that famous personage lived there in such and such a year or years. In this way, a number of valuable historical memories have been revived or recovered; and a walk through some of the older London streets has been rendered not only interesting but instructive.

" 3. Accordingly, after careful consultation with the Local Governments concerned, the Government of India have determined to adopt a similar plan in this country. The buildings which they have decided to commemorate for historical reasons or as having been the residences of famous men are shown in the statements annexed to this Resolution, which indicate the grounds for the decision in each case. The number is necessarily limited, and great care has been exercised in the selection of those buildings whose associations are mainly personal, so as to prevent that which should be an honour to the few from becoming the prerogative of the many. Some of these houses are the property of Government, and no difficulty arises in the placing of a memorial medallion upon them. Others belong to private persons; and the permission of the owner has been sought for its erection. It is understood that in all cases this has been readily given. It has not been found in England that any serious objection has been entertained by individual proprietors to the fulfilment of what is really a public trust; and the Government of India have not been disappointed in their expectation that the standard of public spirit in India would be found to be in no way lower than in Great Britain. The Governor General in Council trusts that the measures now adopted will have the effect of preserving those personal and local associations which in India are peculiarly liable to be forgotten, and that a direct stimulus will thus be given to the more intimate study of the history of the past. The example thus set may perhaps admit of being followed in places where distinguished Indian Statesmen have rendered conspicuous service to Native States."

There were 136 buildings in all in different parts of the country to which inscriptions were affixed ; and of these 33 were in Bengal and 25 of that number in the city or surroundings of Calcutta. They included the houses in which had lived—among Europeans, Henry Vansittart, Lord Clive, Warren Hastings, General Clavering, Colonel Monson, Sir Elijah Impey, Sir Philip Francis (in the house once occupied by whom, W. M. Thackeray, the novelist, lived as a child), Sir Robert Chambers, Bishop Heber, Bishop Wilson, Lord Macaulay, David Hare, and the missionaries, William Carey and Henry Martyn ; and, among Indians, Raja Ram Mohan Roy, Pundit Iswar Chandra Vidyasagar, Keshub Chandra Sen, Rai Bunkim Chandra Chatterji, and Raja Rajendra Lal Mittra.

But among all the houses whose pretensions I explored, those that interested me most were the various dwellings, almost bewildering in their number, that claimed to have been inhabited at one time or another by Warren Hastings or his wife, the beloved and bewitching Marian. I found this study one of extreme but absorbing perplexity, partly because Warren Hastings had undoubtedly invested largely in real estate during his long residence in Calcutta, and had also unquestionably at different times lived in quite a number of different houses, whether official or private ; and also because the evidence was in many cases obscure and baffling, and had been greatly embroidered either by legend or by the riotous imagination of a later day.

I continued to pursue this study even after I had left India, assisted by the researches of Archdeacon Firminger and others who in the last quarter of a century have devoted themselves with such admirable assiduity to the elucidation of the early records of the British in Bengal ; and I now publish a statement which I believe to be as nearly accurate as it is possible to make it.

I.—During the first period of Hastings' residence in Calcutta, and before he sailed for England in February 1765, having resigned his place in the Company's service, he had acquired both a town house and a Garden House in the suburbs. In March 1764 he sold his town house for Arcot[1] Rupees 16,000 to the Council " for the Nabob's reception on his arrival in Calcutta." His country place must have been in the near neighbourhood of the modern Belvedere, for in the Proceedings of Council for June 20, 1763, we find that permission had been

---

[1] An Arcot Rupee was worth double a Sicca Rupee.

granted to him " to build a bridge over the Collighaut (*i.e.* Kali Ghat) nullah on the road to his Garden House." Rev. J. Long in the " Calcutta Review " (1852) and in Vol. I of his " Selections from the Unpublished Records of Government " (1869) is more explicit, for he speaks of Hastings' Garden House as " a house at Belvedere in the rural solitude of Alipur." It is possible that he did not sell his Alipore property, and that it formed the nucleus of the large estate which he afterwards owned in that neighbourhood and of which we shall hear later on. On the other hand, if he divested himself of all property before he sailed in 1765, his acquisition of the Belvedere Estate must have been subsequent to his return.

II.—When he returned to Bengal as Governor in 1772, Warren Hastings occupied successively as Government residences the two buildings better known as Council House and Government (or Buckingham) House, situated side by side on the Esplanade, on the site of the compound of the present Government House. I have already described, in Chapter I, the circumstances in which he occupied or utilised both these residences.

III.—At about the same time we learn from the Register of Leases that he leased a house on the West side of Old Post Office Street (between the modern High Court and the Town Hall) between the years 1775 and 1779. No other mention of this residence exists ; but it has been suggested that he may have taken it as a home for the Baroness Imhoff, after she had separated from her first husband, who left Calcutta in 1773, and before Hastings married her in August 1777.

IV.—When he vacated this house, the Governor General must have sought another town residence where he could live, while using Government House for official purposes. For in February 1779 we find him proposing to the Board " that the house, the property of the late Colonel Fortnom, be taken for the Company on a lease of one year to commence from the 15th of July at the rent of Sicca Rupees 1,200 per month for the accommodation of the Governor General or for such other public purpose as may hereafter be thought proper, if it should not suit the person who may in future fill that office." [1]

This request was granted ; but that the property had only been leased and not acquired, is shown by the fact that in Hickey's " Bengal Gazette " of 29th January, 1780, Williamson, the auctioneer, advertised

[1] " Bengal Past and Present." Serial No. 30, 1917, p. 88.

for sale " The estate of the late Colonel John Fortnom, the elegant house occupied by the Governor General, and the Godowns situate to the South of the Old Burial Ground and Powder Magazine " (*i.e.* St. John's Churchyard). Whether the property was sold or not does not transpire. But that it continued in the occupation of Hastings is certain. Now, where were this house and this property ?

There cannot, I think, be any doubt that they were the house, now 7 Hastings Street, in the occupation of Messrs. Burn & Co., in which it is known that Warren Hastings and Mrs. Hastings lived after their marriage and up till the time of his final departure from Calcutta, and which he was in the habit of calling *her* house, and the Calcutta public of calling " Mrs. Hastings' house." From this rather loose suggestion of feminine ownership all the guide books and memoirs have deduced without exception that the house belonged to Mrs. Hastings before she married the Governor General, that she lived in it at that time, and that after their marriage he shifted his quarters into it. There is no evidence whatever that the house ever belonged to Mrs. Hastings. On the contrary it is evident from the title deeds that it was the town house of Warren Hastings, and in documents in the possession of Messrs. Burn & Co. the house is continually described as having been " formerly in the occupation of the Honble. Warren Hastings, Governor General of Fort William in Bengal." When then he spoke of it as *her* house, this was only the polite euphemism of an affectionate husband, and was used in contradistinction to " *his* house," by which, as we shall see presently, he meant his official residence, *i.e.* Government or Buckingham House.

The house in Hastings Street is now encased in red brick, and the only relic in it in my time of the days of its famous tenants was the old punkah frames, painted with hunting scenes from elephant-back and horse-back.

This is the town house in which Hastings entertained his friends to dinners and concerts, while giving official parties at Government House, and the big Christmas and King's Birthday Feasts at the Old Court House ; and many allusions to it occur in his correspondence with his wife both before and after she had left India. It is the house to which he alluded as containing their sleeping-room in a letter to Marian, who was absent from Calcutta, dated 8th December, 1780. The passage runs :

" I have migrated to my own House ; but the Lyon roars so noisily, that, suspecting that he might disturb my Rest, I am returned to *our* Bed for the Night." [1]

" My own House " was Government or Buckingham House, in the compound of which a lion had been placed that had been brought down as a gift from the Upper Provinces. It was the Hastings Street house also which, on his return from Benares and Lucknow in November, 1784, he described to his wife, already arrived in England, as " your gloomy mansion in Calcutta " ; [2] in which he continued to live up to the date of his final departure in February 1785 ; and where he hung in his bedroom, so that his eyes might fall upon it every morning when he awoke, the full-length portrait of the fair Marian painted in Calcutta by Zoffany. The picture was sent back to him in England after his return, by his secretary, G. N. Thompson, who thought it " a sublime performance." Zoffany, who was still in Calcutta, packed it himself, but did it so badly that when the picture arrived in England Hastings declared that it was " almost spoiled." [3] It was afterwards hung at Daylesford, where, however, Mrs. Hastings, who never liked it, consigned the canvas to a back room. I had the great satisfaction of sending it back again to Calcutta in 1922, having persuaded the Trustees of the National Portrait Gallery in London, to whom it was bequeathed by Miss Marian Winter, daughter of the old Rector of Daylesford, and great-niece of Mrs. Hastings, but who found it too large to hang upon their walls, to give it on loan to the Victoria Memorial Hall, where it will henceforward abide. Thus the elegant Marian, after an absence of over a century and a quarter, is back again near to where she was painted, and a few hundred yards only from the spot where she faced her husband's awakening eyes. A photograph of this portrait will appear in my second Volume.

Some recent writers have supposed that the Hastings Street house was the residence upon which the family of Sir John Macpherson, who succeeded him as Governor General, pounced down as soon as Hastings had left, and took possession with so much haste (according to Thompson) that the sale of Hastings' furniture could not be held there. This however is a mistake. It is evident from Thompson's letter of 18th September, 1787, which draws a clear distinction between

[1] " Letters of Warren Hastings to His Wife " (ed. S. C. Grier), 1905, p. 95.
[2] *Ibid.*, p. 361.
[3] " Bengal Past and Present." Serial No. 30, p. 68, and No. 33, p. 103.

" Mrs. Hastings' house," *i.e.* 7 Hastings Street, and " your own house," *i.e.* Government or Buckingham House, that it was the latter upon which the Macphersons, not illegitimately, descended.

Again, it is a mistake to suppose, as has also been done, that it was in Hastings Street that Hastings thought he had left the bureau containing some highly prized documents and miniatures, about which he continued to write so anxiously to Thompson after his return to England,[1] but which in spite of advertisements and a search that went on for over two years was never recovered.[2] This is clear both from Hastings' first letter of complaint to Thompson of 21st July, 1785, in which he speaks of the bureau having been sent by Dr. Francis, his surgeon, " to the old house," and also from the terms of the adver- tisement itself, inserted in the " Calcutta Gazette " of 6th September, 1787, which speaks of the old black bureau as having been " about the time of Mr. Hastings' departure from Bengal either stolen from his house *on the Esplanade*, or by mistake sold at the auction of his effects." The house on the Esplanade was Government or Buckingham House.

I must now dispose of two other pretenders to the honour of having sheltered the great Governor General, for whose claims I can find no justification. The first of these is a house or houses in Esplanade Row. Mr. Cotton was led by the reference above cited, and by a vague tradition, to believe that Hastings once lived at No. 4 Esplanade Row East, the corner house of Old Court House Street, abutting on the Maidan, which in my time was occupied by Messrs. R. Scott Thompson & Co., Chemists, although the house has since disappeared and been replaced by a towering block of mansions.[3] This legend was said to be supported by the authority of a Dr. G. R. Ferris, who had come to Calcutta in the 'fifties and who declared that the initials of Warren Hastings were to be seen scratched on a pane of glass in one of the windows of this house. Even if this had been the case, it would be no proof that the Governor General had ever resided there. But I could find in Calcutta no one, including the occupants of the building for over thirty years, who had ever either seen the inscription or heard

---

[1] " Bengal Past and Present."   Serial No. 30, p. 74; Serial No. 33–34, pp. 85, 91, 105, 106, 107.
[2] This disposes of that part of the well-known ghost story attached to Hastings House, Alipore, which declares that the Governor General, after driving up in the phantom coach-and-four, proceeded to ransack the house for the missing piece of furniture.
[3] " Calcutta Old and New," pp. 105, 311.

of it ; and I believe it to be a myth. How dubious was the legend is further evident from the fact that another claimant was to be found in the same row of houses, namely No. 9 Esplanade Row East, occupied in my time by Messrs. T. E. Thomson & Co., Ironmongers. Their representative spoke of a panelled room on the first floor, either here or at No. 4, as having been the Council Chamber of Hastings, and of the premises of No. 9 as having been the private office of the Governor General, whence he could walk to the meetings of Council. I investigated the title deeds of this property and found no reference in them either to Government or to Warren Hastings. The legend is without any foundation.

Not far away is yet another pretender whose case I have elsewhere dealt with (Chapter II on the Council Houses), in relation to its claim to have been the Government House or Council Room of Lord Minto, but which—such is the magic attached to the name of his great predecessor—has also been associated in some quarters with the name of Warren Hastings. This is No. 51 Bentinck Street, the site in my time of Messrs. Llewellyn & Co., where I was shown what purported to be the throne-room, waiting-room, anteroom and bedroom of the Governor General. I had the title-deeds of this property inspected. They went back to 1786, when the property, which had belonged to one W. T. Jones, was sold by writ and bought by Col. Peter Murray. Before that date it belonged to one P. M. Dacres. Thus disappeared one more venerable myth. The fact is that, at the close of the 18th and the beginning of the 19th centuries, many of the wealthier houses in Calcutta contained a series of handsome apartments, which it became easy at a later date to identify with the hypothetical Government buildings and residences of an earlier generation.

V.—I now turn to Hastings' suburban residences, as to which there has been a similar and even more active disputation, that may now, I trust, be finally set to rest. We have seen under Heading I. that, in the first period of his residence at Calcutta, Hastings owned a Garden House at Alipore. This was a favourite suburban retreat for the British residents in Calcutta, who went out there in the evening or at weekends from their stifling offices in the town ; although the vast level expanse which is now known as the Maidan, and which they had to traverse before reaching their destination, was then, not a beautiful park, but in parts an unredeemed jungle, infested even at that time with bad characters, and a little earlier with wild beasts.   There were several houses of some size in the Alipore area, as is manifest from the evidence previously quoted of the visits paid by eminent strangers to the Garden Houses of the Governor, whether he were John Spencer,[1] or Verelst, or Cartier.   I see no reason to suppose that Hastings on his return as Governor inherited in his official capacity a Garden House from them, for it appears that he was either already or presently the possessor of a much larger estate there himself.   How he acquired this estate cannot be ascertained with certainty.   But it is believed to have been bestowed upon him by the Nawab Mir Jaffar Ali Khan of Murshidabad, who having come down to Calcutta when he was deposed, and having settled down and made extensive purchases of land and houses at Alipore, when he was restored to his *musnud*, in gratitude made a free gift of a portion of his property to Hastings.

However this may be, Hastings had a house there known as Belvedere, somewhere in the immediate vicinity, if not on the actual site, of the present official mansion ;   and there from his and other correspondence we hear of him as in residence in April 1775, and again as giving a concert in February 1776.

VI.—We now come to the interesting topic of Hastings House, the charming residence in the same neighbourhood where he spent so many happy hours with his newly married wife and which has been the centre of such strange vicissitudes and so luxuriant a crop of legend.

Hastings married Marian Imhoff in August 1777, and I incline to the belief that he only began to build Hastings House when the marriage had already taken place or was in immediate contemplation. A married man would require a different class of residence from a widower,[2] particularly if his wife were so elegant and fastidious a lady as the second Mrs. Hastings, and if he desired, as Hastings certainly did, to exercise a discriminating unofficial hospitality.   The first description that we have of the new house is in the often quoted letter of Mackrabie, the brother-in-law and Private Secretary of Francis, dated February 1778 :[3]—

"Colonel Morison dined with us in the country ; after dinner we walked

[1] India Office Home Miscell., No. 198.

[2] It must be remembered that Hastings had been wedded at an earlier date to the widow of Captain John Buchanan, one of the victims of the Black Hole, but that she had died after little more than two years of married life in 1759.   *Vide* Chapter XII.

[3] The date is sometimes given as 1776.   But the point is unimportant, since it is really immaterial whether Hastings built the house before or after his marriage.

over to the Governor's new-built house. 'Tis a pretty toy but very small, though airy and lofty. These milk-white buildings with smooth shiny surface utterly blind one."

The allusion is of course to the Madras *chunam* with which the interior walls were coated, and the secret of which, as I have elsewhere explained, is now lost.

In November 1779 we read of Hastings inviting Sir Elijah Impey to stay at " his country house with him and Mrs. Hastings "—doubtless the new building ; and in May 1780 we have the well-known visit of Mrs. Fay, who made the pardonable mistake of calling the house Belvedere House, and thus (not without a tinge of malice) described it : —

" The house is a perfect *bijou ;* most superbly fitted up with all that unbounded affluence can display; but still deficient in that simple elegance which the wealthy so seldom attain, from the circumstance of not being obliged to search for effect without much cost, which those but moderately rich find to be indispensable. The grounds are said to be very tastefully laid out."

I have said elsewhere (Chapter I) that I entertain little doubt that it is to Hastings House that W. Hodges, R.A., who came out to India as a personal friend of the Governor General in March 1781, referred when he wrote :—

" For its magnificence Calcutta is indebted solely to the liberal and excellent taste of the late Governor General,[1] and it must be confessed that the first house was raised by Mr. Hastings which deserves the name of a piece of architecture; in fact it is even in a finer style than any that has been built since, although it in on a smaller scale than many others."

In this enchanting spot the storm-tost and harassed man must have spent some of his happiest hours in India with the woman he loved.   There, in the bijou residence, he must often have discussed with her the persecution of his colleagues, the vindictive jealousy of Francis, the clumsy hostility of Clavering, the hesitating support of Barwell, the vagaries of the Judges.   There he found relief from the weight of larger cares.   In the surrounding paddock he bred the Arab horses which they both loved, and in riding which they found a constant recreation.   In the grounds, he, a genuine horticulturist and a trained botanist, planted rare trees from all parts of Asia.   While she was with

---

[1] Hodges' book, " Travels in India during the Years 1780–3," was not published till 1793.

him there, he had no other care. Everything that she did was perfect, a delight for the moment, a precious memory in days to come. When she had gone, the passionate confession burst from him : " I miss you in every instant and incident of my life, and everything seems to wear a dead stillness around me. I come home as to a solitude." When he returned to England, he erected on the banks of the Thames a house on the model of his home at Alipore ; and when they both retired to Daylesford, he laid out the grounds after the fashion of his Indian country seat.

After he had built the new home, Hastings no longer had any need for the older house of Belvedere, and accordingly we find that in February 1788 he had already leased Belvedere House, and an extensive property round it, to Colonel Tolly, the excavator of the nullah hard by that has ever since borne his name ; while in August 1780 the lease was converted into a sale. From that date we need not follow the fortunes of this Belvedere, which, after the death of Tolly at sea in 1784, was leased to W. A. Brooke for £350 p.a., and at the termination of his lease was offered for sale in March 1802. The house and property passed through many hands until in a greatly enlarged and beautified form it became the official residence of the Lieutenant Governor of Bengal, and later still, after the removal of the Imperial capital of India, the temporary official habitation of the Viceroy when he comes down to Calcutta in the winter.[1]

Hastings, however, still retained the greater part of his property, with more that one house on it, and it was upon a spot on this estate between Belvedere and Kidderpore House—which I found little difficulty in identifying while I was in Calcutta[2]—that he fought the famous duel on 17th August, 1780, with Francis, at the close of which the wounded man was carried on a charpoy into Tolly's house at Belvedere.

When Mrs. Hastings sailed for England in January 1784, her husband, who was resolved at all costs to follow her with the least possible delay, and to whom life and duty in India were becoming increasingly burdensome, decided to sell the whole of his Alipore

---

[1] For its history *vide* an Appendix in Vol. II of C. E. Buckland's " Bengal under the Lieutenant Governors." Calcutta, 1901.

[2] From a remark in W. Hickey's " Memoirs " (Vol. III, p. 152), it would appear that this was the recognised spot for such encounters, for he speaks of his own duel with Mr. N. Bateman on " the appointed ground at the back of Belvidere House at Alypore." For an account of this duel, in Hastings' own words, *vide* Chapter XII of this book.

property, and this intention he announced to her in a letter dated 21st January, 1784:

"I passed the last three Days of the Week at Allipoor, and shall continue to go there for the entertainment of my present Guests, as long as they stay with me, on Saturdays and Sundays. When they leave me, I bid Adieu to Allipoor for ever, and I have actually advertised the Sale of it in Three Lots, the Old House and Garden forming One, the New House and Outhouse the Second, and the Paddock the Third." [1]

The property however did not find an immediate purchaser, and was again advertised in the " Calcutta Gazette " of 28th October, 1784, as for sale. On 20th November, 1784, Hastings wrote to his wife:

"I am now writing at Allipoor ; for it has been put up for Sale, and bought in again. . . . I shall continue to make this Place my Saturday and Sunday Residence, until I can find a Purchaser, or leave the Country ; for I find it a relief to my Mind and my Health is certainly the better for it . . . My own Apartments, and the Bed which I once shared with my beloved Marian, are all that I reserve to myself, or care for, and they are sacred." [2]

A few days before Hastings finally left Calcutta in February 1785, he gave a letter of attorney, dated 28th January, to his friends Charles Stuart, Charles Croft, George Nesbitt Thompson and William Larking to sell the still undisposed-of property on his behalf ; and the " Calcutta Gazette " a little later contained an advertisement of the sale to be held on 10th May, 1785. The whole of the property was not offered for sale, for Hastings reserved a lot of 70 *bighas* which he gave to his stepson Julius Imhoff. But the remainder was thus described :

"Lot 1. The House opposite the paddock gate, consisting of hall, a large verandah to the southward, and six rooms. Two small bungalows, large tank of excellent water, and above 63 *biggas* of land, partly lawn but chiefly garden ground in high cultivation and well stocked with a great variety of fruit trees.

"Lot 2. An upper-roomed house consisting of hall and 2 rooms on each floor, a handsome stone staircase and a back staircase all highly finished with Madras Chunam and the very best materials. A lower-roomed house containing a large hall and four good bed chambers : a complete bathing house containing 2 rooms finished with Madras Chunam : a convenient bungalow containing two rooms and a verandah all round : a large range of pukka buildings containing stabling for 14 horses and four coach houses ; other stables also (thatched) for 12 horses and 6 carriages, and 46 biggas of ground.

[1] " Letters " (ed. S. C. Grier), p. 208.
[2] *Ibid.*, pp. 367–8.

WARREN HASTINGS AND MRS. HASTINGS

From the painting by Zoffany.

"Lot 3.   The paddock, containing *52 biggas* of ground surrounded with railed fence."

It is not difficult to identify Lot 1 with the Old House and Garden of Hastings' first letter, and Lot 2 with Hastings House. The lack of correspondence between the description of the latter and the present Hastings House is explained by the fact that the two wings or extensions of the house, as I found it, were clearly a later addition, and that the building, as originally erected by Hastings, consisted of the central block alone.

This is further demonstrated by the Zoffany picture of Warren Hastings and his wife, which I persuaded Miss Marian Winter to bequeath to the Victoria Memorial Hall, and which now hangs there. In the background is the " bijou " residence, as described by Mrs. Fay. On one side of it is the tank as it still exists ; and in front of the entrance are drawn up the Governor General's mounted Body Guard, and a State elephant with howdah.

On this occasion all three lots were sold—Lot 1 to William Jackson for Sicca Rupees 27,500 ; Lot 2 to Captain Samuel Turner of the East India Company and G. N. Thompson for Sicca Rupees 27,000 ; and Lot 3 to Mr. Honeycomb, an Attorney of the Supreme Court, for Sicca Rupees 7,500. The last-named property was sold again in about 1835 to Dr. W. H. Speede, who converted the ground into an arrowroot garden and changed the name to " The Penn." This was situated to the South of the existing Horticultural Gardens at Alipore.

Lot 2, or Hastings House, which is the only one in which we are particularly interested here, had a chequered career, which I ascertained from the title deeds when I bought it in 1901. In November 1788 Thompson transferred his interest to Turner, who sold it, with 69 *bighas* of land, to H. Butler, an East India merchant, in 1796 for Rs. 25,000. In 1806 the property was sold to another East India merchant, S. Wintle, for Rs. 18,500. In 1810 it passed into the possession of a Banian, Gopee Mohun Tagore, for Rs. 24,000, and in 1814 into that of J. D. Alexander and A. J. Macan for Rs. 22,500. In 1816 the property was put up to auction and bought by Gabriel Vrignon for Rs. 23,000, remaining in his family until 1894, when it was bought by a syndicate for Rs. 65,000. I purchased it from them for a price, as far as I remember, of something under 2 lakhs or about £13,000 for the house and 21 acres of ground.

And now it may be asked why, on behalf of the Government of India, I bought it. Soon after I arrived in Calcutta I visited the place because of its associations. The house, so full of wonderful remembrances, was untenanted ; the grounds were bedraggled and unkempt. But the place was alive with memories ; and it seemed to me a scandal that a building with such traditions should be allowed to fall into ruin or be made the victim of successive speculations. It ought, I thought, to be recovered and converted to some worthy use. Further, I was greatly struck by the fact that while the Indian Princes were in the habit of entertaining the Viceroy with truly regal splendour in their respective States, this hospitality was rarely if ever returned, and the Chiefs when they came to Calcutta, as they were rather fond of doing in the winter season, were compelled to put up in mediocre hotels, where they were mercilessly fleeced and encouraged to waste enormous sums of money.

I therefore decided to purchase Hastings House as a Guest House for the Indian Princes, or visitors of great distinction. I took an immense amount of trouble about the place, laying out and planting the gardens, weeding and mowing the lawns, cleaning the tank, and entirely refurnishing the house. I converted one wing into a fine durbar room for the exchange of the obligatory visits with the Princes, I provided a billiard room for those who had modern tastes (a not inconsiderable number), and I arranged the bedrooms and bathrooms is suitable manner upstairs. Above the portico was fixed a tablet which said :

This House known as Hastings House
Originally the Country Seat of
Warren Hastings
First Governor General of Fort William in Bengal (1774–1785)
Was bought as a Guesthouse for Government by
Lord Curzon
Viceroy and Governor General of India in 1901.

For a number of years the Guest House served its purpose right well. There were entertained in it the Nizam of Hyderabad, and the Maharajas of Nepal, Gwalior, Kashmir, Jaipur, Bikanir and others whom I cannot now remember. There at a later date sojourned Inayet Ulla Khan of Afghanistan, and subsequently his father the Amir Habibulla

HASTINGS HOUSE (1924)

himself ; and there also was accommodated the Dalai Lama of Tibet, when he fled from Lhasa, and sought British protection from the invading armies of China.

Nothing could have been better or more successful until, in an evil hour, the Government of India, with the consent of the Home Government, decided in 1912 to move the Capital of India from Calcutta to Delhi.   In a moment the utility and the purpose of Hastings House were destroyed ; the furniture which I had so laboriously collected was sold by auction ; at one time it was even contemplated to sell the place itself.   Public opinion prevented this outrage ; but for some years the house stood derelict, until it was decided to lease it to the Bengal Government as a school for Indian boys of good birth. This venture afterwards collapsed, and the house, which is still the property of the Government of India, is now used as residential quarters for Government officials, providing accommodation for several families. Thus perished my fair scheme, and I suppose that, like most other places in India, Hastings House and its surroundings will gradually relapse into the familiar untidiness of Indian scenes ; and people will forget that in those gardens walked and in those apartments dwelt the most remarkable man and not the least fascinating woman that ever trod the stage of Anglo-Indian life.

There are not many haunted houses in India, but Hastings House was said to be one of them.   The haunting was said to take a double form.   Sometimes in the afternoon an old-fashioned barouche or chariot, hung on high springs, with a coachman in gorgeous livery seated on the box, was said to drive up to the door and then to vanish suddenly from view.   More frequently, after evening had fallen, the crunch of wheels on the gravel and the solemn tramp of four horses were said to be heard approaching the portico, although both equipage and team remained unseen.   A figure, reported of course to be that of the celebrated Governor General, was said to walk in one of the bedrooms. He was even said to be looking for the stolen bureau, which was never here at all.   One person who had lived in the house for many years told me that he had never either heard or seen these phantom visitations. Another couple declared that they had constantly heard the ghostly equipage at night.

In the garden was a hump of brick and plaster overgrown with creepers, by which was also supposed to hang a tale.   Julius Imhoff, to

K

whom his stepfather Warren Hastings had given a large slice of his Alipore property, and who lived upon it for some years until his death in 1799, had had two natural sons by an Indian woman, one of whom was shot dead by a native in the compound, while the other, a child, fell into a well in the garden and was drowned, along with his *ayah* or nurse, who fell in after him. I was led to believe that the well had been filled up and that I was gazing upon the fatal site. But inasmuch as the house and the compound which were presented to Imhoff were assuredly not Hastings House, but were at some distance away, I declined to allow that I was gazing upon the scene of the double tragedy, well authenticated as I believe the latter to have been.

VII.—Among his rather numerous investments in real estate, Warren Hastings also possessed a property, 216 *bighas* in extent, with a house upon it, in the Northern suburb of Chitpore. This property, which was known as Cossipore Garden, had previously belonged to W. Billiers (Chief in Council at Patna, who took his own life in order to avoid a meeting with Lord Clive), and then to J. Lister. Hastings sold it to Cudbert Thornhill,[1] probably when he left India. But there is no evidence to show that he ever occupied it.

VIII.—In days when there were no hill stations, and no railroads to take the town resident to any distance from his daily routine, when the chief means of locomotion were river craft, and the main physical solace of life was the river breeze, it is not surprising to find that those servants of the Company who could afford it kept villas on the Hugli, to which they could resort as a change from the suffocating conditions of existence either inside the city or even in its land suburbs. We have read of the Garden Houses in Garden Reach and of the Governor-General's house at Barrackpore. Similar villas were dotted up and down the river banks, and Warren Hastings, whether he did or did not reside for any length of time in any of these places, at least gratified his taste for the purchase and ownership of real estate by acquiring in more than one locality an interest in riverside property.

Opposite Barrackpore is Serampore on the right bank of the Hugli, and two miles below Serampore is Rishra or Rishera where the Governor General owned a moderate-sized estate. The greater part of it is now in the hands of Messrs. Birkmyre, and there are upon it two jute mills. There is also a house known as Hastings Lodge, approached by an

[1] " Bengal Past and Present," Vol. XIV, Serial No. 28, p. 174.

avenue of mango trees, which are of course said to have been planted by Mrs. Hastings. Her husband may have possessed a house or bungalow on this site ; but it is never actually mentioned in any of his letters, and there seems good reason to believe that the existing building is of later date.

I had the title deeds examined, and found that on 31st August, 1780, three natives sold 45 *bighas* and 16 *cottahs* of land to Warren Hastings for Rs. 1,145. Directly after Mrs. Hastings had left for England, in January 1784, he offered his Rishera estate for sale, and in the advertisement it was described as " An extensive piece of ground, consisting of 136 *bighas* and 18 *cottahs* of Lakheranje Land paying no rent." On 20th November, 1784, he wrote to his wife the letter previously cited, in which he said, " I have sold Rishera for double the Sum that was paid for it. This is a Riddle, and I leave it to your Sagacity to unravel it." [1]

Now let us turn to the deeds. Hastings appears to have been more than justified in his statement of the price obtained, though it is clear that since his first acquisition of the estate in 1780 he had trebled its extent. On 2nd September, 1784, the entire property, consisting of 136 *bighas* and 18 *cottahs*, was sold to W. Bondfield, J. Prescott and R. Riccardo of Calcutta, for Rs. 10,000. Its later history is as follows. Sometime after 1794 the property was divided. The Northern portion containing 60 *bighas* passed into one set of hands and is now the property of the Wellington Mill. The larger portion was sold in 1803 and is now the property of Messrs. Birkmyre. There we will leave it. Hastings may have lived there, and the guidebooks are very confident in the asseveration, but there is no positive evidence to that effect.

IX.—We are on more certain ground with regard to our next site, where he certainly sometimes resided. This was at Suksagar, also on the river, but on its left bank and much higher up than Rishera, being at a distance of 40 miles from Calcutta, and a little beyond the former Dutch factory at Chinsura.

Colesworthy Grant in his " Rural Life in Bengal " (written in 1860) says that the house which formerly stood here and of which he gives two woodcuts—one of the building intact, the other of the same in ruins on the banks of the stream—" was built by Warren Hastings

[1] " Letters " (ed. S. C. Grier), p. 367.

as a country residence for himself and three other civilians, and for the purpose of their having an English farm where experts in the growth of coffee and other products of that nature could be tried."

Forbes in his " Oriental Memoirs " (1813) says that " it was an elegant house of European architecture, highly finished, and the grounds disposed with great taste."

Whether the house and property actually belonged to Warren Hastings, or to his friends, or to both, is not clear. It was, however, a place of favourite resort for Mrs. Hastings and himself. On 8th July, 1780, we learn from the " Bengal Gazette " that they left Calcutta for a trip to Suksagar. There he left her behind, when obliged to return to town for a Council meeting, and thither he addressed to her a letter on 16th July, in which he said he would be coming up the river in his *feelchehra* or houseboat on the following afternoon to meet her off Chinsura and to take her back.[1]

Whatever his interest in the place, Hastings seems to have parted with it when his wife left India ; for after her departure, though he continued to visit Suksagar, it was always as the guest of his friend Charles Crofts, Accountant General in the Revenue Department of Bengal, and afterwards Chief at Chittagong. In a letter to Marian dated 19th February, 1784, he speaks of " poor Croftes with the Gout in his Head, in Defiance of it and of my Entreaties, hurrying after me to make my Reception at his House most welcome and salutary." On 28th February, and again on 8th March, he alludes to it as " Croftes' Bungalo " at Suksagar, but we do not know whether it was in this house that Hastings' colleague for seven years, Edward Wheler, broke a blood-vessel and died at Suksagar on 10th October. Hastings was there again the following month. He was greatly attached to the place, which seems to have been converted *inter alia* into a sugarcane plantation. There was also a rum factory, as Crofts had the contract for supplying the Company's Marine ; and both were flourishing in 1792. Later the property came into the hands of a wealthy merchant, Joseph Barretto, who lived there in princely style, with a Roman Catholic Chapel for his family. He was succeeded by a Spaniard named Laureletta, who converted the chapel into a residence for *mahouts* and fighting cocks. In 1829 it was described as—

---

[1] " Letters " (ed. S. C. Grier), pp. 50–52.

" Silent deserted and sad,
Where the dark tangled grass hides the serpents that hiss
And the jackals alone are now glad."

When I enquired as to the whereabouts of the house, I was informed that no trace of it existed, and that the building and the greater part of the property had long ago been washed away into the Hugli. *Sic transit gloria mundi.*

X.—There was another riverside, or rather seaside, resort named Birkul (Beercool) below Kejri (Kedjeree) at the mouth of the Hugli, and near Midnapur, whither Mrs. Hastings would go for sea bathing. It was in fact a sort of miniature Brighton for Calcutta, and was a place of popular resort between the years 1780 and 1785. It is not, however, on record that Warren Hastings ever lived there or even went there, although he is alleged to have contemplated a visit and to have had a bungalow prepared for his reception.[1]   One authority says that the place was so entirely deserted in later times that in 1823 only one bungalow was left standing, and this had been erected by Warren Hastings. There is no ground for the latter statement.[2]

Thus we come to the end of the Governor General's rather numerous Indian residences and retreats, and, although the study has involved much research, it may be useful in clearing away some of the obscurities that have hitherto overhung the subject, and may interest the not inconsiderable band of those who find a romance in the half-forgotten abodes of great men.

[1] " Letters " (ed. S. C. Grier), p. 88.
[2] W. H. Carey, " The Good Old Days of Honorable John Company," Calcutta, 1906, Vol. I, p. 69.

CHAPTER VII

THE BLACK HOLE AND ITS MONUMENT.

ὦ ξεῖν', ἀγγειλον Λακεδαιμονίοις ὅτι τῇδε
κείμεθα, τοῖς κείνων ῥήμασι πειθόμενοι.—SIMONIDES OF CEOS.

WHEN I went out to India in December 1898 I took with me
and read on board that fascinating book "Echoes from Old
Calcutta," by the late Dr. H. E. Busteed, formerly Assay Master of the Calcutta Mint, which has given pleasure to countless students
of Anglo-Indian history, and which was the first published volume to
lift the shroud from certain aspects of Calcutta history and life, and
to invest them with the romance which is their due.[1] I was very
much struck by the description in this book of the failure to set up
in Calcutta, since Holwell's original Monument to those who had died
in the Black Hole had been demolished in 1821, any memorial to that
little company of Englishmen and one English woman, 123 in all,
whose martyrdom on that night of doom, 20th June, 1756, had laid
the foundation stone of British Dominion in Bengal. Not a pillar,
nor a slab, nor an inscription, remained in Calcutta to preserve their
names or to record their sacrifice. The identity of the Black Hole
prison itself (which had long ago been built over and had disappeared)
was not absolutely certain; although the labours of more than one
indefatigable explorer had established by digging its approximate site.

I resolved that one of my first steps should be to repair this omission,
and to place the identification of the disputed sites, if possible, on an
impregnable basis; and I had not been in Calcutta a month before
a start was made. I was fortunate in finding a valuable coadjutor in
Mr. C. R. Wilson of the Indian Education Department, who was the
latest and the most successful of these explorers, and who had already

[1] The first Edition of this admirable book appeared in 1882, the second in 1888, the third, which was
the copy that I studied and which was presented to me by the author, in 1897. There were considerable
changes, as fresh material became available, in each of the two later Editions. But the fourth Edition,
which was published in 1908 only a few years before Dr. Busteed died, was a still larger and much more
complete work, revising some of the judgments passed in the earlier editions, and containing the results
of the most recent researches.

150

prosecuted his researches to a definite conclusion ; while a little later, when I began to collect the names of the victims, and to endeavour to draw up a final and accurate list, I was equally fortunate in enlisting the help of Mr. S. C. Hill, at that time the officer in charge of the Records of the Government of India. The results of Mr. Hill's studies were embodied in three large volumes of the Indian Records Series, entitled " Bengal in 1756–1757," which were published by Murray for the Government of India in 1905. In the following year there appeared in the same Series two volumes, entitled " Old Fort William in Bengal," by Mr. Wilson, whose premature death in 1904, while I was still in India, prevented him from revising the greater part of his second volume. In these two works however will be found all the information and the documents that are available for that historic period, and to them, in all probability, there will be little more, at any time, to add.

I will first deal with the site of the Black Hole itself, assuming a general knowledge on the part of my readers of the events of that fateful night, as they were recorded not only by Governor Holwell but by other survivors, and as they may be found in every history of British India. All such readers know that the so-called Black Hole was a small low apartment or chamber, ordinarily used as a military prison for the private soldiers of the British Garrison of Old Fort William, into which the survivors of the siege were thrust in the evening of the day on which the Fort had fallen. Its dimensions were 18 feet by 14 ft. 10 in. ; it was the most Southerly of a series of similar compartments built inside the Eastern wall of the curtain, nearest to the South-east bastion ; and it was lighted and ventilated only by two small barred windows in the brick wall, separating it on the Western side from a low verandah that opened through archways on to the Parade Ground of the Fort. In this dark and noisome den 146 men and women were confined from 7 p.m. till 6 a.m. on the following morning, with the result that only twenty-three emerged alive.

After the recovery of Calcutta by the forces of Admiral Watson and Clive and the victory of Plassey, the Old Fort continued to be used for some time as a military barrack, a temporary church for the British inhabitants being improvised in the rooms between the Black Hole and the Main or Eastern Gate of the Fort. After 1767 the latter was converted into a Custom House, and the drawings of the two

Daniells and others show the dilapidated condition into which the walls and battlements had fallen in the latter part of the 18th century. In 1819 the foundation stone of a new and improved Custom House was laid, and the Old Fort was finally demolished. Nor did it ever come to sight again until its foundations were laid bare in the last two decades of the 19th century, just before my arrival in Calcutta.

The first of these explorers was Mr. Roskell Bayne of the East Indian Railway, who, while putting in the foundations of a new Office Building, exposed the greater part of the Northern end of the Old Fort in 1883, and, deducing the remainder from the measurements and drawings given in published works, recreated the Southern part of the building, and believed that he had disclosed the actual site of the Black Hole. A white marble slab was fixed in 1884 on the interior of a great masonry gateway leading into the Post Office (for the latter had in modern times been erected on the greater part of the old Custom House site), and upon it was placed the following inscription :

" The stone pavement close to this marks the position and size of the prison cell in Old Fort William, known in history as the Black Hole of Calcutta."

The stone pavement and tablet, and the gateway (which completely shut them off from the view of persons passing in the street outside), were all *in situ* when I first saw them in February 1899, and they had received the blessing of Lord Dufferin, as recorded in Lady Dufferin's book. A proposal to erect a marble structure or cenotaph with a dome over the presumed site of the Black Hole had been fortunately abandoned.

Meanwhile in 1891 Mr. Wilson, profiting by the discovery in the British Museum in 1889 of Lieut. Wells' map of Calcutta in 1753, which gave an exact plan of the Old Fort, had started a fresh series of explorations, for which the final removal of the old Custom House provided an opening. Beginning with the exposure of the foundations of the Eastern Gate, which had not previously been ascertained, he proceeded to reconstruct the Eastern curtain from the Gate to the neighbourhood of the South-east bastion. He was thus enabled to locate with precision the site of the Black Hole cell, removed by a few feet only from the conjectural site of Mr. Bayne. Dr. Busteed, who had in his earlier Editions accepted the latter's identification, at which indeed he had helped to arrive, devoted several pages in his latest

SITE OF BLACK HOLE

Edition to a criticism, or, perhaps it should rather be called, a commentary, on Mr. Wilson's views. But a careful investigation led me to think that the latter were sound ; and as such they have been generally accepted ever since.

Accordingly, after spending two years in completing and verifying all these researches, I had the ascertained site of the Black Hole, so far as it was not covered by any modern building, paved with polished black marble, and surrounded with a neat iron railing ; and on the wall above it I placed a black marble tablet with the following inscription in gilt letters :

The marble pavement below this spot
Was placed here
By
Lord Curzon, Viceroy and Governor General of India,
In 1901
To mark the site of the prison in Old Fort William
Known as the Black Hole
In which 146 British inhabitants of Calcutta
Were confined on the night of the 20th June 1756,
And from which only 23 came out alive.

The pavement marks the exact breadth of the prison, 14 feet 10 inches,
But not its full length, 18 feet,
About one-third of the area at the North end being covered
By the building on which this tablet is fixed.

I also had the great brick and plaster gateway, which obscured this site from the street outside, taken down, and replaced by an open iron gate and railings, so that both the Black Hole flooring and the tablet can now be seen from the roadway.

I may add, for the benefit of any visitor, that, in close proximity to the site of the Black Hole, there existed in my time, and may still be seen, a low apartment used as a kitchen by the native employés of the Post Office, which presented a striking resemblance to what the Black Hole must have been in 1756, although the dimensions are considerably larger. In those days there was an arcade running along the inside South curtain wall of the Fort, and the apartment that I speak of had been formed by closing in two arches at the Eastern end of this arcade.

At the same time, thinking it would be a pity that the labours of Mr. Bayne and Mr. Wilson in tracing the outlines of the Old Fort should be lost, and regarding the site of the latter as an historical document of the first importance, I had both the outer and the inner lines of the curtain and bastions of the Old Fort, wherever they had not been built over, traced on the ground with brass lines let into the stone of the pavement (some of them are on the main steps of the Post Office), and I caused white marble tablets to be inserted in the walls of the adjoining buildings on which I wrote inscriptions stating what was the part of the Old Fort that originally stood there.

These tablets and inscriptions were as follows, beginning with the group in the neighbourhood of the sites in the Southern part of the Fort, which I have already described.

First, in order to point the way to the intending visitor, a marble tablet with the following inscription was placed on the wall of the Post Office outside the new iron gateway:

> Behind the gateway
> Immediately adjoining this spot
> Is the site of the Black Hole prison
> In Old Fort William.

A little to the South, the big steps of the Post Office, overlooking Dalhousie Square, are practically identical for a portion of their length with the outer wall of the old South-east bastion. Here accordingly are brass lines let into the steps, the space between them being the exact thickness of the ancient wall. A tablet on the adjoining wall thus explains:

> The brass lines
> In the adjacent steps and pavement
> Mark the position and extent
> Of part of the South-east bastion
> Of Old Fort William,
> The extreme South-east point being
> 95 feet
> From this wall.

Entering the new iron gateway and advancing past the Black Hole site to the kitchen chamber which I have described above, we shall see on its outside wall a tablet with the following:

> The two lines of twelve arches
> To the west of this tablet
> Are all that now remains above ground
> Of Old Fort William and
> Originally formed a portion of the arcade
> Within the South curtain.
> The Black Hole prison was a small room
> Formed by bricking up two arches
> Of a similar but smaller arcade
> Within the East curtain
> South of the East gate.

Close to this another tablet explains the neighbouring brass lines :

> The brass lines in the stone
> On the adjacent ground
> Mark the position and extent
> Of the South curtain
> Of Old Fort William.

We will now leave the Southern and South-eastern sections of the Old Fort, re-enter Dalhousie Square, and advance Northwards, toward what was originally the main or Eastern gateway. At the corner of a red brick building opposite the marble replica of the Holwell Monument (to which I shall come presently) is a tablet with the following inscription :

> Sixteen feet behind this wall
> Was the entrance of the East Gate
> Of Old Fort William through which
> The bodies of those who perished
> In the Black Hole were brought and
> Thrown into the ditch of the ravelin
> On the 21st June 1756.

To the North of this, inside the compound of the modern Custom House, may be seen a row of outhouses which are roughly the line of the Long Row, as it was called, in which the forerunners of the present Indian Civil Service, then known as Writers of the Company, resided.   Here is a tablet which says :

> To the West of this tablet
> Extended the range of buildings
> Called the " Long Row "
> Which contained the lodgings
> Of the Company's Writers
> And divided the Old Fort
> Into two sections.

Still continuing Northwards, we come to the North-east corner of the East Indian Railway Office, which was also the North-east corner of the Old Fort. A brass line in the stone pavement and a tablet commemorate the fact, the inscription on the latter being as follows :

> The brass line in the stone
> On the adjacent ground
> Marks
> The position and extent
> Of part of
> The North-east bastion
> Of Old Fort William.

We now turn Westwards down Fairlie Place, the wall on our left hand being identical with the line of the North side of the Old Fort, till we come to a tablet, which records the position of the North-west bastion :

> The brass lines
> In the stone on the adjacent ground
> Mark the position and size of part of
> The North-West bastion
> Of Old Fort William.

A little further on, we enter a gate on the left, and proceeding till we reach the quadrangle inside the East Indian Railway Office, we see on the right hand wall a tablet with the following inscription :

> The brass lines
> In the stone on the adjacent ground
> Mark the position and extent of the
> Northern portion of the West curtain
> Of Old Fort William.
> This tablet marks the position of the
> North River Gate through which Siraj-ud-Daula entered the Fort on
> The evening of the 20th June 1756.
> Behind this tablet to the South of the
> Gate stood the great Flag-staff
> Of the Fort.

The remaining tablets are more difficult of access. If we were able to follow the line of the West curtain of the Old Fort southwards we should come presently to a place where the buildings of the Long Row originally joined the curtain walls. Immediately beyond it was the wharf, and then the river which has now retreated far to the West.

MODEL OF OLD FORT WILLIAM AND THE BLACK HOLE

In order to reach this spot, we must retrace our footsteps and re-enter the compound of the Custom House, until we come to a tablet with the following inscription :

The brass lines in the stone
On the adjacent ground
Mark the position and extent
Of the continuation of the West curtain
Of Old Fort William
Near where it was met by the Long Row.

If, returning from this tablet, we turn to the right and penetrate still further the purlieus of the Custom House, we shall find brass lines marking the position of the North wall of the former Factory, or inner building of the Fort. The tablet hard by has the following inscription :

The brass lines
In the stone on the adjacent ground
Mark the position and extent
Of a portion of the North wall
Of the Factory, the principal building
In the centre of Old Fort William.

We have now completed our perambulation of the Old Fort, in so far as it has been possible to identify and to mark the sites. Several of these, notably the Black Hole, have become places of pilgrimage to all visitors to Calcutta. The remainder will perhaps only appeal to the enthusiast or the historian.

Having thus identified, so far as the circumstances permitted, the main outlines and features of Old Fort William, it seemed to me that the best method of making the subject intelligible to the modern student, would be to have models made for permanent exhibition in the Victoria Memorial Hall. I therefore had two models constructed in teak wood ; the first being of the Old Fort to the scale of 10 feet to 1 inch. The ground plan was based on Wells' map of 1753 and upon the measurements of Bayne and Wilson ; the elevations were based on the still surviving portions of the Fort and upon published views of the building. The second model was an enlargement of the South-east angle of the above model, to the scale of 6 feet to 1 inch, the top being made open so that the spectator could look down into the interior of the Black Hole and adjacent buildings. A third model was made at the same time (to the scale of 10 feet to 1 inch) of the old Church of St. Anne, which stood at the corner of the modern Writers' Buildings (where is now the octagonal chamber of the Bengal Legislative Council), and was the edifice to which the Governor and the Civil Servants marched in procession on Sunday. The lofty spire came down in the cyclone of 1737 and was replaced by a cupola ; the Church itself was finally destroyed in the fighting of 1757.

I now pass to the famous Monument or Pillar which was erected by Holwell over the remains of his companions who had perished in the Black Hole. Their bodies were cast, on the day after the tragedy, into the ditch of the unfinished ravelin, which was an earthwork hurriedly thrown up to cover the main or Eastern Gate of the Fort. Holwell himself after his capture was sent to Murshidabad in irons and kept there till 17th July, when he was set at liberty. He then joined the ships with the fugitives at Fulta, eventually sailing for England in February 1757. There he remained until his return to Bengal in 1758, as a Member of Council, in which capacity as the next senior Member he succeeded Clive in the post of Acting Governor in February 1760. It was probably during his sojourn in England that he resolved to perpetuate the memory of his fellow-countrymen, by erecting a monument over their remains ; though whether he set up the pillar during his brief tenure of the Governorship, or before, or whether he had the tablet executed after his final return to England and sent out to India, there is no evidence to show. Anyhow, when the second Edition of " India Tracts " appeared in 1764, containing his narrative of the Black Hole disaster, there was prefixed to it an engraving of the Monument which had already been erected at Calcutta. His own words in the Dedication were as follows :

"Prefixing, as a frontispiece to this Volume, a Print of the Monument which I erected, at my own expence, to the memory of these unhappy sufferers."

The tense here employed would seem to point to erection while the writer was still in India. The pillar of brick and plaster was clearly of Calcutta manufacture.

The engraving further contained the inscriptions which Holwell had written for the front and reverse sides of the Monument, and in the former of these it was stated that the bodies of the victims had been thrown " into the Ditch of the Ravelin *of this place* "—obviously the

J. Z. HOLWELL

From the painting by Sir Joshua Reynolds.

place where the memorial pillar stood. This engraving is our first indication of the intention of the donor, of the appearance of the Monument, and of the site on which it was raised within a few years of the incident which it commemorated.

So proud was Holwell of this memorial that he had himself painted in oils, holding the sketch of it in his hand, and superintending the work of a native workman engaged in its erection. In the background are visible the base and scaffolding of the Monument. This clearly contemporary portrait, very likely by Zoffany, was, until the year 1892 (when it was purchased by Lord Lansdowne for the Government of India), in the possession of Holwell's direct descendants in Canada, to whom it had come down from Holwell himself. The picture hung in Government House in my time, but was sent by me to the Victoria Memorial Collection, where it ought undoubtedly to find its last resting-place. A further portrait of Holwell by Sir J. Reynolds is in the same collection, and is reproduced here.

Some years later, through the medium of Dr. Busteed, I learned that there is at the present moment in a country house in England, in the possession of a gentleman connected by marriage with one of Holwell's descendants, a model between three and four feet high of Holwell's Monument, executed by, or to the order of, his son, Lieutenant-Colonel James Holwell, who presented it to his father. On one of the sides may be seen this inscription : " To John Zephaniah Holwell this model is most affectionately inscribed by his dutiful son James Holwell "; and on another side are the words : " An exact model of the Monument, erected at Calcutta, Bengal." An illustration is here given of this model. Whether it was made before the pillar was erected, or was a copy of it after erection, there are no means of determining. The Monument consisted of a tall obelisk, with truncated top, springing from an octagonal pedestal or base, the four outer sides of which were each surmounted by a pediment with a funeral urn placed on the apex. The cornices of the remaining or inner sides of the base were straight. This pedestal rested on three steps, which elevated the pillar to a total height of 48 feet from the ground.

Of the eight sides of the pedestal, two alone, on the East and West sides, under the pediments, had memorial tablets inserted in them. The tablets under the two remaining pediments were without inscriptions. In the four remaining sides, under the level cornices, were tablets about five feet high by three feet broad, which contained draped shrouds in relief.

The Eastern and Western tablets were also rectangular, but had semicircular tops like a grave-stone, the head of a cherub with outspread wings being carved in the semicircular portion at the top.

The main inscription on the Western front, looking towards the Old Fort, was as follows :

To the Memory of

Edwd Eyre & Wm Baillie Esq^{rs} The Rev^d
Jervas Bellamy, Me*s*^{rs} Jenks, Revely, Law,
Coales, Valicourt, Jeb, Toriano, E. Page, S. Page,
Grubb, Street, Harod, P. Johnstone, Ballard,
N. Drake, Carse, Knapton, Gosling, Bing,
Dod & Dalrymple ; Milit^y Captains, Clayton
Buchanan[1] & Witherington, Lieuten^{ts} Bishop
Hays, Blagg, Simson, and Bellamy.   Ens^{ns}
Paccard, Scot, Hastings, C. Wedderburn &
Dumbleton ; Sea Captains, Hunt, Osburne,
Purnell, Carey, Stephenson, Guy, Porter, W.
Parker, Calker, Bendall, Atkinson, Leech,
&c. &c., who with other Inhabitants Milita-
ry, and Militia, to the number of 123 Per*s*ons
were by the tyrannic violence of Surajud
Dowla, Suba of Bengal, Suffocated in the
Black Hole Prison of Fort William, in the
Night of the 20th of June, 1756, and promis-
cuously thrown the succeeding morning
into the Ditch of the Ravelin of this place

This
Monument is Erected
by
Their Surviving Fellow Sufferer
J. Z. HOLWELL

The inscription on the reverse or Eastern side ran thus :

[1] This was Captain John Buchanan, whose widow Mary became the first wife of Warren Hastings a few months later, but who died and was buried at Cossimbazar in July 1759.

THE HOLWELL MONUMENT (1784)

From the picture by T. Daniell, R.A.

This
Horrid Act of Violence
was as
Amply as Deservedly
Revenged
on
Surajud Dowla
By his Majesty's Arms
under
the Conduct of
Vice Admiral Watson
and
Colonel Clive
Anno 1757.

It will be observed that there are forty-eight names on the first of these inscriptions. But in his letter to the Council at Fort St. George, Madras, from Hugli on 3rd August, 1756, Holwell gave fifty-one names as the " List of those smother'd in the Black Hole the 20th June, 1756, at Night, exclusive of the English, Dutch, and Portuguese Soldiers, whose names I am unacquainted with " [1]; while in an Appendix to his Genuine Narrative of 28th February, 1757, he enumerated fifty-two ; although, as he gave the number of the soldiers, Militia etc. whose names he did not know, as sixty-nine, there were still two names missing to make up the correct total of 123.[2] The four missing names in these two lists (Abraham, Cartwright, Bleau and Byng) must have been omitted from the tablet by an error, either in the instructions to the sculptor, or of the sculptor himself.

The Monument thus erected, popularly known as The Monument, was a familiar object to all visitors to or inhabitants of Calcutta for the next sixty years. It figures in the engravings of the two Daniells, J. B. Fraser, and others, and was described by every writer of books on Calcutta during that time. In view of the fact that this imposing array of evidence was afterwards challenged, and even the existence of the pillar denied—incredible as it may seem—I will give, before the end of this chapter, the references to which I allude.

In the latter part of its career, the pillar, being only composed of brick and plaster, and no one presumably being responsible for its maintenance, fell into decay. As early as 1782 its misfortunes had

---

[1] " Bengal in 1756–1757." by S. C. Hill, Vol. I, p. 185.
[2] *Ibid.*, Vol. III, p. 153.

begun ; for an extract (here for the first time published) from the
" India Gazette " of 31st August, 1782, ran as follows :

" On Monday last the Monument erected by Mr. Holwell to the memory
of the unfortunate persons who were suffocated in the Black Hole, was struck
with lightning.   A few bricks on the top were knocked off, and the lightning
running down the shart (sic) was attracted by the iron clamps that held the
inscription, a slap (sic) of marble three inches thick, which was broken to pieces.
Some of the natives standing near the Monument were struck to the ground,
but fortunately no lives were lost."

These damages must have been repaired, for the drawings of Thomas
Daniell, executed on the spot in 1786, as well as other drawings and
descriptions of about the same date or a little later, represent the pillar
as intact.   In 1810 however we hear of it as having been again struck
by lightning.   In 1812 a reference, which also has never previously
been noted, speaks of " the inscription as entirely effaced, if ever
there was one."[1]   In 1815 the " East India Gazetteer " described the
pillar as " fast going to decay."

I append here an illustration from an old engraving of the
memorial as it was at that date, with a dark blotch or crack running
down one side of the pillar from top to bottom, and what look like the
creepers of a *peepul* emerging from it.   These black streaks have
evidently been traced in ink on the engraving, and represent the state
of dilapidation of the Monument immediately before its demolition.
The crack was probably the result of the second lightning stroke to
which I have referred.

Finally in 1821 the unhappy ruin was taken down, during the
administration of Lord Hastings ; for in the " Calcutta Gazette " of
6th April, 1821, we read :

" The monument over the well-remembered Black Hole of Calcutta [2] is
at length taken down, and we think should long ago have been demolished."

The Editor of the paper welcomed its disappearance on the ground
that it recalled memories obnoxious to Englishmen.   On the other
hand on 11th April a correspondent signing himself " Brittanus "
indignantly protested against the sacrilege involved in the removal of
the obelisk whose

---

[1] " Journal " (from 1811 to 1815) of Maria, Lady Nugent, 2 vols. (1839), Vol. I, p. 113.
[2] This is of course a slip.   The words should have been " over the victims of the Black Hole."

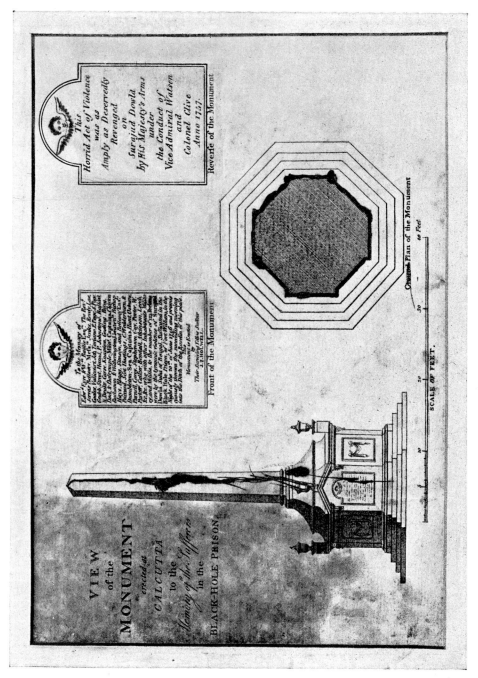

THE HOLWELL MONUMENT (c. 1820)

" dark and weather-beaten appearance seemed to make it contemporaneous with the event which it recorded, and thereby imparted to it a higher interest than any work of later date can possess."

He went on to compare its destruction with the removal of the old Cross at Edinburgh, which so excited the wrath of Sir Walter Scott, and with the carrying away of the Elgin Marbles from Athens : and, with a strange anticipation of my own action 80 years later, added that

" Since the irreparable mischief is done, the only atonement (however inadequate) that can be made by the excellent conservators who have demolished the structure is that they shall forthwith build another as much surpassing the former in size and beauty as it will be inferior in its power of mysterious interest." [1]

No one quite knows why the old pillar should have been taken down in 1821. It may have been that the memories of 1756 were regarded either as obnoxious to the Indians, or as galling to the Europeans. But I think it more likely that, the taste for the conservation of historic monuments being almost non-existent at that epoch, and Lord Hastings being busily employed in beautifying Calcutta, he decided on utilitarian grounds to remove an object which had manifestly become an eyesore, and which no one cared about sufficiently either to preserve or to reproduce.

For eighty years from that date there existed no memorial in Calcutta to those poor sufferers whose bones lay under the soil which had been drenched with their blood, and the pious act of Holwell remained unimitated and all but forgotten.

It is true that in 1883, Messrs. Busteed and Bayne, following upon the discoveries of the latter, proposed that Holwell's pillar should be re-erected in stone as near as possible to the original site. But no one knew exactly where this was, though it was believed to be the spot then occupied by a lamp post at the street-crossing. Almost immediately afterwards this site was usurped by a marble statue of Sir Ashley Eden, Lieutenant Governor of Bengal 1877–1882. The next proposal was to place upon the walls of St. John's Church (the old Cathedral), a facsimile of the names inscribed on the Holwell Monument, omitting the harsh or invidious suggestions. But nothing was done upon this ; and when I came to Calcutta the ground was still untilled.

I resolved at once to erect, not a monument of new design, which

[1] " Old Fort William in Bengal," by C. R. Wilson, Vol. II, pp. 189, 190.

would but have provoked criticism, but a duplicate, as far as was practicable, of the Holwell pillar, constructed of some material more durable than the old brick and plaster ; and in order to escape the charge of spending the money of Government on an object of possible controversy, to present it to Calcutta as my personal gift.

As regards the inscriptions, I felt that it would be undesirable to reproduce either the reference to Siraj-ud-Dowlah in the longer inscription (which was historically untrue, as well as inexpedient) or the brief record of British vengeance in the shorter inscription. But on the other hand I was not content merely with the fifty-two names that Holwell had identified, although he had failed to record more than forty-eight ; and I felt that many others who had died, in the siege, though not necessarily in the Black Hole, were equally deserving of commemoration.

I therefore set myself to a laborious examination of the evidence as regards both the survivors and the slain. This was to be derived from three sources : (a) the letters from Holwell which I have previously cited ; (b) similar letters from other survivors (notably George Grey Junior, June 1756, W. Lindsay, July 1756, and Captain Mills' Pocket Book in the Orme MSS); (c) letters or narratives from Indian correspondents, mostly compiled at Fulta, which appeared in English or Scotch newspapers in the course of 1757, e.g. the "Scots' Magazine" May 1757, the "Edinburgh Society Courant" 14th June, 1757, the "London Chronicle" June, July and August 1757, the "Gentleman's Magazine" February 1758 ; (d) the list of those who were killed in the siege in the Orme MSS in the India Office [1]; (e) Lists compiled from the Bengal Council Proceedings 1752–6, Administration Petitions 1757-8, Ecclesiastical Suits in the Calcutta Mayor's Court, and the Parish Registers of St. John's.

I also put myself in communication with Mr. T. R. Munro, who had spent thirty-three years in Calcutta in the service of the Port Commissioners and had devoted special attention to this subject, having written a good deal about it ; and with Mr. S. C. Hill, who worked simultaneously with myself at the same subject. We each of us drew up independent lists, with the result that of those victims who died in or immediately after the Black Hole we raised the total to sixty, including one woman, Eleanor Weston.[2] Of the great majority of

[1] All these references are to be found in Hill's "Bengal in 1756–1757."
[2] The authority for this is to be found in Busteed, 4th Edition, p. 39.

MODEL OF THE HOLWELL MONUMENT

these we identified the Christian names as well as the surnames. We further recovered the names of 21 others who were killed or died of their wounds either immediately before the Black Hole or after. Thus I was enabled to prepare a list of 81 names for my new inscriptions, in the two categories, as compared with the 48 of the Holwell Monument. Several in the latter's lists, which had no doubt been drawn up in the confusion and anxiety following upon the disaster, were shown by the Fulta Lists to have lost their lives, not in the Black Hole, but in the general fighting, and were therefore transferred by me to that category. At the same time we identified the names of all twenty-three survivors of the Black Hole, whereas Holwell had given only eleven.

I was now in a position to proceed with the ordering of the Monument. But three preliminary steps were still required before it could be erected. First I had to obtain the consent of the Calcutta Corporation, and also of the family of the late Sir Ashley Eden, to remove his statue to an equally fine, indeed I think a finer, position immediately opposite the centre of Writers' Buildings on the North side of Dalhousie Square. This, in both cases, was readily given. Secondly, when the statue was removed, as it was believed to stand upon the exact site of the old Holwell Monument, it was desirable to excavate in order to see if any traces still remained of the interment of 21st June, 1756. Thirdly, it was necessary to have models made and erected on the spot in order to see how a replica of the Holwell pillar would look, in relation to the buildings by which the site is at present surrounded.

When the Eden statue was removed, the excavations were carried down to a depth of nine feet and were taken in every direction. But I was not more successful than Mr. Bayne had been in 1883, when he explored all around the site. He found nothing, although, from the sections of his cutting, he saw that the mould showed signs of animal matter. Long before that date the ground had been frequently disturbed for drainage schemes, water schemes, tramway schemes, lighting schemes. Since his time there had been a renewed turning over of the soil to lay the foundations of Sir Ashley Eden's statue. It was not surprising therefore that I found no traces either of the foundations of Holwell's pillar, or of the dead whose bodies had once lain beneath it.

As regards the models, which were made in wood and painted

canvas, we found that Holwell's proportions were not good, the column (as many of the contemporary illustrations show) being too tall and slender for the base. I eventually settled upon a total height of forty feet from the ground ; and, it being impossible to get the Monument made satisfactorily in India, I gave the order to a firm named De Grelle Houdret, who made the pillar and base of Sicilian marble in Italy, and finally shipped them in the autumn of 1902 to Calcutta. They weighed sixty tons. I made myself responsible for the cost of the Monument. The cost of freight, erection, and fixing the marble tablets, was borne by the Local Government. At first some rather mean pillars and chains were placed round the base, but I had these replaced by a suitable iron railing. Finally I unveiled the memorial on 19th December, 1902, the remarks which I made on that occasion having since been reproduced in Mr. Wilson's book [1] and elsewhere. Ever since the Monument has been one of the recognised sights of Calcutta, and will I hope be preserved by the piety of later generations from the fate that befell its unfortunate predecessor.

I will now give the inscriptions as I rewrote them for the four principal faces and two of the minor faces of the pedestal—which had been reproduced in every particular from the original Monument. The main inscriptions are as follows :—

I
This Monument
Has been erected by
Lord Curzon, Viceroy and Governor-General of India,
In the year 1902
Upon the site
And in reproduction of the design
Of the original Monument
To the memory of the 123 persons
Who perished in the Black Hole Prison
Of Old Fort William
On the night of the 20th June, 1756.
The former memorial was raised by
Their surviving fellow-sufferer
J. Z. Holwell, Governor of Fort William,
On the spot where the bodies of the dead
Had been thrown into the ditch of the ravelin.
It was removed in 1821.

[1] " Old Fort William," vol. I, p. xxviii.

REPLICA OF THE HOLWELL MONUMENT ERECTED BY LORD CURZON

II

To the Memory of
Edward Eyre, William Baillie,
Revd. Jervas Bellamy, John Jenks,
Roger Reveley, John Carse, John Law,
Thomas Coles, James Valicourt,
John Jebb, Richard Toriano,
Edward Page, Stephen Page,
William Grub, John Street,
Aylmer Harrod, Patrick Johnstone,
George Ballard, Nathan Drake,
William Knapton, Francis Gosling,
Robert Byng, John Dodd,
Stair Dalrymple, David Clayton,
John Buchanan, and Lawrence Witherington,
Who perished in the Black Hole prison.

III

To the Memory of
Richard Bishop, Francis Hayes,
Collin Simson, John Bellamy,
William Scott, Henry Hastings,
Charles Wedderburn, William Dumbleton,
Bernard Abraham, William Cartwright,
Jacob Bleau, Henry Hunt,
Michael Osborne, Peter Carey,
Thomas Leach, Francis Stevenson,
James Guy, James Porter,
William Parker, Eleanor Weston, and
Messrs. Cocker, Bendall, Atkinson, Jennings,
Reid, Barnet, Frere, Wilson,
Burton, Lyon, Hillier, Tilley, and Alsop,
Who perished in the Black Hole prison.

An explanation of the above list is given in the fourth tablet.

IV

The names of those who perished
In the Black Hole prison,
Inscribed upon the reverse side
Of this Monument,

Are in excess of the list
Recorded by Governor Holwell
Upon the original Monument.
The additional names, and
The Christian names of the remainder,
Have been recovered from oblivion
By reference to contemporary documents.

There remained the names which I had been unable to identify positively with the Black Hole, and the explanation to be given of their inclusion.

V

The names inscribed on the tablet
On the reverse side to this
Are the names of those persons
Who are known to have been killed
Or to have died of their wounds
During the Siege of Calcutta
In June, 1756,
And who either did not survive
To enter the Black Hole Prison
Or afterwards succumbed to its effects.

VI

To the memory of
Peter Smith, Thomas Blagg,
John Francis Pickard, John Pickering,
Michael Collings, Thomas Best,
Ralph Thoresby, Charles Smith,
Robert Wilkinson, Henry Stopford,
William Stopford, Thomas Purnell,
Robert Talbot, William Tidecomb,
Daniel Macpherson, John Johnson, and
Messrs. Whitby, Surman, Bruce,
Montrong, and Janniko, who perished
During the Siege of Calcutta.

And now I come to a record of two extraordinary events that were either the reward or the sequel of my labours. At about that time there arose a school of native writers, supported by a solitary Englishman, who contended that no such incident as the Black Hole tragedy had ever occurred, arguing, in entire contempt of a testimony, both contemporaneous and subsequent, that is positively overwhelming, (1) that Holwell's narrative must be discredited because it contained

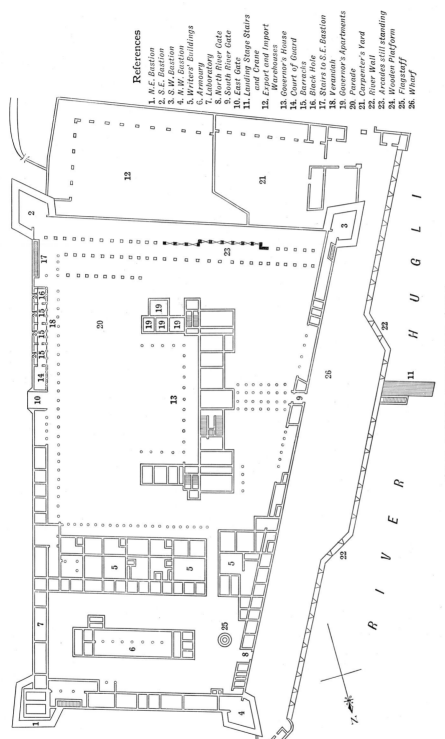

References

1. N.E. Bastion
2. S.E. Bastion
3. S.W. Bastion
4. N.W. Bastion
5. Writers' Buildings
6. Armoury
7. Laboratory
8. North River Gate
9. South River Gate
10. East Gate
11. Landing Stage Stairs
    and Crane
12. Export and Import
    Warehouses
13. Governor's House
14. Court of Guard
15. Barracks
16. Black Hole
17. Stairs to S.E. Bastion
18. Verandah
19. Governor's Apartments
20. Parade
21. Carpenter's Yard
22. River Wall
23. Arcades still standing
24. Wooden Platform
25. Flagstaff
26. Wharf

R I V E R   H U G L I

OLD FORT WILLIAM (1756)

(as is quite probable) many inaccuracies and some contradictions ; (2) that Holwell himself was a notorious liar, who invented the story for purposes of self-advertisement ; (3) that the remaining survivors (who on this theory must also have been a set of shameless liars and impostors) either borrowed their tale from Holwell, or fabricated it independently ; (4) that no mention is made of the tragedy in contemporary Mohammedan histories or in Hindu tradition—a fact which, even if true, is self-explanatory ; (5) that some important British authorities failed to mention it in papers or letters written at the time.

No difficulty was experienced in shattering this preposterous fabric of perverted ingenuity and casuistical manipulation. But no sooner had it disappeared than its authors started the fresh and scarcely less bewildering chimera that Holwell never erected a monument over the place of burial at all, and that all the references to it in contemporaneous literature or documents were either a gigantic hoax or an unprincipled concoction. Holwell was of course the chief and original villain of the piece ; but all the later writers and artists, who either described or depicted the pillar, relied exclusively upon hearsay or borrowed their impressions and their pictures from the perpetrator of the initial fraud. As for the documentary evidence in favour of the Monument it was either a hoax or a forgery.

Although I have little patience with these misguided attempts to rewrite well authenticated and solidly grounded history—which remind me of the efforts of the prolific school of serious comedians, who seek to prove that William Shakespeare was anyone rather than Shakespeare himself—yet having, in the course of the investigations which I have previously described, been led to make a very thorough study of all the evidence relating to the subject—I wrote in the columns of " Bengal Past and Present "—the admirable Journal of the Calcutta Historical Society —(vol. XV, No. 29, 1918) an answer to these critics. I will not reproduce it here, since the demonstration is both too minute and too lengthy. But I will briefly cite the authorities who, at intervals throughout the eighty years of the life of the Monument, testified to its existence and appearance.

I.—1770. Early in 1770 the Dutch Admiral Stavorinus, visiting Calcutta with an official mission, saw the Holwell Monument *in situ*, and thus described it :—

" Near the Great Tank is a stone monument erected in memory of thirty

English prisoners, both men and women, who, when Calcutta was taken by the Nabob Surajah Dowlah, were shut up in a narrow prison, without any refreshment, and suffocated for want of fresh air."

Now the Monument was not of stone, but of plastered brick, and the number of persons commemorated was not thirty. But as to the existence and site of the obelisk the Dutchman's evidence is incontrovertible.

II.—1776. In a grant of land on the North side of the Great Tank, dated 18th November, 1776, " Mr. Holwell's Monument," which as we know, stood there, is expressly mentioned. (Sterndale, " Historical Account of the Calcutta Collectorate," p. 32.)

III.—1782. In the " India Gazette " of 31 August occurs the announcement, which I have previously quoted, that " the Monument erected by Mr. Holwell to the memory of the unfortunate persons who were suffocated in the Black Hole had been struck by lightning."

IV.—1784-5. In this year appeared Colonel Mark Wood's plan of Calcutta, in which the Monument is clearly marked at the crossing opposite the Old Fort.

V.—1786. In this year the two Daniells, uncle and nephew, were painting in Calcutta, and the rather rare series of " Twelve Coloured Views of Calcutta," published there in 1788, contains two drawings by Thomas Daniell in which Holwell's Monument appears—

(a). The first of these, entitled : " Old Fort Street, looking North," shows the South-east angle, with turret, of the ruined Fort, and its Eastern gateway with the Monument opposite it, in the street-crossing at the corner between Writers' Buildings and Tank Square.

(b). The second, entitled : " Mayor's Court and Writers' Buildings," shows the Old Court House, and Writers' Buildings in long perspective, with the same Monument in the same position in the far distance.

(c). A few years later, on the return of the Daniells to England, they brought out in London, over a period of years, the magnificent series of coloured prints, entitled " Oriental Scenery," in one volume of which (dated 1797) there is a third view of Holwell's Monument in the immediate foreground of the picture at the corner of Writers' Buildings. The Monument is surrounded by a railing placed between *chunam* pillars of the conventional Calcutta type.

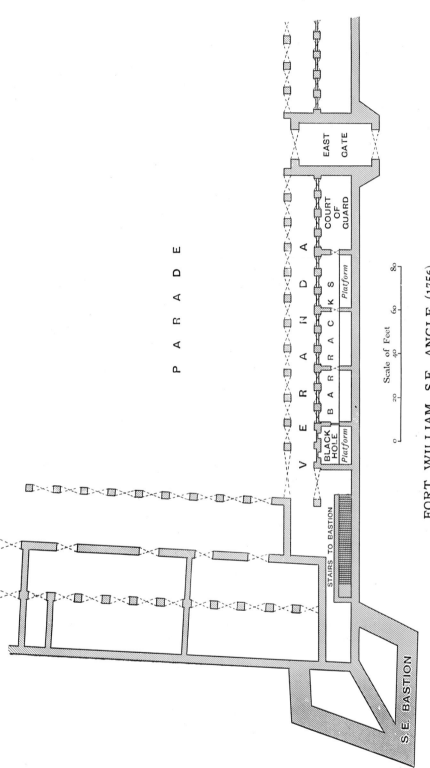

FORT WILLIAM, S.E. ANGLE (1756)

Scale of Feet

0   20   40   60   80

All of these drawings are by the same hand (Thomas Daniell) ; all represent the same Monument, with exactly the same features, on exactly the same, *i.e.* the actual, site.

VI.—1787.   Richard Barwell in a deed dated 15th–16th June, 1787 (cited in " Bengal Past and Present," 1917, p. 167), nominating new trustees for some property belonging to him " on the north side of the Great Tank," describes these lands as " lying and being intersected by the great road leading from Holwell's Monument by the south front of the Court House to the Salt Water Lake."

VII.—1789.   Monsieur de Grandpré, a French officer, who was in Calcutta in 1789, published a book about his travels on his return to Europe, in which he describes what he had seen :—

> " In remembrance of so flagrant an act of barbarity, the English, who were conquerors in their turn, erected a monument between the Old Fort and the right wing of the building occupied by the civil officers of the company, on the very spot where the deed was committed.   It is a pyramid, truncated at the top, and standing upon a square pedestal, having a design in sculpture on each of its sides, and an inscription in the English and Moorish languages, describing the occasion on which it was erected. It is surrounded with an iron railing to prevent access to it, has shrubs planted about it, and exhibits a mournful appearance, not unsuitable to the event which it is intended to commemorate."

Now while the Frenchman's drawing of Writers' Buildings is almost entirely fanciful, being no doubt inserted after his return to France, and while his delineation of the pillar and its base is far from accurate, it affords incontrovertible evidence of the existence on this spot of a monument which is clearly the Holwell obelisk and no other.   For the truncated pyramid of his letterpress is seen in his engraving to be Holwell's pillar after all, with its obtuse apex : the " square pedestal," a mistake which the four pedimented sides might easily suggest to a not too careful observer, is seen in the engraving to have its true octagonal shape ;   the urns and the iron railing are both there ;   the tablets did have sculptured designs upon them, either a cherub's head or the draped shroud known as the Saviour's shroud, which is so well-known a feature in 18th century sepulchral architecture ;   and the only novelty are the shrubs.   As regards the inscriptions, the mention of a " Moorish " name, Suraj-ud-Dowla, is perhaps responsible for this error.   The further mistake that the monument was erected " on the very spot where the deed was committed," is the sort of error that a foreigner relying upon local interpreters might easily commit, and is not after all so very serious, seeing that the obelisk was erected over the ditch into which the dead victims of the deed had been thrown. In fact Monsieur de Grandpré's drawing—probably elaborated and embellished not by himself but by a French engraver—and his descriptions, are, with all their blunders, in reality a very valuable piece of unconscious testimony to the existence of the Monument.

VIII.—1789. The " Calcutta Gazette " of 30th July, 1789, alluding to the celebration in Calcutta of the recovery of King George III from his illness, relates that—

> " The Old Court House, the Government House, the Monument, the Great Tank, and the two principal streets leading north and south, to the esplanade, were adorned by Mr. Gairard."

This is the first of many local allusions to Holwell's pillar as " The Monument "—a title which was universally given to it, for the simple reason that, outside the churchyards and cemeteries, there was at that time no other monument in the city. In William Baillie's Plan of 1792 it is so described in large letters. A Calcutta deed has been published dated 19th–20th July, 1797, in which there is a reference to " The Monument." Again, on 14th August, 1800, there was an advertisement in the " Calcutta Gazette " of a sale by auction of a house at Sealdah, " about twenty minutes' ride from ' the Monument.' " Finally, in Rozario's " Complete Monumental Register," published in Calcutta in 1813, the pillar is once more so described.

IX.—1792. In this year an English traveller named Thomas Twining, whose " Travels " were not brought out in book form till 1893, reached Calcutta. This is what he wrote[1] :—

> " At the angle by which I entered the Tank Square, as the great area was called, stood an obelisk in a neglected ruinous state. As it was only a few yards out of my way, I went up to it. From my very early years few things had filled my mind with more horror than the very name of the Black Hole of Calcutta, although the exact history of its tragic celebrity was unknown to me. With peculiar force was this impression revived when, on deciphering an almost obliterated inscription, I found that the column which I beheld was the monument which had been erected to the memory of the victims of that horrible massacre. A

---

[1] " Travels in India a Hundred Years Ago," by Thomas Twining, 1893.

GOVERNMENT HOUSE, FROM THE HUGLI (c. 1790)

native, who accompanied me, pointed to the part of the fort south of the principal gate in which the fatal dungeon itself was situated."

X.—1792. In the same year William Baillie published his " Plan of Calcutta," reduced from Colonel Mark Wood's map of 1784-5. In this map the Monument is marked again on the familiar site.

XI.—1794. In this year the same William Baillie published, in a series of " Twelve Views of Calcutta," a " View of Tank Square from the East." There once more, at the same corner, is the obelisk with its octagonal base.

XII.—1794. During the years 1792 and 1793, Aaron Upjohn made the surveys of Calcutta and its environs, which resulted in his well-known map, published in April 1794. Again on the identical spot, between the corner of Writers' Buildings and the Great Tank appears an octagon, with the description attached to it, " Monument."

XIII.—1797. There has been published in Calcutta a mortgage dated 19th–20th of July, 1797, in which a house and ground are described as being " bounded on the west by the public street leading from the Monument to the Esplanade, on the north by a street leading parallel with the Great Tank."

XIV.—1800. I have already cited the reference to " the Monument " in an advertisement in the " Calcutta Gazette " of the 14th August, 1800.

XV.—1803. In this year Lord Valentia was in Calcutta, where, as the guest of Lord Wellesley, he attended the great ball, given by the Governor General to celebrate both the Peace of Amiens and the opening of the new Government House. In his " Travels " (published in 1809), after referring to the Black Hole, which he could not see, because it was " filled with goods, being used as a godown or warehouse," he added—

> " A monument is erected facing the gate, to the memory of the unfortunate persons who there perished."

XVI.—1810. In 1824 there appeared a book of " Indian Recollections " by one R. G. Wallace, who had been in Bengal from 1810 to 1812, and who wrote thus of his Calcutta memories :—

> " When I was in Calcutta, the Black Hole was to be seen, and the Monument which commemorated its tragical story, though so much shattered by lightning that I understand it now ceases to meet the eye."

XVII.—1812. Another visitor to Calcutta in 1812 has left in a
letter, signed " Asiaticus," that appeared in the " Asiatic Journal " of
February 1817, a description of a visit paid in that year by himself
and some friends to the Black Hole, then under sentence of demolition. After a very accurate description of the famous chamber, as it
then existed, he added—

> " To the right of the Writers' Buildings a monument is erected,
> with an inscription commemorating the barbarity of the Nuwab. It
> serves as the first attraction to a stranger arriving in Calcutta."

XVIII.—1812. In the same year occurs the reference in the
Journal of Maria, Lady Nugent, which I have already quoted in the
text.

XIX.—1813. I have also already cited the reference to Rozario's
" Monumental Register," published in Calcutta in this year, which
reproduced the inscriptions on " the Monument."

XX.—1815. In this year appeared the " East India Gazetteer "
by Walter Hamilton, the material of which was obviously either supplied, or corrected, by authorities on the spot. I have previously cited
the reference to Holwell's pillar.

XXI.—1817. In this year, a surgeon's mate on a British ship,
named Robert Hull, visited Calcutta and left the following entry in
his MS. journal, since published in " Bengal Past and Present " (vol.
xiii, p. 19, 1916). After describing a visit to the Black Hole, which
still existed, he says :—

> " Opposite it and near the extremity of the Writers' Buildings is
> erected a monument to commemorate the cruelty, and the vengeance
> it subsequently received. It is a plain pyramid, supported by a
> quadrangular base—on the western face of which is an inscription,
> that ' The cruelty of the Rajah was amply revenged in the sequel.' It is
> a mean monument. (Then follows a reference to a passage in Milburn's
> ' Oriental Commerce ' (1813), which had clearly been taken verbatim
> from M. de Grandpré's narrative already quoted. Upon this Mr. Hull
> goes on to remark:) I saw no sculptured designs on either face of the
> pedestal, no inscription in the native language, no iron railings, nor shrubs;
> and so far from its exhibition, in my opinion, of a ' not unsuitable
> appearance,' it appeared totally unworthy of the universal interest
> excited by that most hideous event; nor does it seem to have arrested
> the attention of the natives—none of whom I inquired could point out
> the Black Hole close to it."

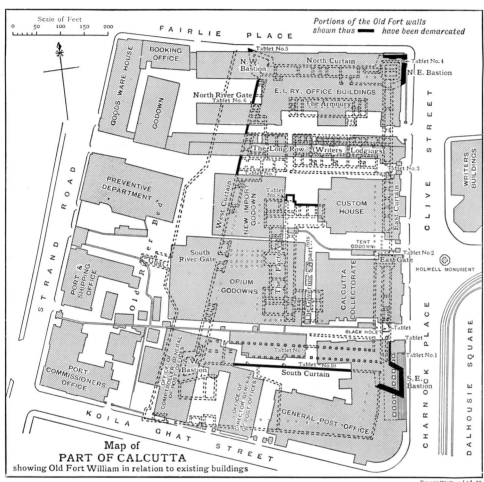

Map of
PART OF CALCUTTA
showing Old Fort William in relation to existing buildings

Emery Walker Ltd. sc.

Clearly the surgeon's mate was bent upon correcting Milburn *cum* Grandpré. But it is evident from his own account that the railing had now disappeared, and that the monument was swiftly lapsing into ruin.

XXII.—Circ. 1818. Somewhere between the years 1815–1821, and probably in 1818, James Baillie Fraser, the well-known Persian traveller, and an excellent amateur artist, was in Calcutta, after travelling with his brother William, a distinguished civilian, subsequently murdered at Delhi. On his return to Europe he published a number of " Views of Calcutta " (1824), in two of which Holwell's Monument appears. The first of these is a near view of the pillar, which is described as " the Monument." It stands upon the familiar site, Writers' Buildings are on the left side of the drawing, the iron railing has disappeared from the monument, and natives are standing or squatting at its base, among whom a barber is plying his trade under a small awning. The other is a more distant view of the pillar, in a plate entitled " A view of Tank Square."

XXIII.—1819. There is in Calcutta (it is published in Vol. II of C. R. Wilson's " Old Fort William ") a " Plan of the Custom House, 1819," which was in course of erection on the site of the demolished fort. On the familiar site at the familiar crossing is inscribed the word " Obelisk."

XXIV.—1820. A Frenchman, named Deville, visited Bengal, and wrote a series of letters to a friend in France, which were published in Paris in 1826. This is what he had to say about the Monument :—

> " Un des plus importans (des monumens de Calcutta), non par la beauté de son architecture, mais par la catastrophe horrible dont il rappelle les malheurs et perpétue le souvenir, se fait remarquer à l'un des angles de squarepond, ou étang quarré.[1] Sa forme est pyramidale, terminé par une boule. On voit à sa base des inscriptions et des bas-reliefs qui représentent les diverses circonstances d'un des événemens les plus mémorables de la ville de Calcutta. Il fut causé par la révolte imprévue des natifs contre les Européens, leurs oppresseurs."

XXV.—1821. Early in this year the " Calcutta Journal," in two numbers, referred to the final removal of the dilapidated, battered, and lightning-stricken pillar of the now almost forgotten Holwell. I have already cited these references.

---

[1] This is obviously the Frenchman's misunderstanding of " Tank Square," which he took to be the same as " Square Tank."

I have thus shown, if indeed it were required, by a continuous series of records covering the entire period from 1760, when the Monument was erected, till 1821, when it was taken down, that Holwell's pillar stood, where he himself had it placed, *i.e.*, outside the Eastern gate of the Fort ; and that for sixty years it was a prominent landmark of Calcutta, described or depicted by over a score of pens or pencils. That anyone should have thought it worth while to argue that all these witnesses were either impudent fabricators and frauds, painting what was not there and describing what they had not seen, or else the innocent victims of the most astonishing series of optical illusions ever recorded, would be deemed incredible were it not that persons were found in India in my day, and have been found since, willing to undertake the task.

The twofold attempt to show, firstly that the Black Hole incident never occurred, and, secondly, that Holwell never commemorated it in the manner described, is however the most barefaced instance known to me in history of the lengths to which political or racial partisanship coupled with a sufficient lack of moral scruple, can be made to go. Nevertheless I am disposed to think that both Holwell's Monument and mine will be found to have successfully survived the shock.

CHAPTER VIII

THE VICTORIA MEMORIAL HALL

Anon out of the earth a fabric huge
Rose, like an exhalation.—MILTON. "Paradise Lost," Book I, 710.

From stately nave to nave, from vault to vault
Through bowers of fragrant and enwreathed light
And diamond-paved lustrous long arcades
Until he reached the great main cupola.—KEATS. "Hyperion," I, 217.

AT the lower or Southern end of the Maidan—that great expanse of level sward, interspersed with clumps and avenues of now considerable trees, which is both the glory and the lungs of Calcutta—there rises into the air a great building of pure white marble. It is built in the Italian Renaissance style with some Oriental features, and is crowned with a dome that soars to a height of 160 feet above the ground. Its gleaming white façade looks straight forth upon the Parade ground, and can be seen from every portion of the Maidan. It is reared upon a marble platform that projects beyond its walls and lifts it from six to seven feet above the garden below. The approach to it lies between two great basins of water—originally irregular tanks or ponds—but now shaped into symmetry, and held in with containing walls and balustrades ; and on every side stretches a wide expanse of lawn and flower bed, which is in process of being converted into what will before long be an umbrageous garden. At intervals over this expanse and along the ceremonial causeway leading to both its Northern and Southern entrances are placed statues or memorial arches to British Sovereigns. This building, which is by far the finest structure that has been reared in India since the days of the Moghuls, and the most splendid concrete monument of British rule, is the Victoria Memorial Hall, erected by the contributions of the Princes and Peoples of India—both European and Indian—in memory of that great Queen. It was begun in 1902, the year after her death. Its foundation stone was laid by King George V, when Prince of Wales, in January 1906 ; it was finally opened by the Prince of Wales in December 1921.

As I happen to have been responsible for the inception of this scheme, and know the history of its earlier struggles better than anyone else, and as, whether in India, or out of it, I have kept a close watch upon its progress, and have had the pleasure of collecting a very large proportion of its contents, it may be well that I should tell the story before it is forgotten. Who knows if, centuries hence, people may not otherwise dispute about its genesis and features just as they still do about those of the Taj Mahal ?

When Queen Victoria died in the closing days of January 1901, there was an outburst of feeling from all classes of the population of India, such as had been evoked by no previous incident since the connection of Britain with India began. Not merely had the Queen been upon the throne for a period that exceeded in duration the lives of the majority of those then living, so that they had known no other Monarch ; not merely had all the great events in the modern history of India been connected with her reign ; but her virtues, her qualities, her well-known affection for her Indian subjects, even her sex, had greatly endeared her to the peoples of India. It was not surprising therefore that a universal desire should at once have found expression to erect a suitable memorial or memorials to the deceased Sovereign ; and it fell naturally to the Viceroy to inaugurate such a movement at the then Capital of the Indian Empire.

During the two years which I had already spent in India, and on the occasion of previous visits, nothing had struck me more painfully than the almost complete lack in that country of relics or memorials of the great events through which it had passed, the thrilling scenes that it had witnessed, the famous men, English and Indian, by whom it had been served. Whereas every European Capital that I had ever visited possessed and treasured in its galleries or museums trophies of such incidents and such men—exercising a potent influence on the imagination and stimulating the patriotism of succeeding generations—in Calcutta and indeed in India, beyond a few scattered statues of Viceroys or Governors or Generals, a few pictures, mostly hidden in Government Houses, and an occasional monument or tomb, there was little to show that the Indian scroll of history had been one on which immortal characters had been inscribed, or that the Victorian Era in particular had witnessed the growth of India from a scattered complex of heterogeneous states and territories into a powerful and consolidated

VICTORIA MEMORIAL HALL, FROM THE NORTH-WEST

Empire. How little anyone seemed to care about, or even to remember, the mighty deeds that had been wrought on Indian soil, or to inculcate their lessons for the sake of posterity. I felt that the lack of this historical sense—the surest spring of national self-respect—was injurious in its effect both upon English and Indian interests. The English hardly realised what their predecessors in India had done. The Indians, unconscious of what a century and a half of Anglo-Indian connection had effected, were disposed, in the rising tide of national feeling, to find a justification for the latter in the memory of a remote and largely unhistorical past, or in dreams of a still more visionary future. Was there not, I thought, in the history of India itself in the past two centuries sufficient to gratify the sentiments both of pride and of hope ? These ideas had already taken shape in my mind, and I had contemplated associating them with the name and reign of Queen Victoria, when her death provided the spark that lit the train.

As the result of a Conference between a number of representative European and Native gentlemen and myself, held at Calcutta immediately afterwards—at which these suggestions met with unanimous approval—I wrote a Memorandum which appeared in the Calcutta Press of 4th February, 1901. This was followed by a speech at a great public meeting, held two days later in the Town Hall, to institute the National Indian Memorial ; and three weeks later by an Address to the Bengal Asiatic Society, explaining with great fulness the character and probable contents of the proposed Hall.[1]

The scheme for which the sympathies and subscriptions of the public were invited was as follows. It was proposed to erect upon the Calcutta Maidan a magnificent building, to be known as the Victoria Memorial Hall, the central feature of which should be a marble statue of the Queen standing under the central dome. In immediate proximity to this would be a hall or halls consecrated to personal memorials of Her Majesty, her family, and her reign. In the remainder of the building would be a number of galleries, corridors, and apartments, which would be filled with statuary, paintings, personal relics, prints and engravings, documents, models and every variety of historical trophy, illustrating the period since the Moghul rule, during which

---

[1] These statements were all published in the " Journal of the Queen Victoria Memorial Fund " No. 1 (April 1901), and were followed up by an article (for readers in England) in the "Nineteenth Century" for June 1901. In these papers will be found a full and accurate account of the scheme, as it was then contemplated, and as it has since been carried out.

British connection with India had begun, grown, and reached its zenith. There was to be a separate gallery or galleries for the contributions of the Indian Princes, who possess treasures of inestimable value, and a Durbar Hall was to be added for the great ceremonial gatherings of the future. Within the compass thus indicated, the test of admission was to be not artistic, or even merely historical interest ; but, in the case of objects or events, exceptional importance, in the case of persons, exceptional distinction or service, irrespective of race or creed. The Hall, which was to be the noblest structure that taste and care and a generous expenditure could produce, was to be an enduring monument of India's place in world-history and of the wonderful record of Queen Victoria's reign.

I need hardly say—as anyone who has had experience in organising such a movement will realise—that there were many difficulties to be overcome on the threshold. The following questions were put and had to be answered—Why should there be an Indian Memorial at all ? Would it not be quite sufficient if India sent her contributions to the great monument that was already in contemplation in London ? A second group of questions followed—Why have a monument in brick and mortar, or even in marble ? Would it not be much better and more in consonance with the character of the late Queen, that her memorial should be of a charitable or eleemosynary character ? Upon this hint every impoverished institution or half completed building in India hastened to advance its claim. A great scheme of Technical Education, a Research University, a perpetual endowment of the Famine Fund—these were among the innumerable suggestions put forward. When these had been disposed of, and it was agreed that something visible, monumental, directly connected with the reign and personality of the Queen and with Indian history, should be preferred, there arose the time-honoured Indian controversy, whether should there be a Central Memorial at all, and if so why should Calcutta be preferred ? The inter-provincial and still more the inter-capital jealousies that exist in India are notorious, and no finer opportunity could have been offered for their vigorous exploitation. I met the former point by at once laying down that the idea of a Central Memorial did not in the smallest degree preclude the erection of provincial or local memorials —on the contrary the latter were to be encouraged—but either the subscribers thereto might be given the option of earmarking a portion of their donations to the central scheme, or the Provincial Governments might set apart a fraction of the sums that they raised, for that object. As to the choice between Calcutta and Bombay, or any other city, I argued (herein committing the single capital mistake of which I was guilty) not merely that Calcutta was the seat of the Government of India during some five months of the year, but that it was now inconceivable that it should be otherwise, that it was useless at this time of day to talk of Delhi or Agra, and that, where the Government of India and the representative of the Sovereign resided, there the Imperial Memorial must, for practical reasons, if no other, be placed. I own that I never anticipated—nor did a single other person in India—that before eleven years had passed, a Government either in India or in England would be found so foolish as to ordain the very change which I derided, and which, after the lapse of a second eleven years, is still only in course of being carried out, at an inexcusable cost to the finances of India, and without any resultant advantage to a single public interest.

However, while my error in foresight has deprived the Victoria Memorial Hall of the undoubtedly great advantage of the support of the Government of India and the personal interest of the Viceroy, it has on the other hand been instrumental in presenting Calcutta with a monument such as no other Provincial capital in India can ever hope to possess, and has definitely marked the metropolitan character of the City on the Hugli, of which no official ukase can ever deprive it.

Another class of objections to the choice of Calcutta was suggested by the alleged unsuitability of the place for any Imperial Monument. Was not the Hugli gradually silting up, and was it not likely that some day in the future the port of Calcutta would be doomed, and the city would relapse into a minor provincial capital, if not a deserted town? And even supposing this did not happen, would the alluvial soil of the delta, on which Calcutta is built and which consists largely of sand, support so heavy a burden, and would not its marble piers, its lofty arches and its soaring dome, gradually sink into the subsoil and come down with a crash? I do not here give the various answers, in each case as I think sufficient, that were forthcoming to all these pleas. I merely record the latter, as among the fences that had to be cleared before we could emerge into the straight run home.

These manifold objections having been answered, there remained the questions—why erect a National Gallery, or Museum, or Hall of Fame ? Who cared for such things ? Were not museums ordinarily deserted, and regarded only as a public bore ? And even supposing the building to be raised and the accommodation provided, from what source would the contents be forthcoming ? What would be the good of gleaming marble halls, if they were to be empty, or of the attempt to commemorate great men and great events, if their relics did not exist ? To answer these doubts I made the speeches to which I have above referred, and the argument of which was summarised in the " Nineteenth Century " article as follows :—

" The collection in the Victoria Hall will fall more or less into the following categories :

" A gallery of sculpture, in which will be collected the statues, busts, and medallions of distinguished men. We fortunately already possess the nucleus of such a collection in Calcutta, though the objects are so widely scattered, and so inadequately placed, that their existence is probably quite unknown to travellers, and is but little known to the majority of Calcutta residents. There is a very fine marble statue of Warren Hastings by Westmacott, which is now effectually concealed from public view in an unused portico of the Town Hall. In the ground floor of the same building, which is rarely used for public purposes, is a colossal figure of Cornwallis by Bacon. There are busts of James Prinsep and the Duke of Wellington in the same building, which has been condemned as unsound, and will probably one day be pulled down. In the Dalhousie Institute, which was named after the great Governor General, and was intended to be a sort of Valhalla for Calcutta, but is now merely an entertainment room, with a small club attached to it, are a number of fine pieces of statuary. A beautiful marble effigy of Lord Hastings by Flaxman stands in the portico. Inside are statues or busts of Dalhousie (which belonged originally to Government House), Havelock, Outram, Nicholson. A number of others that I might name are distributed elsewhere. We shall offer to all these scattered objects a more worthy setting in the Victoria Hall.

" A gallery or galleries of paintings, engravings, prints, and pictorial representations in general, both of persons and scenes. Here, again, we already possess in Calcutta the germs of such a collection, and since the scheme was started, I have received offers or promises of others. Where their owners do not care to part with them alto-

VICTORIA MEMORIAL HALL. SOUTH FRONT

gether, we may hope to obtain specimens on loan.   Oil painting is now almost extinct in India.   But a century ago, a number of English artists of repute, including more than one Royal Academician, came out from England and spent some time in the country, undertaking commissions on a large scale.   Several of their pictures are still trace-able.   One of our objects will be to discover still more.   At about the same time a series of admirable coloured engravings by English artists were published of Indian places and scenes.   These also we shall collect, and where we cannot secure originals, we shall be content with reproductions.

" It ought to be possible after diligent search to present in mezzo-tint and line engravings an almost continuous history of Anglo-Indian worthies, battles, sieges, landscapes, buildings, forts, and scenes during the last two hundred years.

" In view of the great munificence that has been shown by the Native Chiefs in contributing to this Hall, which but for their princely donations would never come into being, I should like to create a Court, or Hall, of Princes within it, where such memorials might be collected as they were willing to offer or to lend.   Statues and like-nesses of notable men among them might be placed here, and might appropriately be surrounded by a collection of the arms and accoutre-ments—spears and battle-axes, swords, shields, horse trappings, and coats of mail—that were once the everyday furniture of their glittering courts, and many of which still survive.

" It should be even easier to amass a first-rate collection, in a gallery set apart for the purpose, which would furnish a complete chronological illustration of the history of British arms in India.   Speci-mens of the various uniforms that have been worn both by the British and the native soldiers, first of the Company and afterwards of the Crown, and of the weapons that they have carried, will be here dis-played.   Military trophies, now locked up in unvisited arsenals, can be brought out into the daylight.   In the same gallery might be placed a collection of British medals given for service in India and upon its borders.

" The documentary illustration of historical events will form an important feature.   In cases or stands we shall collect and exhibit the originals, or where these are not procurable, copies of treaties, sanads, patents, and charters, despatches from the Government of

India with the signatures of successive Governors General and their colleagues, and other documents or manuscripts of personal or historical interest. Maps and plans will form a subsidiary but very necessary feature of the same collection. Seals, newspapers, coins, stamps are all the raw materials from which history is composed, and in time these too may be forthcoming.

"Another very proper content of the Hall will be a collection of models. There are many objects of great historical interest which we either cannot procure, because they have vanished, or could not admit, because of their size and unsuitability, but which might very fitly be represented by small-scale reproductions. I allude to such objects as ships, from the pioneer sloops of the merchant adventurers to the four-masted sailing ships that still lift their spars against the sunset on the Hugli ; forts, sieges, and battlefields ; structures and buildings.

"We shall endeavour to enhance the personal note which is the source of so much interest in any collection, by placing in stands or cases in the various galleries the relics and trophies, the correspondence and handwriting, miniatures, articles of costume or use—in a word, the personal belongings of those who are held worthy of inclusion.

"Finally, we shall hope to decorate the walls of some of the galleries and corridors by fresco paintings of famous events in Indian history. The art of such painting in a manner that is absolutely durable is not yet extinct in India : and even if we are unable ourselves to supply the designs, I think that we can undertake to produce the artificers. Perhaps in other parts of the building we shall resort to the representation of acts or scenes through the medium of bronze or copper plaques affixed to the walls."

To this summary I added a list of the names of those prominent persons, of whom it was hoped to obtain memorials, and the majority of whom are now, twenty years later, commemorated in the building. Apart from the personal representations or mementoes of Queen Victoria and the Royal Family, they included among Europeans,— Pioneers of Commerce and Empire, Governors, Lieutenant Governors, Governors General and Viceroys, distinguished Administrators, great Generals and soldiers, military adventurers, men of letters and science, scholars, antiquarians, jurists, explorers and pioneers, reformers and philanthropists, churchmen and missionaries ; among Indians, similar categories of Ruling Princes, statesmen, fighting men, writers, poets, religious reformers, practitioners of the Arts.

Perhaps, however, the best answer to all the hostile objections and pleas lay in the enthusiastic reception which the proposal met with, and in the overwhelming pecuniary response that was made. While Bombay for a time held aloof and denounced the scheme as a " fatuous project "—its own rival plan having meanwhile made a very halting progress—while hostile critics, even in Calcutta itself, wrote of " Curzon's folly," and while the newspapers teemed with picturesque references to " white elephants," the money continued to pour in. From the principal Ruling Chiefs I received individual offers of 15 lacs (£100,000), 10 lacs, 5 lacs and smaller sums. These I declined to accept in full, feeling that it would be unfair to take advantage of such princely generosity, and that the Memorial ought to be erected by the contributions of the thousands, rather than by the munificence of the few ; nor did I ultimately accept a larger sum than 2½ lacs from any Chief, and that only from a very limited number. Before I left India I had raised nearly £400,000, of which Bengal (including Calcutta) had given over £100,000 ; and the financial success of the project was assured.

Among the Press critics of the scheme none was louder, or more ill-informed, than the English journal " Truth," at that time owned by Mr. H. Labouchere, M.P., with whom I had served in the House of Commons. I have found among my correspondence a copy of a letter which I wrote to him dated 8th May, 1901; and as it gives a very fair idea, both of the nature of the adverse criticism that was rife, and of the response to the appeal which had already been made only three months after its issue (in the preceding paragraph I have given the result after three years), I reproduce the letter here :—

May 8th, 1901.

MY DEAR LABOUCHERE,

I am well aware that all the discontented people all the world over write to your paper : and discontent is not compatible with strict veracity. Nevertheless, your informants, who induced you to denounce our Victoria Memorial Scheme, have been more than usually elastic in their treatment of facts. I will put you and them right in a few particulars.

I see no analogy between our proposed Memorial Hall and the

Imperial Institute. I have visited the latter, and found it to be a bad Club combined with a worse exhibition of products, fabrics, and such like horrible things. We are going to have a building with a statue of the Queen as the central object, and with galleries devoted to sculptures, paintings, and memorials of great men and great events in the past of Indian history. I see no analogy, therefore : nor, I am sure, do you.

You say that some of the Princes have been induced to give as much as five lacs. This is quite untrue. On the day upon which the scheme was unfolded at Calcutta, I received offers by telegram from two Chiefs of 10 lacs and 15 lacs. I declined to accept these amounts, and indicated that I thought one lac would be a more suitable limit to contributions. That limit has not since been exceeded.

You say that the baby Raja of Patiala has been put down for half a lac. Well, he is not quite a baby, being, I believe, about 9 or 10. But as a matter of fact he was not put down for anything. The State is administered during his minority by a Council of Regency, and it was they who subscribed ; and anyone who thinks that the premier Sikh State of India would be willing to stand out of a Memorial to the Queen must know very little of India.

You censure the Commander-in-Chief's Circular. It was issued without any reference to me. But if you think that an order limiting the subscription of the soldiers to one day's pay has benefited the fund, you are strangely mistaken. It has had this result : that where I might have expected Rs. 1,000, I have only got Rs. 100. I can only say that I am desperately glad that no such injunction was issued to civilians.

You call our undertaking fantastic and profitless. Do you think the collections in the National Portrait Gallery, in the Tower of London, in the British Museum, or in Greenwich Hospital, fantastic and profitless ? If you do, I do not agree with you. I regard them as of incalculable value to the education and the patriotism of the nation ; and I should have thought that an Englishman who was trying to present India with the same advantages merited encouragement rather than abuse.

Finally you say that my project has been received with very little enthusiasm in India. Let us apply the test of results. When I started, the scheme was subjected to a good deal of criticism and attack in the various Provinces. They said they did not want to contribute to Calcutta, and would prefer utilitarian or philanthropic memorials of their own. This was very natural. India is a very big place—nearly as large as Europe : and Palermo or Seville might not in any circumstances be enthusiastic about a monument in Edinburgh or Warsaw. Accordingly I said " Very well : have your own monuments, of any kind that you like ; raise your own money, and devote it to what you will. If you can spare a fraction, 10 per cent. or 5 per cent., to the National Memorial, I shall be glad to receive it ; but do just as you please."

They took me at my word. Bombay, which boasts itself the first city in India, went in for a purely charitable memorial, and decided to give me nothing at all. In three months they have raised in the entire Presidency less than £4,000, and are now dry. Madras went in for a Technical Institute, and have raised in the same time exactly £3,000. So it has been elsewhere. I can no more bring pressure to bear upon Burma or the Punjab than you can affect the Sultan in his Seraglio, or the Empress Dowager of Peking. Nevertheless, the collections in all these outlying places, to which no appeal has ever been issued by me, but which have gone on their own lines, have been a failure. Meanwhile my scheme, for which you say no enthusiasm is felt, has elicited nearly £220,000, rejecting the large contributions which you throw in my teeth.

Have you done this at home, and are you in a position to sneer at us ?

There has never been a Memorial to Prince Albert, Mr. Gladstone, or anyone else, that has not elicited contrary opinions, and been the subject of much dispute. I know of no test to apply to success or failure in such a case but the financial one. No official pressure in the world (and here I can assure you that there has been absolutely none) can squeeze money from reluctant pockets : and how I can in three months have got £220,000 (and shall get nearly £300,000) for a scheme to which every one objects, I am at a loss to imagine. I write this not for publication in your paper, but to set you right ; since I know you well enough to be sure that you can have no wish to be wrong.

            I am
                Yours sincerely
                            Curzon.

Though the ground had thus been cleared, and the project had received a good start, there were still formidable obstacles to be overcome.   One of these was local in character, the others were of more general application.

The first difficulty was the selection of the actual site.   Calcutta having been chosen as the *locale* for the Hall, it was obvious that it must be built somewhere upon the Maidan.   Now it needs but the smallest acquaintance with that great city to know that its inhabitants regard the Maidan as a virtuous woman regards her honour, any assault upon which must be repelled as the deadliest form of insult. I had begun by tentatively proposing the North-east corner of that great expanse, between Esplanade Row East and the Ochterlony Monument (in the space now known as the Curzon Gardens), and a hint was at one time thrown out that the tall brick and plaster pillar, which commemorates that hero, might have to be removed.   An explosion of horror supervened.   Then each of the possible rival sites was discussed and in turn rejected : (1) opposite the High Court ; (2) in the Eden Gardens ; (3) behind Prinsep's Ghat ; (4) in the centre of the Ellenborough Course.   The Building Committee, which I had constituted to deal with these and similar problems, ended by recommending a site midway between the Statue of Sir John Lawrence and the Plassey Gate of the Fort.   In this position the Hall would have served as a pendant to Government House, and would have occupied a noble position, visible from all quarters, and yet in close proximity to the town.   But at once it was discovered that any building in such a locality would infringe the vital conditions of Calcutta's honour, would cut off the breezes from the river, would irreparably destroy the amenities of local existence, and render the city a still more terrible Inferno in the summer months !   A strong feeling was then aroused in favour of the site finally selected, which was then described as the Cathedral Avenue or the Jail site, and, the Bengal Government having signified its willingness to demolish the hideous and obsolete structure of the Jail at its own cost, we then referred the matter to a plebiscite of the most representative bodies and organisations in Calcutta, the result of which was an overwhelming vote in its favour.   That decision we at once accepted.   It was, in my opinion, the right one ; and it has been vindicated by all that has since occurred.

Now arose the second group of difficulties, inseparable from the conditions of Indian existence. In that country, with its constant fluctuations both in official and commercial life, its dearth of established professional traditions, its lack of facilities for the erection of any but utilitarian buildings, and the absence alike of architects and artists, how was such a fabric as I contemplated to be raised ? And where were the materials to be found ? And how were the contents, even supposing that they existed, to be brought together ? For all these purposes much forethought, an elaborate organisation, infinite labour would be required. To anyone in London contemplating a similar project, with all the resources of an elaborately organised and complex civilisation behind him, the task might appear not difficult ; and yet even in London, as I write (1924) the British Monument to Queen Victoria is only just completed. In India on the other hand, where none of these advantages exist, where the generations come and go with bewildering rapidity, where all machinery for instance has to be imported from Europe, where nothing like the Victoria Hall had been attempted for centuries, and where the head of the Government, who had made himself responsible for the venture, was for eight months of the year separated by thousands of miles from the scene of operations —the problem was almost bewildering.

As to one point I had no doubt. In Calcutta—a city of European origin and construction—where all the main buildings had been erected in a quasi-classical or Palladian style, and which possessed no indigenous architectural type of its own—it was impossible to erect a building in any native style. A Moghul building, however appropriate for the mosques and tombs of the Moslem Kings, or even for the modern Palace of an Indian Prince in his own State, would have been ridiculous in the commercial and official capital of India, and quite unsuited for the Memorial of a British Sovereign. A Hindu fabric would have been profoundly ill adapted for the purposes of an exhibition. It was self-evident that a structure in some variety of the classical or Renaissance style was essential, and that a European architect must be employed.

I accordingly put myself in communication with my friend, the present Lord Esher, at that time Secretary to the Office of Works, and received from him the recommendation, as architect, of Mr. (afterwards Sir William) Emerson, then President of the Royal Institute of British Architects, who, in addition to his professional distinction, possessed the advantage of knowing India well, and of having designed several important buildings there ; and, in my earliest correspondence with the latter, I traced the outlines of such a fabric as we desired and invited him to submit designs in the Italian Renaissance style. He responded with great alacrity and ability to this appeal ; and firstly on paper, and subsequently during his repeated visits to India, presented us with the noble design which has since been executed.

The next question was that of material. I was beyond measure anxious that the All-India Memorial to the Queen should be erected of Indian marble and stone, and one of our first acts had been to collect specimens of the many marbles in which India abounds, from all parts of that continent, as far East as Burma. But the difficulty then arose that none of these quarries was worked except on the most exiguous scale—and that only by primitive hand-methods—that it was doubtful whether the amount required for so huge a building would be available ; that there were no mechanical appliances for its extraction, and that the cost of transport to Calcutta might be ruinous. So great did these difficulties appear that we were driven to contemplate importing a considerable, perhaps the greater, portion of the marble from the quarries of Pentelikon near Athens. This beautiful material, with its glittering white surface, faintly flushed or streaked with yellow splashes (owing to the presence of iron pyrites in the marble) is that of which the Parthenon and the other most famous temples and statues of ancient Greece were made.

Moreover the quarries were actually being worked at the moment by a British Company. We had nearly concluded an arrangement with the latter, when a dispute as to the cost of the marble arose, which ended, fortunately as it turned out, in the withdrawal of the Company from the negotiations, leaving us no alternative but to depend exclusively upon Indian sources of supply.

A renewed investigation then revealed that the Makrana quarries in the Jodhpur State in Rajputana, from which the marble for the Taj and the principal Moghul buildings at Agra, Delhi and Lahore, had been drawn, were still capable, if worked with modern appliances, of furnishing the requisite amount of material, while the blueish streaks and veins in this marble, which produce such an exquisite effect in moderating a too uniform and glittering surface of white, would, at Calcutta as at Agra, mitigate the blinding glare of the platform and façade, and give them a mellow and restful tone. The next step was to procure a lease of the quarries from the Jodhpur Durbar ; and the next following, to create or arrange with a company for their exploitation. Special arrangements had then to be made with the Railway Companies for the transportation of the blocks of marble, and finally for the preparation, shaping and fitting of them, on the Calcutta Maidan. To diversify the surface, the bonding stones between the larger blocks were uniformly cut from the darker-veined strata of marble.

In the meantime, while all these operations, which, though they are here summarised in a paragraph, consumed months and even years of time, were going on, there remained the task of commencing the collection of the objects that were to be exhibited in the Hall when raised. I have already in my previous summary given a general indication of what they might be, and I will now show the manner in which it was suggested that they should be disposed. As early as February 1902, exactly one year after the Town Hall Meeting at Calcutta, I issued a statement which, after a short description of the appearance of the fabric, gave the desired information.

"The nature of the soil in the Maidan is such that foundations cannot be sunk to a much greater depth than four feet. If a building of great size and weight is to be placed upon it, the foundations will therefore have to be continued above the surface of the ground. In other words, the fabric will have to be raised upon a terrace several feet in height. So far from regarding this as a defect, it seems to me a great advantage. It is an architectural device familiar in the cases of nearly all the Moghul monuments, notably the Taj, and of many of the finest buildings in the world. Height and dignity will be given to the fabric if it be thus lifted ; while the appearance of the white marble terrace, balustraded around, ascended by a great flight of steps, and supporting the main pile, will in itself be one of the main features of beauty. This terrace will probably be from 350 to 400 feet in length, and the building upon it of somewhat smaller dimensions. It is suggested that the form of the fabric should be a parallelogram, of which the main faces will be the northern and southern, terminating in towers, and connected at the ends with curving open colonnades. In the centre of the building will be the Queen's Hall, a circular marble chamber under a lofty dome, rising to a height of some 160 feet from

the floor.   On either side, North and South, of the central hall and dome
will be an interior court surrounded by a two-storeyed *loggia* or arcade.

" We will suppose that a visitor is entering this building from the
main or western front.   Perhaps an idea of its appearance and contents may be conveyed by attempting to follow in his footsteps.   From
the Maidan he will climb the great flight of marble steps to the level
of the terrace.   Upon this terrace in front of him, to right and left,
will stretch the main façade of the building.   In its centre will be a
colossal entrance archway outside which will be placed, upon its pedestal,
Mr. Frampton's bronze statue of the Queen.   To right and left of this
main archway will stretch the white marble front of the building
terminating at the extremities in towers.

" Entering under the archway, the visitor will proceed into an
Entrance Hall or Vestibule devoted to a collection of objects connected with her history, personality, and reign.   Here will be hung
the series of pictures, depicting important incidents in her life, which
have already been presented to us by His Majesty the King.   Passing
through this, he will enter straight into the space under the dome.
In this hall, the centre and core of the building, I contemplate that no
other object shall be placed but a white marble crowned statue of the
Queen as a young woman, raised upon a pedestal.   Outside in the
grounds she will be depicted in bronze in a sitting posture, as she was
in advanced years.   Inside I would represent her standing as she
appeared in her girlish grace, when first she ascended the throne.
Around the hall I would place the inscriptions in different tongues
which were her messages to the Indian people.   Through the domed
hall one will proceed to a similar exit on the Southern face.

" Retracing our footsteps for a moment to the Vestibule of the
Queen's relics, we will suppose that the visitor intends to inspect the
remaining galleries of the building.   If he turns to the left he will
enter the great Sculpture Gallery, where he will see the marble images
of Warren Hastings, of Cornwallis, of Wellesley, of Hastings, of Dalhousie, and of many another *clarum et venerabile nomen*.   If he turns
from the Queen's Vestibule to the right, he will enter the Gallery of
Pictures, where he will see a long procession of likenesses of the men
who have rendered India famous during the last two hundred years.
Through this he will pass to the right-hand tower, where smaller rooms
will be devoted to collections of prints, engravings, coins, and the like.

STATUE OF QUEEN VICTORIA

Sculpt.: Sir T. Brock, R.A.

The curving open colonnades will at either end connect these towers with similar towers at the extremities of the Eastern façade. Should additional internal accommodation ever be required, the colonnade could be filled in, or replaced by separate galleries.

"We will now suppose that our visitor, after inspecting the Queen's statue under the dome, intends to pass out towards the Southern approach. In correspondence with the Queen's Vestibule on the West side, he will enter the Hall of Princes on the Eastern side, where the Indian Princes will be invited to place such collections on gift or on loan as they may be willing to offer. Here, as before, he will be able to branch off to right or to left. If he proceeds to the right he will pass into a two-storeyed gallery, one floor of which will be the Hall of Models (of famous buildings, sieges, battles, &c.), and the other the Hall of Arms, where will be a collection of military trophies, uniforms, weapons, flags, medals, guns. If he passes to the left he will enter the great Durbar Hall, which will embrace two floors, and will occupy the entire North-east wing. This hall will be used for any ceremonial purposes, such as Investitures, that may be held in Calcutta, and it will also be available, under strictly defined conditions, for public purposes, such, for instance, as the meeting held last year in commemoration of the late Queen. It should be by far the finest public hall in India. It will be readily accessible to the town, and can be utilised quite independently of the Victoria Hall, and without any interference with the latter. Such, so far as words, without a plan, can bring it home to the mind, is a rough sketch of the Victoria Hall as I should like to see it planned.

"There remains only to be discussed the question of the surroundings. Here we must to some extent be guided by pecuniary considerations. The enclosure and laying out of a large space of ground as a public garden, the fencing it in with handsome iron railings, and the provision of suitable gates, will be a very expensive affair. But it will be everywhere conceded that such a building, as it is proposed to raise, must in no wise suffer from lack of an adequate setting, and that the grounds must be ample and beautiful. Tastefully laid out and planted with a simplicity worthy of the fabric that it will contain, this garden ought to be a great addition both to the beauties of Calcutta and to the enjoyment of the public."

It was in pursuance of these ideas that in letters to the Provincial

N

Authorities, to the Ruling Princes, to important Societies and organisations, to interested persons in England and India and to the families or survivors of illustrious men, I issued a stream of appeals for contributions and support.

The response was most gratifying. His Majesty King Edward not merely sent paintings of the most important events in Queen Victoria's life, but added some of the furniture which she had constantly used ; and these gifts have since been supplemented by the present King and Queen. The High Court of Calcutta and the Asiatic Society of Bengal lent some of their treasures. The Offices of the Government of India, the Post Office, and the Mint were indented upon for official documents, treaties, sanads, stamps, coins and medals. I loaned or gave many objects from Government House, principally statues and paintings (some of these, having been originally subscribed for by the inhabitants of Calcutta, belonged therefore to the city). The Nawab of Murshidabad presented the black marble throne, on which Clive had taken his seat by the side of Nawab Nazim Nujmud Dowleh, when he took over the *diwani* of Bengal, Behar and Orissa in October 1766 ; the richly embroidered kanat or camp-screen, which had been wrested by Aliverdi Khan from the invading army of the Mahrattas in 1746 ; and many other objects. I had models made, in teak or plaster, of Old Fort William and the Black Hole, of the Battlefield of Plassey, and of Seringapatam.

In the course of 1903 I sent an officer on deputation to the leading Princes of India who possess in their Toshakhanas or treasuries, unique collections of arms, accoutrements, and other historic relics of priceless value ; and they offered on loan and sent to Calcutta many of these treasures. I appealed to every variety of person and interest, possessing historical or family connections with India : and to none with greater success than the late Miss Marian Winter, who, as the daughter of the old Rector of Daylesford, and the great-niece of Mrs. Hastings, had inherited most of the pictures and many of the belongings of Warren Hastings, and who generously promised to bequeath to the Victoria Hall a number of the most important of these articles, including the painting of the elegant Marian mentioned in a previous chapter. I discovered that there was in America, in private hands, the magnificent painting by the Russian artist Vassili Verestchagin (who perished at Port Arthur) of the State entry of King Edward VII,

H.R.H. THE PRINCE OF WALES (KING EDWARD VII) ENTERING JAIPUR (1876)

From the painting by Vassili Verestchagin.

DURBAR HALL IN VICTORIA MEMORIAL HALL

when Prince of Wales, into Jaipur in 1876, and through the good offices of Mr. John Hay, formerly American Ambassador in London, I succeeded in effecting the purchase of this noble painting, which the late Maharaja of Jaipur consented to present to the Collection, of which it is now one of its chief ornaments. An illustration of it is given here.

In the spring of 1903 we passed into law in the Legislative Council a Bill entitled the Victoria Memorial Act, vesting the Hall in a Body of Trustees, and providing them with due powers.

In the course of that summer, elaborate tests were made of the foundations on the Maidan, a solid bed of concrete being laid below the surface, and loads being piled upon pillars specially sunk for the purpose, in order to ascertain the maximum weight which the ground would bear. It was the shallow nature of the soil, terminating at the depth of a few feet in blue clay, quite as much as æsthetic considerations, that necessitated, as I have pointed out, the erection above the surface of the great platform on which the building stands.

By the spring of 1904 so much progress had been made, both in building preparations, and in collection, that having persuaded the authorities of the Calcutta Museum temporarily to surrender a few of their galleries for the purpose, I was able to open there an exhibition of the objects already procured, while Sir W. Emerson gave an interesting account of that part of the work for which he was responsible. He stated that the soil was better than he had anticipated, and that he had spread the concrete so that there would be a weight of $1\frac{3}{4}$ tons on every superficial foot of soil beneath it. The walls, he added, would be of solid brickwork, faced externally with marble, internally with marble, stone and plaster. To resist possible earthquake shocks, iron ties would be inserted in the walls, and the sides of the dome would be sloped, so as to give a better base for vibration. On the top of the dome would be a gilded figure of Victory.

As regards the future of the building the Government of India undertook to bear the charge for the custody and upkeep of the Memorial, and I anticipated that the funds which I had collected would be ample not merely to finish the Hall, but also to provide for the purchase of contents, and for a future endowment.

I should here add that it would have been impossible to carry on the preliminary stages of this great enterprise, had I not been favoured, both then and later, with the active and devoted co-operation of many

persons in India and outside it. Foremost among these was the late
Sir Patrick Playfair, who was at once an ardent supporter and an
enthusiastic collector ; while the Calcutta merchants and some of the
Judges, who both then and since consented to serve as Trustees, lent
an aid that was invaluable. Not the least among the obstacles to rapid
progress was, and has always been, the constant change in the body
of Trustees, arising from the circumstances of Indian life. But a few
steadfast friends endeavoured to atone for this anomaly, and to give
some continuity to the proceedings : and but for the unremitting and
unpaid labours of successive Trustees, the project might more than
once have languished and died.

Such was the point that had been reached when I left India in
November 1905. I fear that it has too often been the experience of
Viceroys, and officials in general, that matters in which they took the
deepest interest have not excited the equal concern of their successors,
and that a change of government has meant a change of policy. So
it was with the Victoria Memorial Hall ; and in England I often had
occasion to repeat to myself almost in despair the poet's lines :

"Though fall'n on evil days,
On evil days though fall'n, and evil tongues ! "

During the ensuing year, 1906–7, I heard in London that the
objects which I had loaned from Government House to the Collection,
and which could well be spared, either because they already belonged
to the citizens of Calcutta or because there were duplicates in the
building, had been resumed by the Viceroy, Lord Minto. The
Asiatic Society had followed the Viceroy's example. The Museum
authorities declared that they could no longer spare the Galleries which
they had lent for the exhibition of the Collections ; Queen Victoria's
relics and a few other objects were alone to be retained in a single
apartment ; the priceless collection which I had made with the aid
of the Indian Princes was dispersed and returned to the donors. The
bulk of the exhibits were taken either to Government House or to
the residence of Lord Kitchener in the Fort, or to Belvedere, or to the
Town Hall. The whole fabric which I had toiled so hard to raise
seemed destined to collapse.

Simultaneously the croakers once more raised the doubt whether
the Maidan could support so heavy a weight ; they suggested that

STATUE OF LORD CURZON AT ENTRANCE TO VICTORIA MEMORIAL HALL

Sculpt.: H. Thornycroft, R.A.

the building should be stopped, and the balance of the fund directed to charitable uses ; and they actually procured the suspension of the work in 1907, on the alleged ground of the subsidence of the foundations.

Realising that publicity was the only means of arresting this movement, I thereupon saw the Secretary of State, Lord Morley, and addressed to him for transmission to India a letter dated 22nd August, 1907, of which he wrote to me that it seemed " difficult to answer," and which was subsequently published in "The Times" of 9th May, 1908, in which I gave the history of these lamentable proceedings, and protested against the dispersal or partial incarceration of the Collection, offering to subscribe £500 towards a temporary building on the Maidan for its accommodation.

The letter had the desired effect. In January 1908 the Museum reopened its Galleries, and the Collection (except that portion which had been returned to the Princes) was resumed. About the same time an expert Committee reported that there was no ground for alarm as to the foundations ; and a little later a contract for the building was signed with Messrs. Martin and Co. of Calcutta. Even so the danger was not yet past, and at intervals in ensuing years the wreckers again lifted their heads, and the echoes of these dismal jeremiads would reach me in England. First came the suggestion that the main design should be abandoned, and a smaller scheme adopted in its place, the proposal to persevere with the original plan being only carried by a small majority in the Committee. Then it was suggested that the Memorial should be transferred to Delhi, that cemetery of dead monuments and forgotten dynasties. Next the Bengal Government tried to back out of its original undertaking to surrender its hideous and decrepit jail, unless it was provided with another at the expense of Government. Finally when, under the Morley-Minto scheme of reforms, expanded Legislative Councils were created, both for the Supreme and the Local Governments, it was seriously suggested that as the Central Hall with the Queen's Statue was rather like the Central Lobby at Westminster the entire building should be appropriated for Parliamentary purposes, and that the two open quadrangles at the sides should be roofed over in order to provide accommodation for the two Councils ! The remaining Galleries were to be handed over to Secretaries or consecrated to Committees. The newspaper attack was also revived with much acerbity, and the " white elephant " reappeared from his ancient stable and lumbered heavily across the stage.

When the Government of India left Calcutta in Lord Hardinge's time, a ray of light filtered across the scene ; for in the consequent evacuation of so many big buildings, including the former residence of the Lieutenant Governor, Belvedere, the latter was for a time offered as a habitation for the Victoria Memorial Collection. But no sooner had this been done, than a subsequent Viceroy announced his intention of occupying Belvedere when he came to Calcutta for the winter, and insisted on the bulk of the collections being moved to an adjoining shed.

While these perturbations shook the air, the building continued to make slow but steady progress under the impulse of the signed contract and the influence of a few faithful friends, principal among whom were Lord Carmichael, the first Governor of Bengal and a man of great taste and enthusiasm, and his successor, Lord Ronaldshay. Sir W. Emerson paid periodic visits to Calcutta ; a commission was given to W. Drury, R.A., to execute the sculptured marble panels for the entrance porches—representing Queen Victoria signing her famous Declaration in 1858, Lord Lytton's Proclamation Durbar in 1877, the Jubilee Procession in London of 1887, and the laying of the foundation stone of the Hall by the present King and Queen in January 1906. The great gilded figure of Victory took its stand on the summit of the dome. When Their Majesties again visited Calcutta in 1912, they further selected the external sites for the Statues of Queen Victoria and King Edward. In October 1913 the jail was finally handed over to the Trustees, and meantime in England I was steadily collecting the objects for exhibition and sending out to Calcutta a yearly consignment of paintings, busts, trophies, and works of art, which are much more likely to be found in this country, as old collections and family possessions are dispersed, than in India itself.

Then ensued the Great War, which had many and serious repercussions on the work in more aspects than one. The great fall in the value of securities, sound as the original investments of the fund had been, entailed a loss that amounted to no less than 8 lacs of Rupees, or considerably over £50,000. Parts of the building, notably the cupolas of the corner towers, had to be suspended and are still incomplete. The rise in prices and in the wages of labour necessitated a partial revision of the contract. It was reported that the supply of marble

STATUE OF QUEEN VICTORIA IN FRONT OF VICTORIA MEMORIAL HALL

was failing, and the stringent conditions hitherto imposed as to the purity of colour had to be relaxed—not altogether without advantage, seeing that the shaded blocks lend a pleasing variety to the surface under the glare of the Indian sun.   In the course of 1920–21 a strenuous effort was made by the Viceroy, Lord Reading, who interested himself greatly in the matter, to complete the work before the visit of the Prince of Wales to open the building in December 1921 ; and as a result of grants from the Government of India and the Bengal Government, and a special appeal to the Princes and public, a sum of 17½ lacs was raised.   On December 28 the Opening Ceremony was performed by the Prince before an audience of 6,000 persons, and those who had laboured so earnestly and amid so much discouragement for twenty years might at length exclaim,"*Hic labor extremus, longarum haec meta viarum.*"

If any surprise be felt at the obstacles which have been recorded in these pages, the answer is I think sufficient, that even in Europe, where the idea of such Museums and Memorials is familiar and popular, and where the æsthetic standard is relatively high, no similar project is ever carried through without exciting a criticism and even an opposition that is as passionate at the moment as it is incomprehensible to those who come after ; while in India not only was the conception new, but the experiment had to be performed under conditions of difficulty as regards material, site, machinery, and labour, which are unknown in the West.   And if further disappointment be expressed at the length of time between start and finish, consolation may be found in the reflection that King Solomon was twenty years building his Temple and his house at Jerusalem, that the Taj at Agra, with all the wealth and labour-resources of the Great Moghul, was not completed under twenty-five years, and that in Europe, while thirty-five years were required for the erection of St. Paul's in London, St. Peter's at Rome was not satisfied with less than one hundred.

And now the Hall is erected, even if it be not finished in every detail, and is open.   Externally the building is a thing of beauty. From far and near can be seen the gleaming outline of the great dome —the fifth largest in the world, floating like an aerial bubble over the dense vegetation in which Calcutta is embowered.   Since it was erected, this dome has been discovered to possess two remarkable interior echoes ; one a reverberating echo—a sharp sound repeated in increasing volume —at the very summit, nearly 170 feet above the ground level ; the other a whispering echo, where at a lower level the gentlest whisper is wafted round the smooth circumference to a hearer on the other side. Much might be said about the external sculptures, one of which on the North side depicts a lion's head with water flowing out of it and passing into four troughs representing the four great Indian rivers—the Ganges, the Krishna, the Indus and the Jumna—thus symbolising the life-giving work of Britain in India. In contrast with the Moghul mosques and tombs, where, as at the Taj, a dusky twilight often prevails within, the internal lighting has here been carefully planned. The exquisite white marble full-length statue of Queen Victoria executed by the late Sir Thomas Brock, R.A., from the model of Sir Francis Chantrey's beautiful bust of the Queen, made in 1839 and standing in the corridor at Windsor Castle—whence it was graciously lent by the King for reproduction—stands in solitary beauty under the dome ; paintings, engravings and memorials of her person and reign stand in the adjacent Hall. Statues of the present King and Queen, presented by the Aga Khan, are hard by. The great marble figures of Warren Hastings and Cornwallis stand in the paved quadrangles ; Clive and Wellesley and Dalhousie are there. Paintings and busts of a long line of statesmen and writers and scholars—a far finer collection than was ever assembled in Government House—adorn the Galleries. The collection of portraits and other memorials of Warren Hastings is unique. Zoffany and the two Daniells, the three painters who, more than any others, familiarised England in the latter part of the 18th century with Indian figures and Indian scenes, are abundantly represented. Indian Princes and Rulers are seen side by side with their European contemporaries. The history of Calcutta is portrayed in a unique collection of paintings, engravings, models and maps. Personal relics recall the great men who have trod the Indian stage.

It is a familiar and easy task to belittle these things and to pronounce them a fantasy or a folly. But Calcutta is already proud of her possession ; and perhaps in time to come, when the concrete triumphs of Western civilisation in India are forgotten or submerged, a breath of remembrance may be reserved for those who held that man does not live by bread alone, and who laboured hard and long to convince India that under British rule her history has been glorious, and that that splendour reached its zenith during the reign and largely under the influence of the great Queen-Empress Victoria.

Two further steps still required to be taken.   When I first raised the £400,000 for the erection of the Hall, I had contemplated setting aside a substantial sum for the creation and adornment of the Gardens, and for the endowment and future purchase of objects for the Hall. But as time passed these allotments were eaten up by the long delays and by the increased cost of the building, and even when the fabric was nearing completion, it seemed likely that the setting would be unworthy of the gem, and that the contents would remain stereotyped from lack of funds.

Accordingly in 1915 I invited my friend, the late Lord Redesdale, who was a noted landscape gardener, to lend me his expert assistance, and together with Sir David Prain, formerly Superintendent of the Botanical Garden at Calcutta and subsequently Director of Kew Gardens, who knew all that was to be known about Indian horticulture, we sat down in my house in London, and with the aid of maps and photographs and plans we drew a design for the Gardens of the Victoria Memorial Hall which was approved without alteration by the Trustees in Calcutta, and has since been put into execution.   In order to complete the carrying out of this plan I have since raised from generous English friends who had lived and prospered in Calcutta and shared with me a loving regard for the Maidan a sum that will enable the scheme of garden embellishment to be completed.

Simultaneously the munificence of other friends, both English and Indian, has enabled me to raise a sum not far short of £20,000 for the future endowment of the building, the annual income from which will provide for the replenishment of the collections.

And so I leave the labour which these pages have attempted to record, satisfied that my " white elephant " is not so exotic or futile an animal after all, and that, though I shall never see its stately form myself, it may not be wholly unworthy of the great service for which it was reared and trained.

Kipling once wrote of Calcutta :

" Me the Sea Captain loved, the River built,
    Wealth sought, and Kings adventured life to hold.
 Hail, England ! I am Asia—Power on silt,
    Death in my hands, but gold ! "

I hope to have bequeathed to her something that will conquer Death, and be better than gold.

CHAPTER IX

FORMS, CEREMONIES, AND ENTERTAINMENTS

" The drums and banners, the turbans and the flowing robes, the spears, the silver maces, the elephants with their canopies of State . . . all these things were to him as the objects amidst which his own life had been passed."—LORD MACAULAY on E. Burke in his Essay on Warren Hastings.

HITHERTO I have dealt in the main with the structure and equipment of Government House, and the other residences occupied by the Governors General. Here I propose to say something about the official and ceremonial life that has been lived in them, and to delineate some of the scenes that they have witnessed. The reader in England, aware that society in India is conducted on somewhat different lines from those which prevail in this country, but not quite certain in what respects, apart from contrasts of climate, this difference consists, has been apt sometimes to exaggerate the symptoms of variation, sometimes to ignore their causes.

From the days when the East India Company acquired the government of India, and appointed a Governor General, the incumbent of that high office has always been expected to maintain a considerable degree of state, to follow a very strict ceremonial observance, and to entertain on a lavish scale. Such a practice was not only in exact harmony with Indian tradition, which associated sovereignty with splendour, but it was also demanded by the British population of Bengal, who expected the head of the Government, and the representative of their own Monarch, to deal with the native Rajas and nobles and also with themselves on a footing not merely of equality, but of vantage, and to hold a Court in Calcutta that should more than reproduce (because of the special requirements of the Orient) the etiquette and dignity of the Court at home. Whatever strictures might be passed upon the habits or tastes of individual Governors or Viceroys, that this standard should be upheld has been a proposition of universal acceptance in India. And while those who have ostentatiously risen above it have excited good-humoured criticism, those who have fallen below it have been severely condemned.

In the social and ceremonial sphere, as in that of policy, there have naturally been sharp oscillations, and the law of reaction has operated with an almost mechanical regularity. One Governor General plays his part in a princely manner ; there is a tendency for his successor to relax ; when the third arrives he is called upon to re-establish the balance ; and so it goes on. In the early days these fluctuations, when they took the form of retrenchment, were sometimes due to direct orders from the Company, who did not like to see too large a portion of their property dissipated in entertainment or parade. Sometimes they were the reflex of personal taste or temperament ; some men being by nature punctilious and observant of form, while others are indifferent or shy. Some men enjoy filling the exalted rôle for which they are temporarily cast ; others do it as an odious duty which they secretly abhor. Again, one man has an instinctive love for entertainment, while others dislike it. Ample private means may enable one Viceroy to do more than another, although the Governors General have not as a rule been rich men. But the salary given has commonly sufficed for the performance of the obligation on quite an adequate scale ; and while there has been a great and inevitable change in some of the external ritual of Government House, as the following pages will show, there remains a residuum of picturesque pageantry and formal etiquette, which is the legacy of a century and a half of British rule in India, and will probably continue as long as that rule endures.

Profuse hospitality, a considerable display, much banqueting and dancing, have always been features of the lighter side of English official life in India ; and the chronicles of the earlier days of the Settlement, even before Lord Wellesley, are full of great entertainments, big dinners, and balls at which the ladies danced furiously throughout the night, and became exceedingly hot. The Governor was expected to maintain no small state and style, and even so unostentatious a man as Warren Hastings, who always wore a quiet costume himself and had no fondness for parade,[1] abated not one jot or tittle of the recognised procedure. In those days the Governor's entertainments assumed a triple form. There were the public breakfasts at Government House,

---

[1] I do not think there is sufficient justification for the remarks of Macaulay in his famous, but too rhetorical, essay that Hastings was fond " of state " and that he " sometimes displayed a more than regal splendour." As a matter of fact, visitors from England whose comments are extant in Memoirs or Letters were invariably struck with the moderation and humility of his equipment. Only on State occasions did he observe the necessary forms.

where in addition Hastings practised a constant and liberal hospitality : the official dances and dinners at the Old Court House, which on its upper floor had the only room in Calcutta large enough for a considerable company ; and the private parties and concerts in Hastings Street or at Alipore.

In the recently published and entertaining Memoirs of William Hickey, who reached Bengal in November 1777, we have an account of the Official Dinner given by Warren Hastings on the King's Birthday, 4th June, 1778. Hickey himself was present, clad in "a coat of peagreen lined with white silk and richly ornamented with a spangled and foiled lace, waistcoat and breeches decorated in like manner, being also of white silk " ; and " everybody malgré the extreme heat appeared in full dress, with bags and swords." Upon the cloth being removed, the Governor General, who presided, gave the toasts

> The King
> The Queen and Royal Family
> The East India Company
> The Army and Navy
> The Commander in Chief
> Success to the British Arms in India,

each toast being followed by a salute of twenty-one guns from cannon drawn up for the purpose in front of the Court House.[1]

In a later volume Hickey gives a very pleasant picture of Hastings at the dinner which, as an old Westminster boy, he gave annually to his former schoolfellows, resident in Calcutta.

" Mr. Hastings, who was by nature uncommonly shy and reserved, always unbent upon these occasions, and became playful as a boy, entering with great spirit into all the laugh and nonsense of the hour, himself reciting a number of ridiculous circumstances that occurred in his time. His health being precarious, he was necessarily abstemious both in eating and drinking, and therefore when he was obliged to preside and give toasts, had a mixture of weak wine and water prepared for himself, with which beverage he went through all the ceremonies, announcing the standing toasts with great regularity and precision. After filling the chair until past midnight, by which time a majority of the Company were incapable of swallowing any more wine, he vacated his seat and retired unnoticed, leaving a few of us to continue our orgies until a brilliant sun shone into the room, and were conveyed to our respective homes."[2]

[1] "Memoirs of William Hickey," Vol. II (1775–82), p. 173.
[2] Ibid., Vol. III (1782–90), p. 245.

Warren Hastings was always accompanied in public on official occasions by the mounted Body Guard, which, as will be seen later, he was the first to place upon a permanent footing, and by the customary native retinue ; and he had as many as eight (Sir John Shore said twelve) A.D.C.s, than whom no 19th century Viceroy had more or indeed as many.

When Lord Cornwallis came out for his first term in 1786, it was with instructions from the Directors to pursue a policy of all-round economy. He abandoned the public breakfasts, dispensed with the country house of his predecessors, and was content with the Commander-in-Chief's small bungalow at Barrackpore. Further, he would never, except on State occasions, allow himself to be followed by the Body Guard.

He wrote soon after his arrival :

" My life is not a very agreeable one, but I have ventured to leave off a good deal of the buckram, which rather improves it."

His own scheme of life was faithfully described in a letter of 11th January, 1789, to his son, Lord Brome, then a boy at Eton :

" My life at Calcutta is perfect clockwork ; I get on horseback just as the dawn of day begins to appear, ride on the same road and the same distance, pass the whole forenoon after my return from riding in doing business, and almost exactly the same portion of time every day at table, drive out in a phaeton a little before sunset, then write, or read over letters or papers of business for two hours, sit down at nine with two or three officers of my family to some fruit and a biscuit, and go to bed soon after the clock strikes ten. I don't think the greatest *sap* at Eton could lead a duller life than this." [1]

It sounds a dull life, and so no doubt in a sense it was : and so is all official life to those who are bound to the wheel of a rigid routine.

But, though abstemious in his own manner of living, Cornwallis did not neglect his official duty as head of the Government, and the customary big festivities with dancing and illuminations took place at the Old Court House in his time. On one occasion he wrote to his son (17th August, 1789) describing a fête which he had given in celebration of the King's recovery. The illuminations were all extinguished by a storm, but

" The supper, which could not be put out by the rain, was a very good

---

[1] " Correspondence of Marquis Cornwallis " (ed. Ch. Ross), 3 vols., 1859, Vol. I, p. 388.

one : some of the gentlemen who stayed late were nearly extinguished by the claret ; seven of the finest ladies in the place and twelve gentlemen sang the Coronation Anthem, so that upon the whole you see that it was a magnificent business." [1]

Hickey describes the same entertainment, and says that " upwards of a hundred thousand small coloured lamps were fixed on the Southern front of the Government House." [2]

Cornwallis did however, both by precept and example, bring about one very desirable change in the moral standards of the time. Before his day there was very little dancing after supper, because the gentlemen were usually too intoxicated to stand upright. Indeed Hickey's and all contemporary memoirs reveal a universal habit of drinking which would be deemed inconceivable now, and which must have accounted in large measure for the sudden or premature deaths that were then so common. However, under Lord Cornwallis, the Indian newspapers remarked that the young bloods who had previously remained at the supper table returned to the ball room, so that the ladies had all due respect. There was also a great diminution in gambling, and a consequent falling off in the number of duels and suicides in the British community.

The Governor General was also an excellent and amiable host in his own house ; but after a certain experience at the table of Mr. William Burke, the Paymaster General of the King's Troops, where he complained that he had been persuaded to take so much claret (this appears to have been the popular drink in Anglo-Indian Society at the time) that he went away very nearly tipsy, he decided to be more chary in accepting outside invitations in future. Listen again to William Hickey :

" Lord Cornwallis entertained most hospitably, having daily a party of from twenty to twenty-five. After his escape, as he termed it, from Mr. Burke's, he determined never to dine from home, except at the Chief Justice's, or places of equal ceremony, which etiquette made it necessary he should do once a year. From my intimacy with the members of his lordship's family, I generally received an invitation once a week. Dinner was served with a scrupulous exactness, the hour being 4 during the hot months, and 3 in the cooler. He sat at table two hours, during which the bottles were in constant circulation. If any one of the company, from being in conversation with his neighbour, or other

---

[1] "Correspondence of Marquis Cornwallis," Vol. I, p. 422.
[2] "Memoirs," Vol. III, p. 349.

cause, inadvertently stopped their progress, or, what was quite as serious an offence, passed them without putting in the corks, his lordship instantly attacked the defaulter in the first instance, calling out sharply, " Pass the wine, Mr.——"; and in the latter, " Fie, fie ! Sir, how can you omit to put the cork into the bottle before you pass it ? " [1]

Another point on which Lord Cornwallis appears to have been particular to the point of Puritanism was as to the celebration of Christmas Day :

" It having always been the custom for the members of Government and the powerful persons of the settlement to dine together at the Court House on Christmas Day, followed by a ball and supper for the ladies at night, the same took place on the 25th of December, 1786, although somewhat against the inclination of Lord Cornwallis, who expressed his disapprobation, as according to his idea the day ought to be celebrated rather as purely religious than in feasting and mirth.   The dancing he particularly objected to, and from that year no public dinner or entertainment of any kind has ever been given on Christmas Day in Calcutta.   At this dinner Lord Cornwallis, as Governor General, presided." [2]

Fifteen years later, when Cornwallis came out for a second time, with the object of curtailing the extravagance, both social and political, of the Wellesley régime, he carried the policy of retrenchment to still further extremes.   The modesty of the stable establishment which he proposed to allow himself is shown from a letter to a friend in India to whom he wrote in January 1797 :

" I shall want a palanquin, a phaeton, and a good coach or chariot, with six carriage horses, two of which must be very quiet and proper for the phaeton." [3]

His successor, Sir John Shore (afterwards Lord Teignmouth), 1793–1798, followed the Cornwallis practice, for he hated pomp of all description.   He only kept three A.D.C.s, he never employed the Body Guard, and he had no attendants, not even men running on foot with his carriage when he drove out. [4]

Just before he assumed office the Old Court House had been pulled down, and the principal official entertainments were henceforward given in the ball room attached to the Theatre, at the North-west corner of Lyon's Range, occupied in my day by the premises of Messrs. Finlay Muir and Company.

[1] " Memoirs," Vol. III (1782–90), p. 294.
[2] *Ibid.*, Vol. III, p. 306.
[3] Sir John Kaye, " Lives of Indian Officials " (2 vols., 1889), Vol. I, p. 168.
[4] " Life," Vol. I, p. 266.

When Lord Wellesley started for India in November 1797, he had already fully made up his mind to fill a rôle, both in the social and the political sphere, which would leave all his predecessors far behind, and would set (as it did) an example that probably few successors would be able or willing to follow. As the " Morning Chronicle " observed : " To such a degree is his frigate encumbered with stores, carriages and baggage, that should the rencontre of an enemy make it necessary to prepare for action, Lord Mornington will inevitably suffer from clearage in the course of six minutes a loss of at least £2,000."

We have seen how, on his arrival at Calcutta, he at once set about replacing his official residence with a magnificent palace, and the same splendour must of course regulate all that passed within it. Pomp and parade were to him the indispensable mechanism of Oriental Government ; and he elevated the spectacular to the level of an exact science. His entertainments and ceremonies and processions, equally with his palaces, were a part of his conception of British rule in the East ; and no sooner was the new Government House open than it became the scene of a series of entertainments such as had never before been seen in Calcutta. All of these were reported to the minutest detail in the Official Gazette, from which we can disinter as much or as little as we please. Indeed Lord Wellesley subsequently made the existence and the size of Government House an excuse for the scale and extravagance of the festivities which were enacted inside it.

There were, it appears, at that time three public entertainments in the year, which were invariably given by the Governor General at the expense of the Company, who allowed him Rs. 8,000 or £1,000 per annum for the purpose. These were the parties on the King's and Queen's Birthdays and on New Year's Day. The Theatre, said Wellesley, was unsuited for the purpose ; besides its hire for two nights amounted to £600–£700 ; therefore to Government House must society come ; and in those surroundings a new order of expenditure must ensue. Further, the successful issue of the wars, whether in India or in Europe, that were a chronic feature of that time, demanded a befitting celebration in the capital of the Indian Empire.

Accordingly his most famous parties, apart from the King's Birthday entertainments, were—a great breakfast on 30th April, 1802, to " above 700 of the principal ladies and gentlemen of the settlement," to celebrate the anniversary of the fall of Seringapatam ; another breakfast on 9th August in the same year, to welcome back General Baird and the officers who had returned from the Egyptian campaign ; a magnificent ball, supper and illumination in honour of the peace concluded on 15th March, 1804, with Scindia and the Raja of Berar; a dinner on 23rd September, 1804, in honour of Major-General Wellesley (afterwards the Duke of Wellington) and in commemoration of the battle of Assaye ; and most of all, the wonderful ball given on 26th January, 1803, to celebrate the Peace of Amiens, the news of which had just reached India.

A brief description of this entertainment will equally cover the remainder, for the programme appears to have been repeated in much the same manner and with the same accessories of symbolical adornment and table decoration on each occasion.   The invited company of 800 Europeans assembled at Government House at 9 p.m. ;   the Governor General, on entering at 10 p.m., held a durbar for the *Vakils* and native gentlemen in the North verandah ;   thence he marched in procession to the upstairs Ball Room, where he took his seat on a crimson and gilt chair of State under a crimson canopy[1] at the Southern end with the chief dignitaries on either side.   The dancing, in which 40 couples led off, then commenced and continued till midnight, when the company descended to a magnificent sit-down supper in the Marble Hall.   At 1 a.m. the fireworks began on the South front of Government House, with huge set pieces, and transparencies, and portraits of the heroes of the hour.   This display was witnessed by the Governor General, the Chief Justice, the Members of Council and the Judges, from the South portico.   Meanwhile the whole city around Government House, and as far as the Fort, including the latter, had been illuminated throughout the evening.   At 2.30 a.m. the dancing recommenced ;   and at 4 a.m. His Excellency retired.

The illuminations do not on this occasion appear to have been quite the expected success, for Lord Valentia, who was present, says :

" The side of the citadel facing the palace was covered with a blaze of light, and all the approaches were lined with lamps suspended from bamboos.   The populace stole much of the oil ; and as it was impossible to light so great a range at one time, the effect was inferior to what it ought to have been.   The fireworks were indifferent, except the rockets, which were superior to any I

---

[1] There is an amusing colour print of a ball at Government House with the crimson State chair and the crimson canopy, as erected by Lord Wellesley, in " Tom Raw the Griffin," p. 149.

o

ever beheld.   They were discharged from mortars on the ramparts of the citadel. The colours, also, of several of the pieces were excellent ; and the merit of singularity, at least, might be attributed to a battle between two elephants of fire, which, by rollers, were driven against each other." [1]

On the other hand the Directors, sitting in complete ignorance at home, were greatly disquieted when, a couple of years later, they got the bill for the illuminations, which alone cost £3,248.

Lord Wellesley excused himself in a letter to Lord Grenville of 18th November, 1798, for the extreme state which he was observing at Government House, by the plea that it was a necessary protection against the " stupidity and ill-bred familiarity " of Calcutta society.

" The effect of this state of things on my conduct has been to compel me to entrench myself within forms and ceremonies, to introduce much state into the whole appearance of my establishments and household, to expel all approaches to familiarity, and to exercise my authority with a degree of vigour and strictness amounting to severity.   At the same time I endeavour, as much as is compatible with the duties imposed on me by the remissness of Sir John Shore, to render my table pleasant to those whom I admit to it, and to be easy of access to everybody." [2]

I prefer to excuse this rather foolish and unmannerly explanation by the fact that it was given when its author had only been for six months in India.   That he could and did unbend is shown by the testimony of a young officer named Captain George Elers of the 12th Regiment of Foot, who, as a friend of Colonel Arthur Wellesley, brother of the Governor General and afterwards Duke of Wellington, went to Calcutta with an introduction to Lord Wellesley in December 1804.   Calling at the Fort upon Colonel Calcraft, the Town Major, who was a noted gourmet, the young officer received from him a very unfavourable account of the Government House chef.

" You had better not go there.   You will not get anything worth eating. His cooks don't understand the thing."

Nevertheless the Captain went, dined, and was conquered.

" The immense hall was brilliantly lighted.   After drinking a moderate quantity of wine, coffee was introduced, after which the Governor General took my arm and walked about.   At length he sat on a sofa and said :— ' Captain Elers, I shall never give you any more formal invitations ; from this

[1] " Voyages and Travels," Vol. I, pp. 61-2.
[2] " Fortescue MSS.," IV, 381.

day a knife and fork will constantly be placed for you during your stay in Calcutta at my table.' "[1]

In memory of Lord Wellesley's kind hospitality at Calcutta, the Captain attended the dinner that was given to the returned Proconsul at Willis's Rooms in March, 1806, when two hundred persons sat down to dinner, at a cost of 2,250 guineas, the share of Elers, who must have done himself well, amounting to 15 guineas. Wellesley, strange to say, seems to have been very little affected by the compliment of this banquet, which most men would have regarded as great, and to have treated it as no more than his due.

As to the cuisine at Government House, excellent as are the native *bawarchis* or cooks, the Governor General has almost invariably maintained a European chef, as their Memoirs or correspondence show; and some of the most amusing minor episodes of Viceregal existence used to be the reconciliation of the habits and ideas of these foreigners with the conditions of Indian life. One of my French chefs, when angry, used to throw the kitchen utensils out of the window. His successor improved upon the precedent by throwing out the native cooks.

With Lord Wellesley's departure, the law of reaction demanded a sharp retreat, and this was the more certain when it became known that Lord Cornwallis was being sent out again to replace him. During the few months that elapsed before his death at Ghazipur in October, 1805, the economical old soldier went resolutely but rather stupidly to work. He dropped the title of His Excellency and the courtesy prefix of "Most Noble," usually attached to the holder of a marquisate, and asked to be addressed as "Honourable" only; he preferred a carriage and pair to the coach and six; he reduced the Body Guard, and dismissed the greater part of the servants, divesting the remainder of their turbans and badges. In fact, as William Palmer, formerly Military Secretary to Warren Hastings, wrote to the latter in England:

"Government House is quite a desert, and his Lordship himself has been seen to come out of his room to hunt for a *hircarrah*."[2]

His successor Lord Minto, as Sir John D'Oyly wrote to Warren Hastings, endeavoured to " establish a mean between Lord Wellesley's

---

[1] "Memoirs of George Elers" (1777–1884) (edited from the original MS. by Lord Monson and G. Leveson-Gower), 1903, pp. 156–7.

[2] *I.e.* a messenger, corresponding to the modern *chuprassi*. " Letters of Warren Hastings " (ed. S. C. Grier), p. 424.

expense and parade, and the parsimony of Lord Cornwallis," [1] or as another witness put it : " Next came Lord Minto, who preferred (and gave full scope to his preference) to live the life of a private gentleman of fortune than as a Viceroy over a hundred million fellow creatures." [2]

Nevertheless the law of alternation compelled him to revert to the immutable fashion of his predecessors ; and we find him driving to Barrackpore, as they did, in a carriage and four, and attending the funeral of Begum Johnson at St. John's Church in February, 1802, in the State Coach with six horses and a detachment of the Body Guard ; and he seems, as Lord Amherst after him, to have been quite unable to escape the obligatory escort of gold sticks and silver sticks and the like. This is what he wrote in 1807 :

" I drive out almost every morning and evening. The formality of these airings is uncomfortable to a degree that I cannot at all accustom myself to. I am always followed by an officer and six troopers of the bodyguard. These cannot be dispensed with. Four syces or horse keepers with fly flappers ran alongside of the horses until I positively rebelled against this annoyance. It is still worse with a palanquin. Thirty people go before in two lines, which extend a great way forward. They carry gold and silver maces and halberds and embroidered fans, and cows' tails to keep the flies off. . . . All these run on foot at a round trot, some of them proclaiming my titles : which, as the proclamation is rather long, I imagine must be Hindostanee for Gilbert Elliot, Murray of Melgund and Kynynmound of that ilk." [3]

There is printed as an Appendix to the Indian Journal of Mrs. Maria Graham, who visited Calcutta in 1810 in the time of Lord Minto, a most amusing account of a Disputation or Speech Day of the Hindu College held at Government House by that Governor General—which was written by one Ibrahim, the son of a Malay merchant, who, being in the capital, was invited to the function.

" At the end of the hall there is a throne, superlatively beautiful, supported by four pillars of gold, and having hangings of the colour of blood, enriched with gold fringe ; it is beautiful in the extreme, and the elegance of the drapery is surprising. Within the throne there is a golden chair with hanging and fringe of gold, in which the Rajah sits when he receives other Rajahs and Vakeels. [4]

[1] "Letters of Warren Hastings" (ed. S. C. Grier), p. 425.
[2] " Bengal and Agra Guide," 1841.
[3] " Lord Minto in India," p. 29.
[4] These were the State chair and canopy of Lord Wellesley.

" When the Court was full the Rajah entered and everyone moved different ways. But as soon as the Rajah seated himself, the *muntries* and high officers of state arranged themselves according to their rank. On that side of the hall which was to the left of the Rajah, and within the pillars, all the wives and family of the Rajah were arranged in a row one by one ; and it is impossible to forget their beauty, for who could look on them without feeling unhappy at heart ! And when everybody was seated . . . the Rajah looked down from time to time, and often cast his eyes on the ladies—when I could perceive that his heart was gladdened, for his countenance glowed with satisfaction, giving pleasure to all.

" Among all the ladies there were six who were most beautiful, seated in chairs, being pregnant, some two, others six, months ; but there was one of the wives of the Rajah beautiful to excess, and she was eight months gone with child. She was kind and beautiful to look at, of a beautiful small make, and she sat in front of a large pillar, while a Bengalee moved a large fan behind her. Whoever gazed on her felt kindness and love and became unhappy."

As a matter of fact, the Rajah's wife, Lady Minto, was never in India at all ; and the ladies in question, whose numbers the susceptible Malay must have exaggerated, were the wives of Lord Minto's two recently married sons and of his Military Secretary, all of whom lived in Government House, and I believe did present their husbands with offspring while there.

When Lord Minto left, and Lord Hastings (then Lord Moira) succeeded, we revert at a bound to the palmiest days of Wellesley ; and the state and style were even such as to excite a certain amount of local criticism. Palmer now wrote to his old chief at Daylesford :

" A Formality and stately Etiquette is introduced at the Government House not at all suited to the Habits and Manners of this Community. Whether Custom will reconcile it is doubtful ; at present it rather disgusts. The Society is accustom'd to an intercourse with its Governor of dignified affability on his part, and of respectful freedom on theirs, and will not, I apprehend, readily adopt the relations of Sovereign and Subjects. A Household Establishment is formed resembling that of Royalty—probably modelled on that of the Castle of Dublin. Be that as it may, the Transition is too abrupt to please." [1]

Charles D'Oyly was even more emphatic than General Palmer :

" I am sorry both Lord Moira and Lady Loudoun are so enveloped in formality and grandeur, for there is no approach to anything like intimacy, and she in particular seems inclined to give general satisfaction to everybody. We have lately been accustomed to so little state that the present system assumes

[1] " Letters of Warren Hastings " (ed. S. C. Grier), p. 427.

a character not at all partaking of the usual advantages of novelty in general, but of confinement and restriction wholly foreign from our idea of comfort. I believe they both seek popularity, but the mode of acquiring it varies much in different countries, and that which forms its model on the Rules of a Court in Europe is the least calculated to impress Indian Minds which have always been accustomed to the exercise of a freedom the most unrestrained."

Lord Moira had, it appeared, appointed a Chamberlain and other officers about his person, " purely for Show and State," at large salaries, the Chamberlain receiving, it was alleged, £3,000 a year. Doubtless this figure was exaggerated, but the general information is corroborated by Miss Emma Roberts, who, contrasting the régime of Lord William Bentinck with that of Lord Hastings, said :

" An attempt was made by Lady Hastings to establish a more rigid system of etiquette ; she had her Chamberlain and her train was held up by pages. An intimation was given to the ladies that it was expected they would appear in court plumes, and many were prevented from attending in consequence of the dearth of ostrich feathers, the whole of the supply being speedily bought up ; and as it was not considered allowable to substitute native products, there was no alternative but to remain at home." [1]

Lord Hastings himself justified his procedure in a letter to Warren Hastings, on the ground that " All appearances of Government had been strangely let down : and the consequences had a worse effect upon the minds of our own people than on the conceptions of the natives. Slight toward Government had become much the fashion and entailed many practical embarrassments." However this might be, the natives, at any rate, did not object to the increased state maintained at Government House, for they were said to believe that the soul of Warren Hastings had been reincarnated in his namesake and successor, on the ground that the latter " loves the Natives of India, and thinks highly of the Company's servants."

There is no doubt that this revival of grandeur was a deliberate policy on the part of Lord Hastings. When he came out in the " Stirling Castle," society was thrilled to hear that he had brought with him nearly 600 cases or packages of goods ; and when his vessel halted at Madras he himself was at pains to inform the Governor of that Presidency that he intended to " hold up the Government at Calcutta with more form and state than had heretofore been maintained." [2] In his Journal he

---

[1] " Scenes and Characteristics of Hindostan," Vol. III, p. 75.
[2] " Private Journal," Vol. I, p. 6.

THE GOVERNOR GENERAL AND BODY GUARD OUTSIDE GOVERNMENT HOUSE (1820)

constantly reiterates his intention to maintain a higher level of style. If he went out driving, it was in a carriage and four, each horse being attended by a syce ; and I reproduce a picture from Fraser's " Views of Calcutta," in which he is depicted as seated in an open barouche with a white wig, a red coat, and a cocked hat in his hand. Two officers or A.D.C.s in uniform and wigs sit opposite him.   The native coachman, in white with a scarlet *cummerbund*, is seated on a red hammer cloth, and drives the four horses ; a syce, similarly clad, runs at the head of each horse, while two more run behind the carriage.   Half a dozen *chobdars* with silver maces on their shoulders march in front.

It was in keeping with the same conception of his exalted position that Lord Hastings, unlike the majority at least of his successors, always " handed in " Lady Hastings to dinner (she was Countess of Loudoun in her own right and was so called until he received a step in rank in 1818), *i.e.* the Governor General and his wife preceded their guests.   Elsewhere we shall see the style which they observed when they went up the river on tour ; and the same rigour of etiquette and lavishness of display characterised all their public proceedings.

It must not however be inferred from the excessive attention to ceremonial that Lord Hastings was a pompous or unkindly being. Far from it.   He was both a conscientious administrator and a warm-hearted man.   Henry Thoby Prinsep, one of the famous Prinsep family, and father of yet another of the same name, who was a Judge of the High Court at Calcutta in my day, was Political Secretary to Lord Hastings, and in his unpublished Memoirs, which were shown to me, left the following pleasant portrait of his Chief :

" Lord Hastings was a most agreeable man to do business with, so considerate towards other people's feelings that I cannot call to mind a single harsh word that he ever addressed to any one of those officially connected with him. He was so unwilling to express dissatisfaction that even in the matter of etiquette, when he thought one day that I ought to have come in full dress to assist at an important reception, his mode of drawing my attention to the circumstance was to show me his own sword and, drawing it, to point out that it was one that had been used at Agincourt, and that he had obtained it in his capacity of Constable of the Tower.   I knew his ways and of course took the hint."

And again :

" He was a proud man, stiff and formal in his manners, admitting very few to personal intimacy, and not mixing with society at large, or with those whom he received at his table. . . . With his Staff and household he maintained the same stiff manner as with Secretaries and officials. The only person who ventured to converse with him with perfect frankness on all topics was his aide-de-camp Captain George FitzClarence, afterwards Lord Munster. . . . In the Society of Calcutta he was very popular, though no one could boast of enjoying much of his personal intimacy. He kept a good table and entertained very frequently ; and he managed the roster of his invitations so that everybody felt they had a fair share of his consideration."

The "Bengal and Agra Guide" for 1841 says that " In Lord Hastings' time full dress balls, masquerades, crowded dinner parties, military show, and uniforms amongst the Civil functionaries in immediate connection with the Government was the order of the day." It was in his time that the news of Waterloo, won by the brother of a previous Governor General, and himself a soldier who had first climbed to fame in India, reached Calcutta in November 1815. On 14th December the town was illuminated in honour of the event and a local newspaper recorded that " the scene of the most conspicuous splendour was of course the Government House, the North front of which was peculiarly brilliant, and embellished with a variety of well-known devices. The transparency of the Duke of Wellington was exhibited over the gateway, and had a grand effect. The lights were disposed with great effect over every part of the building." An instance of the very different social habits of the time may be seen in the ' Calcutta Gazette' of 21st October in the same year, which announced that after the Drawing Rooms " two parties sat down to play at Commerce, Lord Moira presiding at one table, and the Countess of Loudoun at the other."

The amusing Guide already quoted introduces the next Governor General with the observation : " We then come upon the Amherst era, and may pass it by with the remark that it resembled, with the exception of an immense *penchant* for silver sticks, in every respect that of Lord Minto." If this were so, it would indicate only a qualified revulsion from Lord Hastings' régime. But the question of gold and silver sticks, which I have already noticed in the case of Lord Minto, seems to have been a serious one, for it attracted the attention of more than one contemporary observer. The same authority whom I have already quoted (H. T. Prinsep) was particularly severe about the silver sticks. He wrote of Lord Amherst :

" He had extraordinary notions of the importance of a very punctilious ceremonial. He never moved from one room of the Government House to another without a long train of *chobdars* (i.e. servants with silver maces) preceding him.   When he rode out with Lady Amherst, it was a rule that she should never advance beyond his horse's quarters : and in all things he required similar formal observances.   But he was remarkably obliging in his manner, and the readiest man in conversation and in the oratory of a dinner of public entertainment that I have ever fallen in with.   He was also highly educated and accomplished, but wanted altogether that confidence in his own judgment and power of correct and prompt decision which is required to govern men and command their respect and confidence."

But in respect of the silver sticks the Governor General, though the chief, was not the sole, culprit.   This ceremonial was not confined to him, although his equipment in this respect doubtless much exceeded that of his inferiors in official rank.   Bishop Heber constantly alludes to the subject.   Lady Amherst, on the occasion of their visit to the Botanical Gardens, was, as might be expected of her exalted rank, accompanied by gilt sticks and maces, and preceded by two men with gilt spears, and two more with swords and bucklers.   But all members of Council and others down to the rank of Puisne Judge were similarly preceded by two men with silver sticks and two with heavy silver maces. The Commander-in-Chief and the Chief Justice were accompanied in public by silver sticks and four or five spears, very elegantly worked poles of silver and blades generally gilt, with crimson velvet on the pole for the hand, and crimson fringe where the staff and blade join.[1]

Though all this sounds rather ridiculous and obsolete now, one can understand the importance, in the first half century of British rule in India, of investing the Representative of the Crown with all the emblems that had from time immemorial been coupled with sovereignty in India.

In my time, eighty years later, and I expect for long before, these processional formalities had ceased.   But on occasions of ceremony such as Levées, Drawing Rooms, Investitures and Durbars, and official openings, as also in the Elephant Procession at the Delhi Durbar, the native attendants of the Viceroy, with all these insignia, which were kept in the Tosha Khana or Treasure-room of the Foreign Office, would reappear ;   and this induced me to enquire rather closely into the character and meaning of these picturesque regalia.

They are, of course, of very ancient origin and have always been associated with the Oriental conception of supreme authority, having

[1] " Narrative of a Journey in India," by Bishop Heber, Vol. I, p. 70, Vol. II, p. 289.

been adopted in consequence by the British rulers of the country.   The gold mace, as far back as in Sanscrit literature, was a symbol of honour, gold being regarded as a scarer of spirits.   Kings and Royal Princes could alone be allowed to have *chobdars* (or mace-bearers) carrying a gold stick.   The silver stick was granted as an honour to their nobles or sirdars.   Another regal emblem is the *sinha-mukha* or lion-faced club, which signifies Royalty combined with Justice.   The *chowri* or fly-whisk, made of a yak's tail, is a further mark of authority, the *chowri* being waved about the head of the august person, not, in its original conception, for the prosaic purpose of keeping off flies, but to gather together and dispose of any evil spirits who might be hovering about. As to spears, long spears were defensive in origin, being intended to keep the riding elephants in order, if they became restive ; but short spears, with long heads, called *ballam* and adorned with tassels, are carried in front of Rajas as emblems of dignity.   Another sign of Royalty is the fan or punkah, the waving of which in Oriental symbolism is not designed merely to give a breath of much wanted air to a per-spiring prince, but to drive away depression from the Royal brow. The peacock feather brush (*morchal*) is also an appurtenance of Indian Royalty, the eye in the plumage being supposed to guarantee special protection against the Evil Eye.

But among these emblems the one that is most closely associated in the East with Royalty is the Golden Umbrella, which would be brought out on great State occasions and held over the head of the Viceroy or his wife, whether in a carriage or on elephant back.   The King of Burma was always the Lord of the White Umbrella, and the Lord of the Umbrella-bearing Chiefs.   Golden umbrellas were conferred upon Princes of the blood royal, and eminent Chiefs.   The title of the Maha-raja of Kolhapur (Chatrapati) also means the Lord of Umbrellas.   As the inscriptions in Assyria and Persia show, the umbrella was universally held over the head of the King ; and the same practice or belief is widespread in every part of Asia and Africa.   I have never seen the carrying of the gold embroidered umbrella mentioned among the ceremonial observances of the Indian Viceroyalty, perhaps because it is taken for granted.   But it is one of its most ancient and venerated symbols.

From this digression I return to Lord Amherst.   It is only fair to him to state that another observer thought the turn-out of the Governor

General on the Course (*i.e.* the Maidan) at Calcutta rather disappointing :

" The appearance of Lord Amherst on the scene did not exactly correspond with what might have been expected from the Governor General of India. He rode in plain clothes, on a white horse, not remarkable for its beauty, attended by a single aide-de-camp, and a couple of troopers of the bodyguard, who were dressed in red hussar jackets, with silver lace, leather breeches, and long boots, caps and feathers. Lady Amherst appeared in a better style, accompanied by her daughter and an aide-de-camp, in a smart carriage and four. An escort of the bodyguard attended in front and rear." [1]

The official entertainments in Lord Amherst's time were conducted with becoming formality, and in their celebration of martial triumphs recall the performance of Lord Wellesley's reign. There was a great banquet at Government House to the heroes of the first Burma war, and a magnificent fête, in April 1828, in honour of the fall of Bhurtpore. On the latter occasion, the external decorations showed Lord Combermere, the captor of Bhurtpore, and Bhurtpore itself, in lamps on the right, Sir A. Campbell, the Commander in Burma, and Ava in coloured lamps on the left, wreaths round the pillars, George IV in the centre also in lamps with star and crown. In the great Ball Room were transparencies representing Combermere leading the young Raja into Bhurtpore, followed by his staff, while a figure of Victory waved a laurel wreath. Also Campbell on horseback, with his steamer in the background, the Shwe Da Gon Pagoda, and a nymph scattering olive branches. India, Peace, Victory, and other appropriate inscriptions were liberally scattered about ; and the company danced till 3 a.m. [2]

After two such reigns as those of Lord Hastings and Lord Amherst, the hour for reaction had evidently struck ; and the next comer, Lord William Bentinck (1828–1835), was well qualified, both by temperament and conviction, to inaugurate it. He had a natural taste for simplicity, much disliked ceremonies and forms, and was resolved to widen the circle of Government House society and to extend an equal patronage to all. Lord Macaulay, who served under Bentinck, placed upon the pedestal of his statue at Calcutta this fine tribute : " Placed at the head of a great Empire, he never laid aside the simplicity and modes of a private citizen." When he attended Church service on Sunday at St. John's he walked in, with his wife on his arm, in morn-

[1] Alexander, " Travels from India to England," 1827.
[2] " Lord Amherst " (Rulers of India Series), p. 158.

ing dress and took a seat on one side of the pulpit, his Private Secretary and A.D.C.s who followed him, occupying a pew behind.[1]

On the other hand, there were people who scoffed at this contrast to the practice of his predecessors, and Government House, if it opened its doors more widely, seems to have gathered in a somewhat promiscuous crowd. Victor Jacquemont, the French Naturalist, who stayed with the Governor General, was emphatic in his praise : " The man who perhaps does most honour to Europe in Asia is he who governs it." Nevertheless he also wrote :

"Lord William Bentinck on the throne of the Great Mogul thinks and acts like a Pennsylvanian Quaker. You may easily imagine that there are people who talk loudly of the dissolution of the Empire and of the world's end, when they behold their temporary ruler riding on horseback, plainly dressed and without escort, or on his way into the country with his umbrella under his arm."

The critics of the social observances of the new régime were more vocal, and in this respect there seems to have been a palpable falling off in the splendour and even in the dignity of Government House. Christina Pringle, dining there on 4th December, 1829, wrote :

" Yesterday we dined at Government House. There was very little state or show (I suppose Lord and Lady William keep up less than any of their predecessors), the dinner was good enough but Frenchified, as they keep French cooks, but they had no varieties or particularly fine wines, but everything economical." [2]

Altogether the dinner party is described by this lady as a very dull and stiff affair. Each lady was handed in by two gentlemen—such was the curious practice of those days, indicating a great plethora of the male sex in Calcutta—and scarcely anyone spoke.

Miss Emma Roberts is much more minute and also more instructive in her narrative :

" There is nothing like a Drawing Room held at this Court ; no Lord Chamberlain or noblemen in waiting, or any functionaries corresponding with these personages, except the aides-de-camp, who are seldom very efficient, being more intent upon amusing themselves than anxious to do the honours to the company. In these degenerate days, so little State is kept up that, after the first half hour, the representatives of Sovereignty quit their dignified post, and mingle with the assembled crowd.

[1] " Journals of Victor Jacquemont," Vol. I, p. 160.
[2] " Bengal Past and Present," Vol. IV, 1909, p. 469.

" There is no Court dress, or scarcely anything to distinguish the public nights at Government House from a private party, excepting that until lately no gentleman was permitted to appear in a white jacket.

" Where shall I walk at Government House, formed an interrogatory to which, a few years ago, the suitors who could not give a satisfactory answer had little chance of success.   The enquiry now is seldom made; the reply having lost much of its importance.   At the State dinners, ladies sit according to their rank, and they are as nearly paired with male attendants of equal pretensions as circumstances will admit ; but at balls and suppers, after the Governor General has led the wife of the greatest personage to table, the rest of the party follow in an indiscriminate manner.

" Government House is the only place in which the guests are not allowed to introduce their own attendants ; the servants of the establishment are numerous, and perfectly equal to the duties required.   They are handsomely clothed in livery according to the Hindustani fashion ; wearing in the hot weather white muslin vests and trowsers, with cummerbunds or sashes, twisted with scarlet or some other colour, and the crest in silver in their turbans.   In the cold weather the vest is of cloth of the livery colour.   They are all fine-looking men, and the uniformity of their appearance gives them a great advantage over the promis-cuous multitude usually in attendance at large parties, though the absence of the personal domestic is considered by many a heavy grievance, and more es-pecially by those who are deprived by the existing regulations of the indulgence of the hookah.

" There is no established rule respecting the entertainments at Government House; no service of plate, or decorations for the table belonging to the estab-lishment.   The grandeur of the banquets depends entirely upon the tastes and liberality of the person who holds the appointment of Governor General for the time being ; and it is whispered that there are not always a sufficient quantity of silver forks for all the guests, and that the side tables are sometimes supplied with a manufacture of steel of no very tempting appearance."

Miss Roberts, who though critical was not unfavourably disposed towards the new régime, would seem after her return to England to have received less complimentary reports :

" Latterly, invitations to Government House have been very widely extended amongst the natives of rank; and the introduction of men, ignorant of the rules and regulations of European society, has given offence, and occasionally disgust, to those who do not consider the measure to be expedient, or who refuse to make allowance for early notions and rooted opinions, which nothing but more intimate associations can dissipate.

" The latest accounts from Calcutta state that the present Governor General has determined to break through ' the unjust and aristocratical distinctions ' which, as the writer terms it, ' have for so long a period *festered the feelings* of those in the less elevated grades of Indian society,' by extending the invitations to Government House to persons who, previous to his appointment, had not been considered eligible to so high an honour. Whether this measure, which relates to the European portion of the community, will produce the good effect which the commentator of the *India Gazette* so fondly anticipates, is exceedingly questionable. He tells us that it will ' strengthen the attachment to the Government, and enable individuals in different stations of life to form intimacies engendered by merit.' Few persons above the very lowest orders are desirous to destroy all the distinctions of rank; an unlimited *entrée* into Government House to Europeans of every description would not, we believe, be considered advisable, and wherever the line of demarcation shall be placed, there will be discontent. Those who are most anxious to gain admission for themselves feel equally desirous to exclude the class immediately beneath them ; and on enquiry it will be found that those shopkeepers who complain of the prejudices which kept them out of the best society refuse to associate with trades which are not considered so genteel as their own. The reception-room at Government House may be crowded by all sorts and conditions of men, but so far from engendering friendships between them, the only effect of such indiscriminate assemblages will be to bring the public parties into disrepute, and to render private society more rigid and exclusive than ever.

" Cards of invitation to the balls and parties of Government House have been lately sent to persons in the pilot service ; very respectable men, no doubt, but from their habits, education, and manners, scarcely fitting guests for the circle of a court. It is said that even the stewards of ships found entrance into these promiscuous assemblies, and that the company altogether made a strange appearance. Some of the gentlemen chose to appear in deshabille, wearing white calico jackets, and carrying white beaver hats under their arms ; others were requested to withdraw in consequence of the unruliness of their demeanour; while those who were too well conducted to transgress the bounds of decorum spent their time in a very uncomfortable state of restraint. On one of these guests being asked how he was amused at the party, he replied, ' Pretty well; five or six of us got together and sat down.' This person brought his invitation with him to England in order to convince the incredulous.

" The position of Indo-Britons at Government House is somewhat singular, and it perhaps would have been advisable to have extended invitations to respectable persons of that class.

" For a very long period, no half-caste was admitted into Government House. Nevertheless, the charm of the dark-eyed beauties prevailed; a man of high rank contrived to introduce his wife; other married ladies were admitted, there being no longer any plea for their exclusion; but it was still a long time before exceptions were made in favour of illegitimate daughters. Several succeeding Governors General positively refused to admit them ; and it is not exactly known how their entrance was effected at last.

"Notwithstanding the exclusions which are described to be so 'festering to the feelings,' the walls of the Government House have witnessed an odd *mélange* of guests ; many have strutted in great importance along its lighted saloons, whose pretensions to such an honour would have been considered more than doubtful in England.

"The *entrée* is extended to captains of free-traders, some of whom seem rather out of their element in fashionable parties ; but the honours paid to merchants in the naval service are, in the present day, as nothing compared to the glories of their reception before the trade was open, and when they brought intelligence ardently looked for, and supplies of still greater importance. Formerly, the commandant of an Indiaman was received in Calcutta with a royal salute ; his colonial rank was equal to that of a post-captain in the Royal Navy, and he was not less of a bashaw in the state-apartments of Government House, than on the boards of his own quarter-deck.   Skippers of chartered vessels trading to India were aspirants for seats in the direction ; they made enormous fortunes by the sale of their cargoes ; and a passage home in their floating hotels amounted to a sum, the interest of which would have maintained a moderate person in comfort for life.   Old Indians are fond of reverting to those glorious days ; when money was plenty and news scarce; when vessels were a year upon their voyage, and their freight, always insufficient to supply the demand, sold at the most extravagant prices ; when people contrived to get in debt upon princely fortunes, and accustomed themselves to so lavish a profusion of money, that they found they could not return home unless they had the Bank of England at their command.   It was in these days that the parties at Government House were in their glory ; when the visitants felt their importance, and were looked up to by the inferior orders of the community as kings and princes.

"The presence of the Governor General is not always productive of the gaiety which is generally expected to be the accompaniment of a viceregal court."[1]

A good deal of this is gossip, and perhaps not always very good-natured gossip.   But it is not without value, as reflecting the prevalent impression of the day, and as marking a stage in the history of Calcutta Society which, though not permanent in many of its phases, was yet responsible for a definite expansion of the Government House list.   Indeed the efforts of Bentinck and his wife—a very excellent lady whose praises were sung by Greville—to multiply the points of contact between European and Native society, are regarded by his friendly biographers as one of his main titles to praise.

With the retirement of Lord William Bentinck and the arrival of

---

[1] "Scenes and Characteristics of Hindostan," Vol. III, *passim.*

Lord Auckland and his charming sisters in 1836, there was no diminution of hospitality, but there was a marked return to the old observances, the disappearance of which had been viewed by Calcutta Society with annoyance and regret.   The *chobdars* brought the silver sticks out of their hiding places, and escorted the Governor General when he went out to dinners ; and the postilions in new liveries of scarlet and gold once more bestrode the horses that drew the Governor General's carriage, while the syces ran alongside again.[1]   Lord Auckland and his sisters sat on their velvet chairs in the middle of the aisle in St. John's Church, with an open railing round, and a space railed off behind for the staff.   Greater show once more prevailed, and the mixture of affability with reasonable state seems to have won general acceptance.

Miss Eden's letters tell of many great State parties at Government House, a Ball to Sir Charles Metcalfe (who had acted as Provisional Governor General for a year before the arrival of Lord Auckland) to which one thousand people were invited, while a sit-down supper was provided for six hundred and fifty, big balls for the Queen's Birthday, and the State Ball, with three bands, the hall being lined with soldiers who lowered their colours and presented arms as the Governor General walked in.[2]

In the long and weary summer months which were then spent by the Governor General in Bengal, for the most part at Barrackpore, there was a great deal of entertainment on a more moderate scale and the house was seldom devoid of guests.   In those days also, private theatricals, fancy dress balls, conjurers' exhibitions, and the like, were much more frequent than now, as the sole relief to the torrid monotony of existence.

On these occasions a device was adopted that seems to have been peculiar to India.   The ball-room floor had depicted upon it in coloured chalks either the arms of the illustrious individual whom it was desired to honour, or the arms of the Queen, the Governor General, and the Company.   Presumably these pictures were soon effaced by the assiduous soles of the dancers.

There was another fashion which existed as far back as the days of Lord Cornwallis and perhaps earlier, and remained popular up to

[1] " Letters from India," by Hon. Emily Eden, Vol. I, pp. 135–141.
[2] *Ibid.*, Vol. I, pp. 103, 174 ; II, pp. 162, 239.

the middle of the last century, though it has now all but disappeared. On the occasion of the King's or Queen's Birthday or of some other public rejoicing, it was the regular custom to illuminate the exterior of Government House and Grounds, and to have fireworks on a very extensive scale. The Indians, with the humblest of appliances, excel in the art of illumination ; and Miss Eden tells us of the whole outline of Government House picked out with lights, and the dome covered with lamps fixed by over two hundred workmen upon bamboos, on the occasion of the marriage of Queen Victoria with Prince Albert in 1840. She tells also of a sad fiasco in Lord William Bentinck's day, when the native fireworks, which were said to have cost £5,000, were ruined by the damp following upon rain, and the Governor General's family were smoked out of Government House. In my time we had one such illumination to celebrate the Coronation of King Edward VII ; but on this occasion the native *chiraghs* were supplemented by electric light, which had only recently been installed in Calcutta.

In the second quarter of the last century there was inaugurated as an episode what afterwards became a normal practice, and ended by making a vast difference both in the life of the Capital, and in the social obligations of the Governor General. This was the retreat of the Government of India and its head during the summer months to some distant and more temperate part of the country. Previously the Governor General had spent his summers at Barrackpore, and, so far as the heat permitted it, entertainment of some sort went on. Only when he was away, as was Lord Hastings, on a prolonged tour in the Upper Provinces, would he be absent for an entire season from the seat of Government. But in 1829 Lord Amherst for the first time spent the hot weather at Simla. Lord William Bentinck followed his example, and occupied a residence there which was called Bentinck Castle after him, until at a later date it was submerged in the more capacious form and designation of Peliti's Grand Hotel. He even bequeathed his name to a prominent peak in the neighbourhood, which, from its resemblance to the profile of his countenance, was for long known as Bentinck's Nose. Lord Auckland spent the summers of 1838 and 1839 at Simla, and also bequeathed his name to a house which still retains it. Lord Ellenborough paid one visit to Simla in 1842, and so, after Sobraon, did Lord Hardinge in 1846. Lord Dalhousie spent

P

there the three summer seasons of 1849, 1850 and 1851. Lord Canning only visited Simla once, in 1860, the year before his wife's death. It was while on a march in the interior from Simla in 1863 that the first Lord Elgin died. It was reserved for his successor, Sir John Lawrence, who first went to Simla as Viceroy in 1864, and took his Council with him, to convert what had become an annual habit into an official routine, and to obtain the consent of the Home Government to the permanent location at Simla of the summer headquarters of the Government of India. From that date onwards until Calcutta ceased to be the official Capital of the Indian Empire, the annual migration from Bengal took place at the end of March or beginning of April, and Calcutta did not see the Viceroy again till November or December.

It will readily be understood what an effect these migrations, beginning with Lord Amherst, had upon the observances of life and society at Calcutta. Indeed in the early days of the practice, when there were no railways, the Governor General, when he started for the Upper Provinces, might be away for the best part of a year or even more. The Barrackpore entertainments in the heat of the summer gradually dropped out, and except during the four winter months after his return from tour, Calcutta had to do without Viceregal hospitality.

To return to the Capital and to the traditions of Viceregal residence there from the point at which we left them, Lord Ellenborough (1842–1844) was in India too short a time, during much of which he was absent from the Lower Provinces, and was far too busy with schemes of war and conquest to make any alteration in the social system which he inherited ; and to Calcutta he bequeathed no other legacy than the so-called Ellenborough Course to the South of the Fort on the Maidan, which was made a fine turfed ride for equestrians, while he also added some inscriptions to the rather incongruous Memorial Hall, or Temple of Fame, erected by the first Lord Minto at Barrackpore. No Governor General was ever more fiercely attacked during his short reign—and not wholly without reason—and on one occasion, when he left Calcutta for Upper India, a hostile critic, who subsequently published his vitriolic correspondence, wrote :

" His Lordship's departure had no effect upon the gaiety of Calcutta, for he disliked it too much to add to the *agrément* of Society. There was a mutual cordiality of indifference, which rendered separation rather a relief than otherwise." [1]

The next Governor General, Sir Henry (afterwards Viscount) Hardinge, except for his first few months in India in 1844, was never at Calcutta, until after a three years' absence he returned at the end of 1847 to make his final departure. Almost his entire term of office was spent in the field, or in the Punjab, or at Simla ; so that the Capital knew little, though what it knew it liked, of the great soldier who had carried British arms in so glorious a manner to victory.

Lord Dalhousie, perhaps the most laborious of the long list of Governors General, though he was most scrupulous as regards what the French call the protocol, had little taste for entertainment, and performed his social duties with punctilious accuracy but with no enthusiasm. He preferred collecting around him those who were engaged with himself in the great task of governing India, to entertaining in tedious succession the same people at Calcutta over and over again. Lady Dalhousie and he—neither of whom enjoyed good health—did their duty with dinner parties and balls at Calcutta and Barrackpore : and the Governor General observed with minute fidelity the old forms of state. He came in to the State Balls alone, with the men holding the silver maces and the peacock feathers marching on either side of him, and the Body Guard Officers and his Staff in front. Lady Dalhousie came in later by a side entrance. He also used to walk into dinner first and alone. He never went out with Lady Dalhousie except in a carriage and four. But there was none of the vast entertainment or the prodigal display of earlier years, and the spirit in which the host regarded his obligatory guests may be judged from a passage in a private letter from Calcutta of 8th April, 1850.

" Like a fool I gave the people a ball, where they danced in a temperature something under boiling water till past 3 in the morning." [2]

Calcutta Society, enraged at the absence of its official head for three summers in succession, vented itself in newspaper attacks upon the fugitive Governor General ; and to these he replied, if not publicly—for he always knew how and when to observe official silence—at any rate with mordant satire in private letters to his friends.

[1] " Letters to Friends at Home," by An Idler, Calcutta, 1844, p. 139.
[2] " Private Letters " (ed. J. G. Baird), p. 116.

On 1st February, 1851, he wrote from a camp in the Punjab to Sir George Couper as follows :

" You ask the cause of the altered tone of ' The Friend.'   I can't tell you, unless it be displeasure that I did not remain at Calcutta.   When the G.G. remains at Calcutta, the up-country journals abuse him for wallowing listless and inactive in ' The Ditch.'   When he goes up to the N.W. Provinces, the Calcutta papers abuse him for amusing himself wandering about the country, and enjoying cool leisure in his ' mountain retreat.'   Hit high, hit low—stay up or go down—there is no pleasing them." [1]

In the ensuing summer the attacks were renewed by an Indian Correspondent in "The Times," charging Dalhousie with extravagant outlay at the expense of the Company, particularly in respect of his gorgeous silver howdah, but with meanness in his personal expenditure on entertainments.   This stung the peppery Scotsman to fury, and he replied to his friend Fox Maule (afterwards Lord Panmure) on 18th August, 1851, in the following terms :

" Next, I am *said* to be fond of show and parade, ' silver howdahs and so forth,' at the expense of the Company.   A more malignant lie was never voided.   From the hour I landed I have husbanded the Company's money as I never did my own at the poorest.   Though the Government Houses at Calcutta and Barrackpore are furnished as no servant of the Company at the Presidency would endure his own, and though urged, I may say by the whole community, to render them fitting the residences of the head of the Government, I have refused to this moment to do so.   I do not believe that in nearly four years I have expended 20,000 Rs. on all the appurtenances of furniture, etc., which are allowed me.   I have ordered no plate, no ornaments, no china—nay in camp last year, the service was actually made up with blue delft soup-plates of which I was myself ashamed.   But then there is the silver howdah !   It was ordered in prospect of meeting with Gholab Singh.   Not a third-rate sirdar who comes out to meet you on the road but comes on his elephant with a silver howdah.

" The howdah of the G.G. was one of *wood painted like a street cab*, so that the very mahout was ashamed to sit in front of it.   Accordingly one was ordered at Calcutta, and on this extravagance, amounting to £1,500 sterling, I am pilloried to the English public as fond of parade—silver howdahs *and so forth*— at the expense of the Company. [2]

" When, as representative of a sovereign, I go to meet a sovereign in his state, it is my duty to go in a manner fitting the character I represent.   It would

---

[1] " Private Letters," p. 151.   " The Friend " was the famous Calcutta newspaper "The Friend of India," afterwards designated "The Statesman," which was edited by the younger Marshman.
[2] *Vide* Chapter X of this book.

be as indecorous to neglect such state as it would be to go into a gentleman's drawing-room without my coat and my stockings about my heels.   But because I do my bare duty I am slandered as fond of parade at the Company's expense. Such are the rewards of public servants.   But then to heighten the antithesis, while indulging parade at the Company's expense, I am *said* not to offer the hospitality which is expected of a G.-G.   This, again, is the return for entertaining as much (I will venture to say) as any man who ever was head of a Government in East or West.   Last month I told you I cared as little as most people for newspaper attacks.   Well, I confess I do care for this.   To be fond of show, to be careless of the Company's money, to be stingy of my own, are meannesses so odious to me that I own it cuts me to be held up to England as guilty of them all.   It frets me to know that all England will believe me to be guilty, and will hold me to be justly unpopular in consequence ; nor does my consciousness of the injustice of the charge in this case comfort me, because the truth never can be known.   I can't feel indifferent under a charge of meanness, even though false."

Perhaps the exact truth about Lord Dalhousie's attitude towards ceremony may best be found in the admirable pen-portrait drawn of him by his faithful physician and friend Alexander Grant.

" Like Wellesley he never discarded the State and personal considerations due to his position."

And again :

" It must be confessed that he liked to be surrounded by a general atmosphere of deference ; homage even was not unpleasant to him.   He may also have been a little too sensitive of the dignity of his position, seeing it was so well assured.   There was however the smallest amount of ceremony in the life of the household.   There was no full-dress uniform as in times very recent. Even in Lord Auckland's time no one in camp was allowed on the march to precede the Governor General.   No such irksome formality was required during Lord Dalhousie's long reign." [1]

From these rather composite pictures it may be deduced that Dalhousie was punctilious and even exacting in his observance of what he regarded as the necessary forms of State ; but that this attitude sprung not from any inherent love of display but from a sense of duty and a temperament inured to command.   The information which may be found in Dalhousie's published Life and Correspondence shows indeed that no Governor General was more conscious of the value of ceremony as a factor in Indian government.   The forms and

[1] " Physician and Friend," 1902, pp. 149 and 166.

the attention which he rather grudged than otherwise to the European community in Calcutta, of whom he was frankly bored, he lavished with deliberate prodigality upon the Princes, Chiefs, and nobles whom he encountered in his long and exhausting Provincial tours. No one held more frequent or more stately Durbars ; none was more profoundly convinced of their political importance.

We next come to Lord Canning. The social and ceremonial history of his régime (1856–1862) is writ large in the " Story of Two Noble Lives," which tells the tale of Lady Canning and her gifted sister. So large had Calcutta Society now become that we read in May, 1856, of a Ball on the Queen's Birthday for 1100 people, and on New Year's Day, 1857, of the State Ball, to which 1050 were invited and 450 sat down to supper. Later we hear of a Durbar for Scindia in the Marble Hall, with admission for 600 guests, and a Ball for the same Prince in the upstairs Ball Room. Abandoning the practice of Lord Dalhousie, Lord and Lady Canning invariably, and rightly, entered the Ball Room side by side. Even during the Mutiny Government House had seldom been more crowded, for there were constant arrivals and departures ; great steamers and sailing ships lay packed in the Hugli ; and streams of ladies and refugees poured into the town. Dinners were frequent, and to Government House came and went Lord Elgin, on his way to China, Sir Colin Campbell, Sir Patrick Grant, Sir James Colville (Chief Justice), Captain William Peel (destined to so premature an end), General Havelock, Sir James Outram, and many another whose name was afterwards written in undying letters on the scroll of fame.

Lord Canning is said by one writer to have been the first Governor General or Viceroy (he became the latter in 1858) to accept an invitation to dine outside of Government House, and this only as a special compliment to Mr. James Wilson who, besides being a Privy Councillor, had been sent out from England as Finance Member of Council with a special mission.[1]

This story is certainly not true, for we have seen many occasions on which previous Governors General allowed themselves this innocent relaxation ; although, as far back as Warren Hastings, we have the authority of W. Hickey for the statement that " etiquette did not allow of the Governor General to accept any private invitations or to

[1] Colonel J. H. Rivett Carnac, " Many Memories of Life in India," etc., 1910, p. 46.

dine with anyone but the members of Government or Judges of the Supreme Court." As time went on the list varied slightly, and the custom in my day had been stereotyped by long usage in favour of the Commander-in-Chief, the Chief Justice, the Bishop, and of course the Lieutenant Governor of Bengal. The Viceroy used to welcome his dinners with these high officials as a relief from the paralysing monotony of Government House. In the freer atmosphere of Simla he could accept the hospitality of his colleagues in Council (who rarely had houses in Calcutta); and these were most agreeable and welcome relaxations.

The first Lord Elgin was in India too short a time, before his premature death in 1863, to leave any definite mark. But during the first year of his term of office, the greater part of which was spent at Calcutta or Barrackpore, he made himself very popular, being a man of social tastes and cheery disposition. He had to recover the influence with the British residents which his predecessor Lord Canning had at one time forfeited; and this he accomplished so successfully that when he started on the journey up country, from which he was never to return, the European inhabitants of the capital gave a public entertainment in his honour at the Town Hall.

When Lord Elgin's successor, the celebrated John Lawrence, became Viceroy in 1864—the first and till now the last Indian Civilian to hold that office—we are once more back in the region of revulsions and contrasts. The stern and rugged nature of this great man, simple in his rectitude, but unbending and even uncouth in his social or rather anti-social predilections, rendered him profoundly unsuited for the ceremonial aspect of his duties. He abominated dinners and parties and balls, and official civilities. An era of remorseless economy and retrenchment was inaugurated at Government House. The Staff was reduced, the French chef was abolished, the Viceroy declined to encourage racing and withdrew the annual gift of the Viceroy's Cup; he laid down the not unsensible rule that native gentlemen should not be asked to Government House dances, unless they were in the habit (which of course but few were) of bringing their wives. He used to walk off quietly to church in the Scotch Church or at St. John's; he liked rambling on foot in the native bazaars; and the true bent of his fervent spirit was shown in the institution at Government House of Family Prayers.

It may be imagined that, great as was the admiration of every Englishman for this remarkable man, and unshakable as was and is his hold upon the heart of the British people, his administration of Government House did not add to his popularity. On the contrary he was made the object of unsparing newspaper attacks ; and the manner in which he was thought, not without justice, to have " let down " his exalted office, was one cause of the prejudice which has existed ever since against the elevation of any member of the Indian Civil Service to the supreme post of Viceroy of India. All these minor foibles have long since been forgotten; and rightly was the statue of John Lawrence placed in the finest position on the Maidan, where it gazes straight upon the great palace to which he climbed by his unaided force of character and his transcendent services. But they cannot be altogether ignored in the context in which I have referred to them here.

Rooted as was his aversion from anything like display in his domestic life, Sir John Lawrence loyally conformed to the traditions of the Viceroyalty in its official and spectacular manifestations. His great Durbars at Lahore, Agra and Lucknow were conducted with all the old time ceremony. " No one," says his biographer, " understood better than he that in the East, pomp may often be power ; and no one accordingly was more ready, when occasion required it, to drop his ordinary self, and to exchange the privacy, the simplicity, the unceasing desk-work of his ordinary life, for the gorgeousness and circumstance and magnificence of a great Eastern monarch. The splendour of his Durbars was, undoubtedly, all the more impressive from the force of contrast which they presented to his daily habits." It was the austerity, and what was regarded as the parsimony of the latter, that earned him so large a measure of criticism from his fellow-Englishmen.

It was, as I have already narrated, in the time of Lawrence that the migration to Simla, to which his immediate predecessors had become increasingly prone, became a rule of Government, justified not so much by the need of a cooler and healthier climate during the great heat of summer, as by the Westerly expansion of the territories and responsibilities of the Government of India, and the necessity for a more central position than the Bay of Bengal. The only Viceroy, since the days of Canning, to spend a summer at Calcutta, was Lord

Northbrook, in the year of the Behar famine in 1874 ; and he left on record that a heavy price had to be paid for this act of self sacrifice in the ill health of many of the officers of Government and of the principal members of his own Staff.

We now come to the days of Viceroys still living or not long dead, in whose time the changes that have been made have been inconsiderable, while the violent fluctuations and contradictions of the past have shown no tendency to reappear. The fact is that the observances of Government House, whether at Calcutta or Simla, or now at Delhi, have become stereotyped by long practice ; and although some Viceroys will be more tenacious of form or more profuse in entertainment than others, the general standard remains at a fairly uniform level. Calcutta has of course been shorn of her ancient glory, and can hardly reconcile herself to the sentence that has been, as she thinks, so cruelly and unwisely passed upon her ; and certainly those who go there and see that vast and glittering palace, the stage of so great a drama, and the scene of so much bygone splendour, no longer occupied by the chief representative of the Crown in India, and denuded of the greater part of its former contents, will not be consoled by the fact that another palace is springing up in another place which, if it has been the seat, has also been the grave of Empires.

In the last half century there have however been certain changes, in respect both of customs and ceremonies, which have been the result, partly of the great growth of the English community in India and the large number of visitors who come from outside, partly of the ever growing tendency to reproduce in the East the habits and even the hours of life at home. Whereas we read of Lord Wellesley at the beginning of the 19th century entertaining at Government House parties of 600–700, and of Lord and Lady Canning in the middle of the century, exceeding the number of 1000, in my time (1899–1905) the number present at the Levées (confined of course to men) was, as a rule, over 1600, and on one occasion over 2000 ; at the State Evening Party, mainly given for Indian guests, it was 1500 ; at the State Ball 1600 of both sexes. A calculation was made for me showing that in the month of January the number of meals served to visitors, guests, or residents in Government House, which only seven years before had been 2700, had risen to 3500. It may be imagined that the task of entertaining these great masses of people involved no small organisation and could not be done in any slipshod or niggardly manner. On the other hand the social habits of our age in respect of dancing and other matters, rendered a good deal of the former ceremony obsolete, and beyond the State Procession and the State Lancers, with which the proceedings opened, I cannot recall that there was anything to differentiate a State Ball in Calcutta from other entertainments.

Another notable change, brought about by the conditions to which I have referred, was to be seen in the character and hours of the Viceroy's Levées. A hundred years ago they were held, whether for the European or the Indian community, early in the morning, usually at 10 a.m. in the upper Ball Room at Government House. Bishop Heber described one such Native Levée held by Lord Amherst on 7th February, 1824; and the incorrigible Tom Raw provides a metrical account of a similar European function given either by Lord Amherst or his predecessor Lord Hastings. The Governor General entered the room, heralded by trumpets and flourishes, and preceded as now by glittering A.D.C.s in pairs. He then walked round and conversed with the principal guests, saying a few words to each.

> " Smiling with courtly air the great man bowed
> To our still shaking hero—asked some trifling
> Question—the same that he had asked the crowd."

He even tells the story of the Governor General, who seeing the same officer yearly at his Levées, and remembering nothing more of him than that he rode a fine white horse, always asked him how the animal was.

> " He, tired to death to hear this always said,
> Next Levée roared out first, " My Lord, my horse is dead."

In this context I recall an experience of my own. An Englishman, whom I had not seen for many years, having written his name at Government House, and been invited to dinner, I asked him, when the presentations were made before going in, how was his father, whom I had once known well. " Dead ten years," was his reply in sepulchral tones.

We read of a Native Levée held by Lord Canning in the same room in Government House on the Queen's Birthday in May 1859, at which the Viceroy first walked round the room and conversed with a few individuals, then received an Address from the Bishop and Clergy, to which he made a reply, and finally stood before the Throne, while the non-entrée company walked by.

This practice of morning Levées, whether held at a very early hour or, as later, at noon, lasted till the time of Lord Lytton, when there was substituted for it the English fashion of Levées held at night. So they were held in my day, in the Throne Room on the marble floor, the practice followed being identical with that of the London Court. The only difference for which I was responsible was this. The numbers that attended at the Levée and Drawing Room in my first year were so great—1920 Europeans and 610 Indians—the former Ceremony lasting for nearly one and three-quarter hours, that I was obliged to divide the Levée into two, and to ask one half of the alphabet to come on one occasion, and the other half on the next. About four hundred ladies used to attend the Drawing Room—but for these a single function sufficed. A much more sensible practice as regards dinners prevailed in modern times, having been introduced, I believe, by Lord Lytton. The Viceroy, with or without his wife, no longer went into dinner first, but escorted the leading lady ; his wife following with the leading male guest. Before going in, they were both taken round the room where the guests, frequently one hundred and twenty in number, were assembled, and each of the latter was introduced by an A.D.C. who had studied a printed list in advance and was presumed to be acquainted with the names. This sometimes gave rise to unexpected developments, as for instance when, one of my A.D.C.s losing his head, and having already presented no fewer than four ladies under the same, and that a quite unpronounceable name, the next lady, anticipating a like fate, and unable to accept the affront, cried out in indignant tones " I am not Mrs. Petrocochino ! "

The main functions of the Viceregal Court, while I was in Calcutta, were the following. Two Levées, Drawing Room, State Ball, State Evening Party, Garden Party ; together with several balls of five hundred to six hundred persons, and a weekly dance in addition ; Official Dinners of one hundred to one hundred and twenty, and smaller dinners two or three times in the week. The principal outside functions were the Proclamation Parade of all the troops in the garrison, held on New Year's Day on the Maidan, the annual Convocation of the Calcutta University, of which the Viceroy was

Chancellor, the review of the Body Guard at Ballygunje, and countless minor ceremonies or functions. Like some of my predecessors I once gave an Eton dinner at Calcutta (and always on 4th June at Simla) at which no fewer than thirty-seven Etonians were present. The outstanding entertainment at Government House in that period was the Fancy Dress Ball which we gave on the exact Centenary of Lord Wellesley's Opening Ceremony, *i.e.* on 26th January, 1903, and at which we all appeared, or tried to appear, in the costumes or uniforms of our predecessors a hundred years before.

Readers of the earlier pages of this chapter will recall the great part that was played in the Government House entertainments in the first half of the 19th century by fireworks and illuminations on a colossal scale. Enormous sums were spent by Lord Wellesley and his successors upon this form of rejoicing, which was always supposed to be particularly acceptable to the native population. Their fireworks however were then, as they have been ever since, of a very mediocre order of merit ; and when I wanted an exceptional display at the Delhi Durbar in 1903, I had to turn to Messrs. Brock in England to provide it. On the other hand, illumination by *chiraghs* or small oil lamps flickering in an earthenware cup and following the outline of the building, or even of the gravel paths and lawns, is an art in which the Indian excels; and from time to time Calcutta, upon some great occasion, would burst once more into an orgy of flame. Lord Dufferin held one such illumination to celebrate the first Jubilee of Queen Victoria in February 1887 ; and I held another after the Delhi Durbar, to commemorate the Coronation of King Edward, when with the assistance of electric light upon the principal public buildings and places of business, Calcutta was converted for one night into a truly fairy scene.

The last half-century witnessed a novelty in the scheme of official entertainment at Calcutta which at an earlier date would have been impossible. I allude to the visits of members of the Royal Family to India. The first of these to come was the Duke of Edinburgh, who landed from H.M.S. " Galatea " at Prinsep's Ghat in December 1870, in the Viceroyalty of Lord Mayo, and in whose honour a great Durbar or Ceremony of Investiture was held under a *shamiana* on the Maidan —a scene which was depicted in an oil painting hung in Government House. Five years later, in December 1875, the Prince of Wales, afterwards King Edward VII, coming out in the " Serapis," was welcomed at

Prinsep's Ghat by Lord Northbrook, who had become Viceroy in 1872, and for a fortnight Calcutta indulged in every form of public rejoicing in honour of the Royal guest.   In 1890 Prince Albert Victor, the Heir to the Throne, paid a similar visit in the Viceroyalty of Lord Lansdowne.   In 1905 the present King, then Prince of Wales, arrived at Calcutta in the opening days of Lord Minto's term, arriving by train but embarking at the Howrah bridge in a boat that took the party down to Prinsep's Ghat.   He took part in many functions, and, *inter alia*, laid the foundation stone of the Victoria Memorial Hall. But the culminating honour was reserved for the years 1911–12, when in Lord Hardinge's time the present King, fresh from his great Coronation Durbar at Delhi, appeared at Calcutta—the first British Sovereign to visit the Capital of his Indian Empire.   Ten years later, in 1921, his example was followed by his son, the present Prince of Wales, who, in the time of Lord Reading, opened the now completed Victoria Memorial Hall, the noblest monument that has been raised in India since the days of the Great Moghul.   Thus it may be taken for granted that no future occupant of the British throne, no King Emperor of the Indian Empire, will fail to visit his Indian Dominions, or to honour its former Capital with his presence.   Each of these incidents has been made the occasion of memorable festivities at Calcutta, and on each the Royal visitor has stayed in the house which Wellesley reared as a fitting abode either for the Monarch or for his representative.

If I may look back upon the seasons that I spent in Government House, and the official ceremonies that took place there, I am inclined to think that the most impressive were, not the great parties in which the European Community, official or unofficial, were the main participants, but the Durbar or reception of some great and powerful Indian Chief, who came to pay his respects to, or to be entertained by, the Viceroy.   In this ceremony none but the Viceroy's Staff and the suite of the visiting Prince took part ; no strangers were admitted, except perhaps the personal guests of the Viceroy, concealed behind a screen in the corner of the Throne Room.   But the ritual was simple and imposing.   The Viceroy would enter the room preceded by his Staff and by the officials of the Foreign Department who were responsible for the arrangements, and would take his stand on the steps of the canopied Throne.   On this occasion Tippu's howdah would be replaced by the silver chair of state with the lion-arms, and at its feet would lie the great scarlet and gold embroidered carpet. On either side of the Viceroy in the background stood the *chobdars* with their gold and silver maces, the men with the yak tails in their embossed handles, and the men with the peacock feathers set in gold.

From there he looked down the long vista of the Marble Hall with its gleaming white pillars, absolutely empty save for the Body Guard in their magnificent uniforms, standing like statues on either side. In the distance could be heard the music of the band playing upon the great exterior staircase. An intense silence prevailed, broken at length by the crunch of wheels on the gravel and the horse-hoofs of the Body Guard, as they escorted the carriage containing the Prince to the foot of the steps. At that moment thundered out the guns from the distant Fort, giving to the Chief his due salute. One—two—three—up to the total of seventeen, nineteen or twenty one, the reverberations rang out. Not until the total—carefully counted by the Chief himself—was completed, did the procession, which was being formed on the terrace at the top of the staircase, attempt to move forward. Then he would be seen to advance along the crimson carpet laid outside and to enter the Marble Hall in all his panoply of brocades and jewels, the Foreign Secretary leading him by the hand. As they approached at a slow pace along the polished floor, not a sound was heard but the clank clank of the scabbards on the marble. At the stated distances the Prince, who was followed by his retinue, gave the stipulated bows. He then entered the Throne Room, where the Viceroy, according to the rank of the visitor, either descended from the steps of the Throne to greet him or awaited him on the dais. The guest then took his seat in the nearest of a row of chairs, arranged on the right side, with his nobles and attendants in the order of their rank beyond him. The Viceroy's Staff took the corresponding seats on the left, with the Foreign Secretary at their head. The Chief then rose, came forward while everyone stood, bowed low and presented the *nazar* or ceremonial offering of one or more gold *mohurs* laid upon a white silk handkerchief, which were touched and remitted by the Viceroy. The principal members of his retinue were then successively presented by him. Seats were resumed, and a conversation ensued, on the visit of the Chief, the circumstances of his family, the condition of his State. At the end the Viceroy's turn for the offer of ritual hospitality came ; and from a silver gilt platter, presented to him for the purpose, he took the *pan*, a small triangular packet containing a composition of the areca nut cut up in small pieces powdered with lime and wrapped in a leaf of the betel (a pepperplant) covered with gold leaf.   This he handed to the Chief who accepted it in the hollow of his hand.   Next the Viceroy sprinkled a few drops of attar of roses from a gold and silver flagon on the extended handkerchief of the guest.   The Foreign Secretary offered the like compliment to the principal Sirdars.   The conversation was then resumed for a few moments, at the end of which the Prince arose and retiring backwards, slowly retreated to the threshold of the Throne Room, where the regulation bows were once more exchanged, and he then walked back the full length of the Marble Hall to the outside steps.   There once more the sharp order of the officer commanding the escort rang through the air, the clatter of the horse hoofs resounded, the State Carriage, specially sent by the Viceroy for the purpose was re-entered, and the procession rolled away.

The entire performance would occupy from fifteen to twenty minutes.   But in its simplicity and dignity of form, it was the most stately of the many functions at the Capital in which the representative of the Sovereign was frequently called upon to take part.

During the course of this narrative I have several times alluded to the Body Guard and the Band of the Viceroy ; and as these are among the most time honoured of the appanages attached to him in virtue of his position, it may be well that before I close this chapter I should say something about them, since their history is but little known, and with the exception of the former, of which an official record has been published,[1] cannot anywhere be found.

For nearly a hundred and fifty years the head of the Government of India, whether he was Governor, Governor General, or Viceroy, has had attached to him a mounted escort known as the Body Guard which figures in every official record or private narrative that has dealt with his functions or appearances at Calcutta ; and the present Corps, with its splendid *sowars*, each over six feet high, in their striking uniform, holding their long lances with fluttering pennon and mounted on magnificent Australian chargers, was always one of the sights of the city.   The history of the Corps is, however, a curious microcosm

---

[1] " Historical Records of the Governor General's Body Guard." Compiled by Lieut. V. C. P. Hodson, 1910.

of the history of British rule in India ; for like the ceremonial whose story I have already told, it has reflected with remarkable parallelism, in its expansions or reductions, the policy pursued by successive Governors General, of display or simplicity, of lavish expenditure or abrupt retrenchment.

The Body Guard was formally constituted by Warren Hastings when at Benares in 1773. But for a decade before that date the Governor of Bengal had had a European Body Guard, composed of two troops of Dragoons and one of Hussars, which was the first cavalry force on the Bengal establishment, and which took part in the battles of that time. When the Dutch Admiral Stavorinus visited Calcutta in 1770, " Six of the Governor's Life Guards on horseback, dressed in blue, with gold lace, rode by the side of the Coach, in which the Director (Vernet) was." Clive reduced this force in 1765 ; and the Court of Directors in 1772 gave their sanction to a mounted troop of one hundred men.

Warren Hastings, however, converted this European into a Native force, under an English Commandant, which consisted of one hundred rank and file, and was intended as a Body Guard to the Governor General in time of peace, and to accompany the Commander-in-Chief in war. In his Minute to the Board of 6th January, 1774, in which he proposed the establishment, Hastings said :

" I am uninfluenced by the desire of adding to my own consequence. I can safely aver that I feel a repugnance in my Disposition to every form of Ostentation, and it was owing to this Cause, added to a desire of avoiding every unnecessary expense that I have made so slow a progress in forming the number of Horse which have always been considered as necessary for a Guard to the Governor—that at the time of my journey to Benaris I had no more than eight Horsemen."

The first stables of the newly constituted Body Guard were near the new Fort William, and Rs. 500 (then worth about £50) were allowed for the purchase of each horse (country bred). At a later date Arabs were sometimes purchased.

The first of the sharp zigzags of fortune occurred when Warren Hastings left India in February 1785. Thereupon his successor, Sir John Macpherson, who held office until the arrival of Lord Cornwallis, and was burning to curry favour with the parsimonious authorities at home, reduced the Body Guard in the first fortnight of his

LEVÉE OF LORD CORNWALLIS

(The Governor General stands in the doorway on the right)

administration from 100 to 50, and abolished altogether the Infantry Contingent, composed of Sepoys belonging to the force of the Nawab Vizier of Oudh.

Lord Cornwallis, arriving in September 1786, accepted these reductions, but took the Body Guard with him when he went to the Mysore Campaign in 1792.

Lord Wellesley was not likely long to acquiesce in this diminished scale; and his passion for display was soon shown when, on the occasion of his visit to Madras in 1799, he wrote back to Sir Alured Clarke to ask that his Body Guard might be sent after him. The Commander-in-Chief prudently declined, on the unanswerable plea that the distance was too great for them to go by land, and that they would arrive out of condition if sent by sea.[1]

However, Wellesley was not to be defeated; and he was so much impressed with the Body Guard of the Madras Governor, that he took back with him to Calcutta 166 Madras troopers, and added them to his own 50, making a total of over 200, whom he reviewed on the Maidan in May 1800. At the same time he appropriated for their use the Ballygunje Lines, which remained the headquarters of the Corps for more than a century, until the Viceroy and the Government of India left Calcutta for good in 1912.

The magnificent Marquis, however, was not yet satisfied. In 1802 he had increased the native strength to 300, with two light guns, and in the next year he added another 100 and a Band.[2]

When Cornwallis came out for a second time in 1805 he was not likely to accept this expansion. He preferred a carriage and pair to the stately equipages hitherto in use; and he had already issued orders for reduction of the strength to 125, to take effect from 1st January, 1806,[3] when he died.

Lord Minto (1807–1813) sent the entire Body Guard in 1811 to take part in the war against the French in Java, and they returned the compliment by giving him a farewell Breakfast at Ballygunje before he left India in 1813.

His successor Lord Moira (soon to become Lord Hastings), who, as

---

[1] Torrens' "Wellesley," Vol. I, p. 181.

[2] There is a water-colour drawing in the India Office of Wellesley reviewing this enlarged Body Guard at Ballygunje, which is reproduced here.

[3] Lord Wellesley somewhat exaggerated when, at a Drawing Room after his return to England (18th January, 1806), he remarked that Cornwallis had dissolved the Governor General's Body Guard the day after he landed.—" Diary of Lord Colchester " (Speaker, 1802–1817), 1861, Vol. II, p. 26.

Q

we have seen, was also Commander-in-Chief and had great ideas of state and style, was invariably attended by the Body Guard in his extended tours up country, and he took them with him to the Mahratta campaign of 1818. An excellent illustration of the uniform of the Body Guard at this period may be seen in the engraving which I have reproduced in this volume from Fraser's "Views of Calcutta." In it the Governor General's State carriage is accompanied by two of the Body Guard galloping in front, and three behind. Their uniform is a busby of blue with white badge, a red jacket, white breeches, and black boots. By 1814 Lord Hastings had increased the strength to 240 of all ranks, and in 1818 to 400 : and this was their approximate strength when they were reviewed by his successor Lord Amherst on the Maidan in December 1823. Sir Charles D'Oyly, in "Tom Raw the Griffin," described them as on duty in the Entrance Hall of Government House, at a luncheon party in 1824, " bescarleted and silvered."

By this time the Directors in England were again becoming nervous, and in 1826 strict orders came out for a reduction to the original strength of 150. Lord William Bentinck, who had very homely tastes, gladly accommodated himself to this point of view ; and the discursive Miss Emma Roberts, on her visit to Government House in 1835, was proportionately disappointed.

" Guards are stationed at intervals ; those which were formerly attached to the Governor-General were a splendid and picturesque set of men, clad in strange and striking costume ; warlike as became a military power, and particularly ornamental as the appendages of State. The spirit of retrenchment, which has lately descended to petty savings, unworthy of the masters of so magnificent a territory, has removed and abolished this appropriate guard of honour, and the natives, already astonished and disappointed by the contrast afforded by the simplicity and plainness of their European rulers with the pomp and pageantry of Oriental Courts, viewed this last innovation with disapprobation and regret." [1]

The next Proconsul who was disposed to prance was Lord Ellenborough, under whose martial reign the numbers increased rapidly to 300 ; while his successor, Lord Hardinge, who was a professional soldier and who took the Body Guard with him to the Sikh war in 1845–6, raised the total to 500. This was too much for the suffering Directors, and orders were issued for a progressive reduction to a final

[1] " Scenes and Characteristics of Hindostan," 1835, Vol. III, p. 72.

LT.-COL. F. A. DANIELL IN THE UNIFORM OF THE BODY GUARD (1802-1806)

From a painting by Sir R. Ker Porter.

total of 130 men. Lord Dalhousie, who was also of an ambitious temperament, managed to keep them for a time at 300 ; but when Lord Canning succeeded in 1856, the Corps was reduced from four troops to two, and, at the outbreak of the Mutiny, had been brought down to the stipulated 130.

The records of that time[1] reveal with pathetic iteration the confidence of the Governor General in his Body Guard, his refusal at first to disarm them, and his final and reluctant consent in August 1857, when their arms were removed and they were replaced on the staircase of Government House by European pickets at night. Attempts had been made to tamper with the loyalty of the force, and although it is quite probable that these might have failed, yet the blind confidence of British officers in their men met with so many cruel and bloody rebuffs at that period, that Government House could not afford to run risks.

Sir Seymour Blane, who, after being A.D.C. to Lord Canning, became Military Secretary to the first Lord Elgin (1862–3), and afterwards for a time to Sir John Lawrence, told me that previously the Body Guard had worn the uniform of British Cavalry, but that, after a prolonged struggle with the Commandant, he succeeded in getting them armed with the lance, and dressed in high boots, a long scarlet *chapkan*, a purple and gold *cummerbund*, and a *pagri* (*puggaree*) with aigrette to match.

The Body Guard having now become in the main ceremonial, Lord Mayo in 1869 decided to reduce the strength from two troops to one ; and in the time of his successor, Lord Northbrook, the number was finally fixed at 120 of all ranks, which total has ever since been observed. War-loving or vainglorious Viceroys have ceased to be a likely phenomenon ; and the old era of ups and downs with the Body Guard has come to a peaceful end. The only change that the last half-century has produced has been that in 1877 Australian Walers were first purchased, and that in 1882 the colour of the horses was confined to bays. I believe that trumpeters have since been added, though when and why they trumpet I do not know. I have never seen a finer body of men, more splendidly mounted or more efficient in the discharge of their duties, than those by whom I was served ; it was a source of pride to me to review them every March on the Ballygunje

---

[1] *Vide* particularly " Story of Two Noble Lives," Vol. II, pp. 169, 185, 256, 263, 376, 378.

Maidan, since taken over for Indian Cavalry lines; and I was not surprised when my English guests told me at the Delhi Durbar of 1902 that the Viceroy's Body Guard was better mounted and better turned out than the Household Cavalry at home.

Some of the ablest officers in the Indian Army have served in the Body Guard, among the best-known names being those of Field Marshal Sir Neville Chamberlain and General Sir William Birdwood.

I next turn to the Band. Visitors to Government House have always noticed, and as a rule expressed much admiration for, the Viceroy's Band; and undoubtedly it was a great alleviation, after a hard day's work, to sit down to dinner to the sound of the best music, rendered by competent performers. There was always, however, a difficulty in recruiting the Band, and this led me to look into the history of the institution, which has never before been given.

I found no record of a Band as having been attached to any Governor before the time of Lord Wellesley; and we may be sure that he would not for long have tolerated the absence of so necessary an adjunct of Proconsular state. At his Party in the new Government House to celebrate the King's Birthday on 4th June, 1803, we read in the Official Record that " The Governor General's Band played several loyal and martial airs during supper." Again, when Lord William Bentinck came up from Madras to visit Lord Wellesley on 27th June, 1805, he was " met by the State Boats and the Band of the Governor General." When Lord Hastings made his big tour in the Upper Provinces in 1814, almost entirely by river, he had a special boat or barge for the Band which he took with him, and which, we learn from the Diary of Emily Shakespear, was supplied by " His Majesty's 44th Regiment." At this date the Band was not a separate Establishment, but only a Band borrowed from the Regiment stationed in Fort William by the courtesy of its Commanding Officer. Sir Ch. D'Oyly, in the disguise of Tom Raw, describing a Levée at the beginning of Lord Amherst's reign, speaks of " the band of some King's Regiment " in the North room of Government House. The Governor General's request for the loan of the Band was always granted; but after a while it was felt that it was hardly right for the Governor General to be continually under an obligation to the Regiment that might happen for the moment to be on garrison service in Calcutta—all the more so if he showed a disposition to take it away with him when he proceeded on tour.

LORD WELLESLEY REVIEWING THE BODY GUARD AT BALLYGUNJE

Accordingly in the term of Lord Amherst (1823–1828) an attempt was made for the first time to place the constitution of the Band upon an assured basis ; and sanction was obtained for the formation of a separate Band, which consisted at first of four sergeants (including the Bandmaster), four corporals, two gunners, and seventeen native boys. The Band, which at that date (hill stations and the annual exodus being unknown) rarely left Calcutta, was placed under the jurisdiction of the Town Major, who was given an annual allowance for the repair or renewal of instruments.

When we come to Lord Auckland's day (1836–1842) we find his sister, Miss Eden, in one of her attractive letters, dated 16th March, 1836, speaking of "our own band as a very good one which plays every evening when we have company." [1]

Lady Canning, in the dark days of the Mutiny, laboured hard at improving the Band, and thus wrote of it :

"We have never given relâche to the band, because it wants work and to be brought into good order; it is so much inferior to the Bombay Band and even to that at Madras." [2]

In 1872 under Lord Northbrook (1869–1872) the Band was reconstituted and its establishment was fixed at a total strength of thirty.

Throughout this period the Band had been a Brass Band, essentially military in character, being drawn from regimental bands in different parts of India. But, owing to the inadequate rates of pay, it never rose much above the level of a second-rate regimental band ; and the guests at Government House in the third quarter of the 19th century frequently denounced it as unworthy of the representative of the Sovereign. At this period it used to play for large dinner parties on the top of the steps of Government House, or on a raised platform on the East side of the house, where an enclosed tennis court was made later on.

Lord Lytton (1876–1880) was the first Viceroy to endeavour to remedy this state of affairs. Having regard to the duties required of the Viceroy's Band, he considered that it should be a private orchestral, rather than a military, band, and with this object he engaged and brought out at his own expense six German musicians. The expenditure incurred in purchasing instruments and fitting out these persons was subsequently paid from the public funds, and the entire charge

[1] "Letters from India," Vol. I, p. 107.
[2] "Story of Two Noble Lives," Vol. II, p. 58.

on account of the Band was then transferred from the military to the civil estimates. The Germans were highly trained musicians ; they joined the Band at dinner parties and balls, and frequently played quartets in the drawing-room at Peterhof, then the Government House at Simla, after dinner. In those days the Band was not present every night at dinner, but only when there were dinner parties. The experiment of bringing out these men was not, however, a success. They objected to being classed with the ordinary military bandsmen, although they received much higher pay, and they soon found that they could do much better for themselves elsewhere in India. Accordingly, at the end of their three years' contract in 1880, some of them declined to renew the engagement, thus rendering the others useless. The Band now once more became a brass band, and so continued until an English Bandmaster named Waterson was brought out, who insisted upon stringed instruments, which he put into the men's hands and required them to play. The Band has remained a combined string and brass band ever since.

I have said that the main difficulty experienced was in procuring a good Bandmaster and in keeping the Band up to strength. I engaged a very competent German Bandmaster from the Hyderabad Contingent, and he remained for some years, until the feeling aroused in the Great War brought about his retirement. As regards recruiting, the various regiments in India did not like surrendering their best performers, and all sorts of experiments were made for obtaining juvenile recruits from schools and other sources, both in India and England. The strength of the Band in my day was twenty-seven. My successor, Lord Minto, raised it to thirty-six.

Since Simla became the official seat of the Government of India during the summer in the 'sixties of the last century, the Viceroy's Band always accompanied him there. But they do not go on tour. Once a year they gave a concert in the Town Hall at Simla, which was always largely attended, and where they rendered music that might have done credit to the best European orchestra. Government House without them would be a very different place both to the Viceroy and his family as well as to their guests ; and I hope that the axe of no future economist will ever be laid at the root of this most excellent and indispensable institution.

Before I leave the subject of the trappings of the Indian Viceroyalty, I should like to say something about an institution that was for long its most prominent and certainly its most picturesque feature, namely the Boat Establishment of the Governor General. The fact that it has now wellnigh, if not altogether, disappeared, renders it all the more desirable that its story should be told by one—probably the only one—who has enjoyed the opportunity of studying it.

In my chapter on Barrackpore I have spoken of the trips up the river to Barrackpore, accomplished in my day in a little seventy-ton steam launch called the " Maud " (from the Christian name of Lady Lansdowne), followed by a smaller eighteen-ton boat, the " Lytton," dating from the time of that Viceroy. These were the then available means of river locomotion ; while by land there remained the carriage and pair or the train.

But what a difference from the times, a century before, when the excursion was made in fanciful boats, gorgeously painted, richly furnished, and manned by scores of men ! In nothing has the march of events, the progress of mechanical invention, and the remorseless desire to economise time, left a deeper mark upon Calcutta life than in the supersession, by later and more prosaic means of transport, of the picturesque and stately riverain pageantry of the past. Those who read of Calcutta in the days of Warren Hastings, and indeed till after the Mutiny, will find pictures of the river alive with gaily caparisoned craft, as beautiful a spectacle as were the great four-masted sailing ships that crowded the Hugli, and made their towering spars a pattern of lacework against the sky. Even in my time these were fast dwindling, to give place to hideous steamers and tramps, belching forth volumes of sooty smoke into the crystalline air, and I expect that by now they have pretty well disappeared.

Everywhere it is the same. The Thames at London—once adorned with every variety of rowing boat and pinnace, when the palaces of the great nobles lined the banks, when people moved to and from their residences or places of business by water, when even up to the middle of the last century the annual Lord Mayor's Procession took place on the river, and when Constable could paint his glowing picture of the opening of Waterloo Bridge—has lost its pristine vogue, and hears only the shriek of the penny steamer, or the hurtle of the pedestrian barge. Never, I fear, in London shall we see that ancient glory again. Never more will the Hugli see the Governor General's fleet of boats dancing on the waters, or moving in picturesque procession up the stream. But before the memory even of the scene has passed into complete oblivion, let me here recall it as it was, and acquaint my readers with the manner in which the Governor General of a bygone age moved to and from the Indian Capital.

Let us first listen to Mrs. Fay, who visited India in the time of Warren Hastings:

" The noble appearance of the river also, which is much wider than the Thames at London Bridge, together with the amazing variety of vessels continually passing on its surface, add to the beauty of the scene. Some of these are so whimsically constructed as to charm by their novelty. I was much pleased with the snake boat in particular. Budgerows, somewhat resembling our city barges, are very common ; many of these are spacious enough to accommodate a large family. Besides these, the different kinds of pleasure boats, intermixed with mercantile vessels and ships-of-war, render the whole a magnificent and beautiful moving picture, at once exhilarating the heart and charming the senses : for every object of sight is viewed through a medium that heightens its attraction in this brilliant climate." [1]

If this was the common spectacle, how much more splendid was the Governor General's establishment ! Hastings' letters to his wife are filled with references to his *feelchehra*, to a pinnace, to the *budgerows*, and to the " great yacht."

What then were these craft ?

Some years later Sir Charles D'Oyly, in his " European in India " (published in 1813), gave a coloured illustration, which is reproduced here, of the Governor General's principal Pinnace or Yacht, the *Sonamukhi* (*i.e.* golden face), and his *feelchehra* (*i.e.* elephant face) with the liveried *dandies* or boatmen. The author of the accompanying letterpress—Captain T. Williamson—said that the larger vessel or State Yacht was built by Warren Hastings[2] of teakwood, sheathed with copper. It was a mixture of European and Oriental naval architecture, and cost Rs. 45,000. It was manned by thirty oars, but was too heavy to be rowed, and was commonly pulled by a large number of towboats or sailed (having two masts) and tracked. More than half the boat was constructed so as to represent cabins, saloons, etc., with green venetians. It had a flat roof and awning.

---

[1] " Original Letters from India " (ed. 1821), pp. 238–9. There is a new edition by the Rev. W. K. Firminger, Calcutta, 1908.

[2] This, as might be expected, was a mistake for Lord Wellesley.

THE VICEROY'S FLOTILLA AND BOATMEN (1813)

Its attendant *pheel cherrah* (as it is spelt in the book), was a long narrow boat, so shaped in the stern as to resemble the fore part of an elephant. It was pulled or paddled by *dandies* or boatmen in scarlet and gold livery with turbans, and had a small cabin in the after part of the boat.

Another favourite form of boat in those days was the *morpankhi* or *moorpunkee* (i.e. peacock-tailed), more commonly spoken of as snakeboat, because the large paddle with which the boat was steered from the stern was frequently shaped in the form of a peacock or a snake. These boats were very long and narrow, not more than eight feet broad, and often a hundred feet long, and were propelled by thirty or forty rowers. There was also a row boat or skiff called the *bhauliah* or *baulia*, with a cabin amidship, which was very light and swift. One Governor General was said to have made the voyage from Lucknow to Calcutta, a distance of 400 marine leagues, in his *baulia* in eight days. Another variety was the *pansi*, which in the early days of the Company was always transliterated *paunchway*, where the rower as a rule stood, and the passenger was accommodated in the middle.

The *Sonamukhi* in particular figured in the State arrival of all Governors General, while the *feelchehra* was placed at the disposal of guests of distinction. Lord Valentia in 1803 was sent for in the State Barge, which was

"very long in proportion to its width; richly ornamented with green and gold; its head a spread eagle gilt, its stern a tiger's head and body. The centre would contain twenty people with ease, and was covered with an awning and side curtains; forward were seated twenty natives dressed in scarlet habits with rose-coloured turbans, who paddled away with great velocity."[1]

When, on 14th February, 1803, Lord Valentia visited Barrackpore, the water was " covered with the State barges and cutters of the Governor General. These, painted green and ornamented with gold, contrasted with the scarlet dresses of the rowers."[2]

On the great Fête nights at Calcutta in which Lord Wellesley indulged, we read in the Official Records that " The Soonamooky yacht and the Government State-boats were illuminated and produced a most happy effect."

At this stage it seemed to me so unlikely that, despite the reappear-

[1] " Voyages and Travels," Vol. I, p. 60.
[2] *Ibid.*, p. 65.

Q*

ance of the same names, this grandiose establishment could have been a legacy from Warren Hastings, or his immediate successors, and it bore upon its surface so unmistakably the Wellesley stamp, that I began to make search in the Official Records; and there, after much trouble, I unearthed the real history, which has never before been told.

Warren Hastings did, as his letters have shown, have a State house-boat called the *Sonamukhi*, and a pinnace for Mrs. Hastings called the " Mary "; but the furniture in both belonged to him and was about to be sold with the rest of his effects, after his departure, when the Government intervened and bought it at a valuation. At the same time the *feelchehra* was also purchased for the Government.

When Wellesley appeared upon the scene he was far from content with this humble establishment. A new *Sonamukhi* was built, and this was the boat that cost, with furnishing, Sicca Rupees 47,000; and a new *bhauliah* was also ordered which, with carving and gilding, cost Sicca Rupees 2,600. In 1801 three more pinnaces and three more *bhauliahs* were added, and the Governor General's Yacht establishment presently consisted of nine pinnaces, four *bhauliahs*, and a number of cook-boats and tow boats, as well as a Band-boat. There is an interesting coloured engraving of one of Lord Wellesley's *dandies* or Boatmen, wearing his State livery, in the collection of Drawings published by Sir Charles D'Oyly.[1] It is reproduced here.

The next stage was reached when Lord Hastings arrived in 1813. He also had large ideas. The old *Sonamukhi* was forthwith condemned and sold, and a new one ordered, at a cost of Rs. 45,000. Certain boats of the old establishment were retained, others were replaced; and the fleet was presently on a level not much, if at all, inferior to that of Wellesley, while a yacht named the " Nereide " had now been added, at a cost of Rs. 90,000, for the Governor General's journeys by sea.[2]

Lord Hastings' " Private Journal " contains numerous references to this flotilla. When he and Lady Loudoun arrived at Calcutta in October 1813, they came up the river in " the *Sonamuchkee*, a beautiful pleasure vessel, which was towed up the river by men."[3] From this, in order to land at Chandpal Ghat, they moved into " the *Feelcherry*, a highly ornamented barge." In the following year, when he started on his

[1] " The European in India," 1813. Plate XII.
[2] She was sold in 1832 for Rs. 21,000.
[3] This was Lord Wellesley's *Sonamukhi*.

LORD HASTINGS

From the painting by Hoppner, at University College, Oxford.

prolonged tour up the river, he and his wife occupied the new *Sona-muckhee*, which he found " remarkably convenient," and which " sailed very well," while they frequently transferred to the *Feelcherry* " with thirty-two stout paddlers " for minor excursions.   To the flotilla were also attached *bhauliahs*, i.e. " a barge with eight to ten oars, attached to a pinnace with a low cabin like that of a Venetian gondola."

An interesting account of the start of this expedition is left by an independent witness, Emily Shakespear, wife of J. T. Shakespear, of the Bengal Civil Service, and aunt of the novelist Thackeray, who thus described the departure of the Governor General from Barrackpore :

" The Soonamookee is a beautiful vessel lately built for His Lordship's accommodation.   The exterior is painted a dark green and is richly ornamented with gold; the apartments, which consist of a Drawing Room, Bed Room, and two Dressing Rooms with marble baths attached to each, are white and gold, and are handsomely fitted up with green morocco furniture.   Another pinnace, of equal dimensions and almost equal beauty with the Soonamookee, is appropriated to the conveyance of His Lordship's children and their Governess, and a third, called the Castle, for a banqueting and audience boat.   A splendid barge for the reception of the Band, a *Fulchurah* or State Barge ; and a large vessel fitted up with all the conveniences of a kitchen, are also in attendance, the whole of them painted green with gilt mouldings to match the State Pinnace. The fleet consists of about 400 boats." [1]

Some slight check is placed upon the exaggeration of the lady by the statement of the Governor General himself [2] that the flotilla consisted of " something more than 220 boats."   What is more interesting in his narrative is the revelation of the painful inadequacy and slowness of this method of locomotion.   The progress was almost entirely dependent upon the wind ; long hours were spent in tracking across the stream ; the progress was often " miserably slow "—only a few miles in the day ; the boats were always running aground, and accidents were frequent.

The Official Records of this period show that the State Boat Establishment, as it was called, was kept at Barrackpore, where additional ground was purchased in 1814 for its accommodation.

I have more than once referred in this book to Bishop Heber's

---

[1] " Bengal Past and Present," Serial No. 12 (1910), p. 136.   Compare Sir W. Hunter's " The Thackerays in India," p. 149.
[2] " Private Journal," Vol. I, p. 72.

arrival at Calcutta in the time of Lord Amherst (1823). He too was impressed with the splendour of the Governor General's flotilla.

" Of the two State Barges the largest is called the Sunamookee, and is a splendid but heavy gilt and painted barge, rigged like a ketch, with a dining-room and a bedroom. The other is the Feel Churra, elephant bark, from having its head adorned with that of an elephant with silver tusks. It is a large, light, and beautiful canoe paddled by twenty men, who sit with their faces towards the head, with the leg hanging over the side of the boat ; and the great toe through a ring attached to its side. They keep time with their paddles, and join occasionally in chorus with a man who stands in the middle, singing what I was assured were verses of his own composition, sometimes amatory, sometimes in praise of the British nation, the Company Sahib, and the Governor General. In the forepart of the boat is a small cabin, very richly ornamented, like the awnings in English barges, but enclosed with venetian blinds; and between this and the head the mace-bearers of the Governor General stand. The Union Jack is hoisted at the head and the stern of the boat, and the Company's flag in the centre." [1]

In Lord Amherst's day the scale of the up-river excursions had been somewhat reduced, for we find him describing a health trip in June 1825, in the *Sonamukhi*, accompanied by " pinnaces, budgerows, paunchways,[2] and baggage boats, to the number of about 50, with a staff of 500 men."

The attempt at sailing or tracking had now for some time been abandoned, and when the Frenchman V. Jacquemont went up to Barrackpore with Lord and Lady William Bentinck, in June 1829, the pinnace, described as a magnificent and comfortable boat, was towed up by a slow tug, and occupied three and a half hours on the journey. It was reserved for Lord William Bentinck here as elsewhere to make a substantial reduction. He wrote a Minute (17th July, 1828), reviewing the whole case, and placing the Boat Establishment on a new and greatly curtailed basis. The *Sonamukhi* was to be unrigged, and only maintained with such a crew as might be necessary to take her up to Barrackpore and back, towed by a steamer (river steamers had now come in). The *feelchehra*, which had survived till this date, was sold ; and the entire establishment was reduced to ten boats.

The agreeable Miss Emily Eden, whose letters I have so often

---

[1] " Narrative of a Journey in India," Vol. I, p. 51.
[2] The *pansi* or *paunchway* was the common native boat of the period.

quoted, frequently describes the *Sonamukhi*, which she and her brother (Lord Auckland) invariably employed for their trips to and from Barrackpore under the new conditions. She adds the detail that "This is a beautiful boat to live in, five excellent cabins, and fitted up with every possible comfort. She cannot sail a bit, but floating about is all that is necessary, and we have plenty of boats to tow her."

It was during Lord Auckland's time that the exiled Afghan Amir Dost Mohammed came down to Calcutta, and was greatly struck with the fittings of the *Sonamukhi*. "The furniture is all white and gold and very showy, which delighted him, and the oilcloth on the floor was a new invention to him, and he thought it beautiful."

Poor innocent Amir ! Is there now a living man who has seen a beautiful oilcloth ?

Lord Dalhousie still used the *Sonamukhi*, which seemed to have an immortal existence, and in a letter to Sir George Couper of 28th February, 1848, he wrote :

"Nothing can be more luxurious than this style of travelling, in a yacht all green and gilding, with no crew, towed by a steamer, with sofas and punkahs, and bedrooms and luxuries of all sorts : one sits as much at ease as in a room, with the advantage of catching every breath of air which can find its way to you in this incipient frying-pan." [1]

When the Cannings arrived at Calcutta in 1856, they were similarly towed up the river from Garden Reach in the *Sonamukhi*, which Lady Canning subsequently described as follows :

"It is a sort of barge, with a little gallery all round, and contains a good drawing-room, dining-room, five cabins, and five bath-rooms of different sizes. We have besides a great retinue of servants—tailors, washermen, etc., many of whom at night spread their beds on the upper deck. In the day we sit there a good deal under an awning. A steamer with three guns and forty English soldiers tows and defends, and a shabby native boat astern of us has the kitchen and sheep, poultry, cows, goats, etc. Another small boat to land in closes the procession, or rather tail, and a long heavy one it is to drag, so no wonder we get on slowly ! " [2]

I think that this river journey of Lady Canning to Allahabad in 1858, in the course of which the above words were penned, was the

[1] "Private Letters," p. 20.
[2] "Story of Two Noble Lives," Vol. II, p. 459.

last time in which the once famous flotilla of the Governor General appears in literature upon the scene.

After the Mutiny the old *Sonamukhi* still retained a fitful existence, and was towed up and down the river at Calcutta, until, twenty years later, she was lent by Lord Northbrook to the Chief Commissioner of Assam, from whose hands she never returned. There, I believe, she still exists, just as we sometimes read in history of the obscure twilight of some erstwhile beauty of the stage.

Meanwhile a steam launch called the " Gemini " was given to the Viceroy for his Barrackpore excursions, assisted by the " Lytton " (1876) ; and in 1892 the former was replaced by the " Maud," which, strange to say, cost exactly the same sum as the great painted and gilded pinnace of nearly a century before, *viz.* Rs. 45,000. The " Maud " has since been replaced by a launch with the more august designation of the " Empress Mary "; and in this boat the Governor of Bengal makes his excursions up-stream to Barrackpore. Thus does the tale of the great Flotilla of the Governor General, which began in so much glory, end—not in metaphor only—in smoke.

Among the other amenities of Viceregal residence at Calcutta, I must not omit to notice the Race Course. It is superfluous to say that there, as elsewhere throughout the wide circuit of the world, the British were not content to rest for long without a race course, any more than they will now subsist without golf links ; and this is one of the Calcutta amusements in which the Viceroy has always been expected to take, and as a rule has taken, a lively interest.

It was not always so. In the early days racing met sometimes with official indifference, occasionally with the official frown. As far back as 1780 racing seems to have been popular in the Settlement, and the first race course is said to have been opened at Akra, at the bottom of Garden Reach, on ground which was afterwards given, in or near 1830, to the Agri-Horticultural Society for an experimental farm. There was also a race meeting at Baraset, 13 miles from Calcutta, beyond Dum Dum. Here Richard Barwell had a hunting lodge for pig-sticking ; and here was a Military College for the young British Cadets on their arrival in Bengal. This institution, which was probably responsible for the race course and the race meeting, was a hotbed of gambling, drinking, duelling, and every form of rowdy dissipation, until eventually it had to be closed.

But Calcutta was not content to be without its own course, and this was laid out on the plain to the South of the New Fort. There in 1780 a plate of Rs. 2,000 was advertised to be run. I have come across a record in January 1781 of a match on the course between Mr. Touchet's Gorgon and Mr. Henkle's Match-'em-Peter, which the former won with great difficulty. Thereupon the company retired to Mr. Livius' Garden-house near Belvedere, where their host, after regaling them with tea, coffee and lemonade, produced a band, to the music of which they danced country-dances on the green. W. Hickey speaks of the race course and the stand on the Maidan in 1783. There is also extant a record of a Calcutta race meeting in January 1794, when, after early morning racing, breakfast was served in tents to a company of over 150, and was similarly followed by dancing until 2 p.m.[1] There was a similar three-days' meeting in 1795, and another in 1797.

For some reason, whether because it conflicted with his ideas of Sunday observance (for the Calcutta races were at that time usually run on that day), or more probably because of the frantic gambling to which it gave rise, Lord Wellesley set his face firmly against horse racing. A lead had already been given to him in this respect by the Court of Directors, for in May 1798 they sent out a letter to the Governor General in Council, calling attention to the flagrant profanation of the Sabbath by horse racing and other pursuits, and on 9th November of the same year Lord Wellesley issued a Proclamation " ordering and directing all magistrates and officers commanding at military stations to prohibit horse races and all other meetings for the purpose of gaming on the Sabbath day within the limits of their respective jurisdictions and commands ; and if any person or persons shall be guilty of disobedience to such prohibition, the magistrates and officers are hereby strictly commanded to report the name or names of any person or persons so offending to the Right Honorable the Governor General in Council ; and the latter hereby declares that the person or persons so offending shall be liable to forfeit the protection of the Honorable the East India Company and to be sent to Europe."

Calcutta, however, was too strong for the autocratic Governor General. The Bengal Jockey Club was started in 1803, and in Novem-

[1] H. F. Rainey, "Calcutta Review," 1852. W. H. Carey, "Good Old Days of Honorable John Company," Calcutta, 1906, Vol. I, p. 137.

ber of that year we hear from Lord Valentia that " a three-days' meeting was held at a small distance from Calcutta," probably at Akra or at Barrackpore, at which " very large sums were betted, and of course were lost by the inexperienced."

Lord Minto also discouraged the sport, and in his time the Calcutta Maidan was deserted for the Barrackpore course, which was close to the gates of the Governor General's Park.[1]

It was in Lord Hastings' time that the sport appears to have been firmly established. In March 1816 there were two races on each of three days at Calcutta. They were run in the morning, after the fog had dispersed. There was also a meeting at Barrackpore. In 1818 there were five days' racing on the Maidan in the month of December, and the third Calcutta Derby (run for the first time in 1816) was won by a horse named Trumpeter. In this year the races were held for the first time in the late afternoon. The present race course was commenced in 1819, and Mrs. Fanny Parkes in her gossipy " Wanderings of a Pilgrim " speaks of races as in full swing both at Calcutta and Barrackpore in 1823, and later in 1835 and 1837, in which year the " Auckland Cup " was run for.

From about 1820 onward the sport never looked back. There were in my day two stands—the Grand Stand, almost resembling Ascot in its size and splendour, looking straight down the Maidan ; and the old and more primitive stand on the Eastern side of the course, erected near the old Presidency Jail. This was afterwards used for the summer races, which are run when Calcutta is empty, and amateurs ride their own horses. It has since been taken down.

Successive Governors General and Viceroys have patronised the sport—with the solitary exception of Sir John Lawrence, whose serious soul was revolted by anything so immoral—and have given an annual cup or trophy of the value of £100 for the principal race. This is run about Christmas time, and was always attended by the Viceroy and his wife, driving in full state up the course. Like the Melbourne Cup in Australia, it is the great sporting event of the year in India, and attracts an enormous crowd to Calcutta. A remarkable feature is that the natives appeared to me to be no less interested in the races than the Europeans, pouring across the Maidan in thousands, and pressing up to the rails.

[1] Mrs. Maria Graham, " Journal of a Residence in India," 1812, p. 147.

From racing, the so-called " Sport of Kings," it is a natural transition to pass to *shikar*, which in modern times has become the traditional sport of the King's representative in India.   It is curious how little notice we find of tiger-hunting or game-killing of any kind in the records of the earlier Governors of Bengal.   They would seem rather to have indulged in the doubtful amusement of looking on while wild animals fought each other in captivity.   Great entertainments of this sort used to take place.   In the Official Records of 1765 I came across an account of fights on 18th December, at the New Fort, between a tiger and a buffalo, between two camels, and between an elephant and a rhinoceros.   The rhino having declined to fight, the indignant elephant ran wild, charged the ring of spectators and killed six persons. Two days later a notice was issued by His Lordship (Lord Clive) that he intended to hold an elephant fight on the Maidan ; and on this occasion, under such distinguished patronage, there was a fierce encounter.

We are told that Warren Hastings once shot a tiger on the site of what is now the Cathedral, in the South-east corner of the Calcutta Maidan, and the " India Gazette " of 1784 recorded a bag of four of these beasts by the Governor General's party near Chinsura ; but in the whole of Hastings' published correspondence I have only found one reference to that form of sport.   Barwell had a hunting lodge at Baraset, though this was not for tiger-shooting but for pig-sticking, and we hear more of his boon companions there playing high and drinking deep than of any sporting excursions.

In the whole of the voluminous Correspondence of Lord Cornwallis, during his first term of office in India, lasting for seven years, there is not a single mention of a tiger or deer or buffalo hunt, although these animals abounded within a few score of miles of Calcutta.

As a matter of fact, the Company's servants led a very sedentary life in Bengal, seldom leaving the town (unless on official duty) except to take the air on the river,[1] or on rare occasions to profit by a sea trip to Chittagong ; and although the Sunderbunds were then, even more than now, infested with tigers, we read of no expeditions to kill them. Lord Wellesley, who would have loved a Viceregal shoot on the present magnificent scale, does not appear to have been a sportsman.

---

[1] Sir Philip Francis, during his five years' residence in India, never went more than 100 miles from Calcutta.

But there is a plate in Sir Ch. D'Oyly's " European in India " depicting him and his suite looking on at an elephant fight, if that could be called sport—which it certainly was not—at the breakfast table of the Nabob of Oudh.

It is not till we come to Lord Hastings' time that, in the course of his long and tedious river journeys to the Upper Provinces, we read of the Governor General, who was insufferably bored by the slowness of the progress, turning aside to indulge in *shikar*. The two volumes of his Private Journal record many such attempts in 1815, and again in 1817 and 1818 ; [1] but compared with modern experiences they seem to have been singularly tame and unsuccessful. Perhaps, as he explained, when out after antelope in Datia, the game was frightened away by his red coat.

Other Governors General did a little mild shooting on their long marches to the North-west. We read for instance of Lord and Lady Amherst on their journey from Allahabad to Cawnpore in November, 1826, " hunting and hawking as they go, to beguile the way."

The mid-century Governors General appear to have similarly indulged in occasional sport. But there was nothing in those days analogous to the organised big shoots of modern times. The change came first with the spread of British rule over distant areas to which the early Governors had no access ; secondly, with the extension of the railway, enabling the Viceroy to proceed easily to parts of India where, in the days of marching or river-tracking, he could never penetrate ; and thirdly, with the fondness developed by the modern Raja, equipped with up-to-date weapons of precision and possessing a hereditary sporting instinct for preserving wild game in an organised fashion in the jungles of his State, both for his own enjoyment and that of his friends, and most of all for the entertainment of the King's representative. The sporting tours of the modern Viceroy, with their wonderful adventures and often prolific results, are an experience which no one who has enjoyed them would willingly have missed, or can ever forget. But it is not in the neighbourhood of Calcutta that they can be obtained ; and therefore they find no place in this Volume.

Among the minor sports, however, in which the Calcutta Englishman, and the Viceroy's Staff in particular, have never failed to indulge, have been the early morning paper-chases and the hunt of the jackal.

[1] Vol. I, pp. 259–263, 269, 272, 301–308 ; Vol. II, pp. 307–310, 315, 318.

In my chapter on Barrackpore I have referred to the jackal hunts that took place there in the times of the first Lord Minto and of Lord Amherst, and have narrated how the present Duke of Bedford (then Lord Herbrand Russell) kept a pack of jackal hounds while on Lord Dufferin's Staff, as did the late Earl of Suffolk when on mine.

As for Polo, were not the contests between the Viceroy's Staff and the Commander-in-Chief's Staff, whether in Calcutta or at Simla, among the great historic features of the season ? But Polo is outside the scope of this book.

So also is Golf, which was started at Calcutta in 1839, and has since swept everyone along in its victorious train.

PRINTED BY
CASSELL & COMPANY, LIMITED,
LA BELLE SAUVAGE, LONDON, E.C.4
5.525